The Ethnic Groups of Houston

New Series, No. 3

T H E

Ethnic Groups of Houston

Edited by Fred R. von der Mehden

Rice University Studies   Houston, Texas

Printed in the United States of America

First Edition, 1984

Requests for permission to reproduce material
from this work should be addressed to:
Rice University Studies
Post Office Box 1892
Rice University
Houston, Texas 77251

Library of Congress Cataloging in Publication Data
Main entry under title:

Ethnic groups of Houston.

   1. Minorities—Texas—Houston—History.   2. Houston
(Tex.)—History.   I. Von der Mehden, Fred R.
F394.H89A24   1984   976.4'1411   84-60485
ISBN 0-89263-255-0

Published in cooperation with the Houston Center
for the Humanities

The photographs in this volume are from the collections of
E.C.M. Chen, the Houston Metropolitan Research Center, the
Institute of Texan Cultures, Mrs. C. Y. Chu, G. J. Sham, Cary
Wintz, Donna Collins, Beulah Menutis, Helen Pitsaros, Fofo
DeClaris, the Voinis family, the Peteriotes family, Gus Frees,
Congregation Beth Israel, Congregation Beth Yeshurun, Con-
gregation Emanu El, Mrs. Rose Keeper, Dell Bush, Eloise
Loonam, the San Jacinto Museum of History Association, Bank
of the Southwest (Schlueter Photographic Collection,
Houston Metropolitan Research Center), the Gulf Coast Scan-
dinavian Club, the Linneas of Texas, SVEA, members of the
Augustana Lutheran Church, the Schlumberger Companies,
and the Houston Museum of Fine Arts (Bayou Bend Collection). Grateful acknowledgement is made for permission to
use these materials.

C O N T E N T S

PREFACE

This volume grew out of a four-year project by the Houston Center for the Humanities under the sponsorship of the National Endowment for the Humanities. From the beginning it had three broad objectives: to increase Houstonians' understanding of their rich ethnic heritage; to help the city's ethnic groups increase their awareness of their own experiences; and to develop a means of retaining that heritage for posterity. In order to accomplish these goals, research and public programs were melded. As overall coordinator and supervisor of the research aspect, I designed a project that ultimately covered ten ethnic communities. Coordinated with this research was a series of public programs under the general supervision of Mary Schiflett of the University of Houston, Central Campus.

This collection rises out of the research and writing prepared for this project. Each ethnic group was studied by a Houston scholar already knowledgeable about that community. These faculty and research staff from Rice University, the University of Houston, the University of St. Thomas, Texas Southern University, and the Houston Metropolitan Research Center were guided in their work by advisory groups from the communities that we studied. The paucity of published materials on Houston's eth-

nic character made this advice invaluable. It was with the cooperation of the various communities themselves that the authors were able to obtain the interviews and often ephemeral papers that form much of the empirical data for this volume. Of particular importance was a series of lengthy oral histories given by ethnic group members who were particularly well informed about the history and attitudes of their communities. These systematic oral histories will now give Houstonians direct access to their past. Copies have been deposited in the Houston Metropolitan Research Center of the Houston Public Library.

The authors wish to extend their special appreciation to the National Endowment for the Humanities for funding this project, to the Houston Center for the Humanities and its director, June Holly, for giving a home to the study, to students at the School of Architecture of the University of Houston, and to the Houston Metropolitan Research Center for helping us to obtain many of the photographs. Above all we thank the members of the ethnic communities who so graciously helped us to understand their people and cultures.

Fred R. von der Mehden
January 1984

Introduction
Houston's Ethnic Heritage

Fred R. von der Mehden

The intensity of ethnic influences on Houston's population has surged, ebbed, and resurged over the years since the establishment of the city on the banks of Buffalo Bayou. Of course, throughout the city's history our leaders have pictured Houston as an international gateway, a center of cosmopolitanism, and a preview of what the world is to become. Houston's first promoters, the Allen brothers, forecast boastfully that the metropolis would be a "communication with the coast and foreign countries and with different portions of the Republic." *The Standard History of Texas,* written before the First World War, said that "one must look to Manchester and to Hamburg to even presage the future commercial supremacy of Houston." Others extolled the many cultural attractions of the city. Naturally, not all foreign observers saw Houston in quite the same light; many viewed the town with jaundiced eyes, such as the Frenchman who commented in the 1840s that "Houston is a wretched little town composed of about twenty shops, a hundred huts, dispersed here and there, among trunks of fallen trees. It is infested with Methodists and ants."

Yet that "wretched little town" could vaunt an international flair even in its first decades. About one-third of its citizens had come from abroad, principally from Germany, Ireland, England, and France. The handwritten census of 1850 shows pages with more European-born than American-born residents. Those were the frontier days when new colonists from throughout the world were drawn to Houston and Texas as individuals, families, and whole communities. In those first decades Houstonians gathered in the muddy streets to watch with fascination as hundreds of Chinese passed through to work on railroads to the west and north. A sizable German population lived in and about the town; one observer noted that "the Germans, who are very numerous and well to do in the city, have their Volk-fests and beer-absorbings, when the city takes on an absolutely Teutonic air." The first Jewish congregation, Beth Israel, founded in 1859, had a large German-Jewish membership. Attracted by the promise of the new land and highly imaginative advertising (one picture showed mountains in the immediate background), Houston saw continued foreign immigration through the century.

By the first half of the twentieth century, however, the city had settled into a somewhat parochial mode. International commerce did expand with the opening of the ship channel, but trade was largely in bulk products based on agriculture and petrochemicals. The city's businessmen had not become the globe-trotters that they were in the next decades. While in those years the new smaller ethnic communities of Japanese, Greeks, Scandinavians, and Chinese grew, the number of Houstonians born abroad or of foreign parentage was quite small when compared with northern cities of comparable population. By 1950 we had only about 17,000 foreign-born residents and 28,000 of foreign parentage out of a population of some 600,000. Cities such as Minneapolis, Milwaukee, Buffalo, and Pittsburgh, then our rivals in population size, had three to four times those numbers. Against our less than 8 percent of citizens foreign born or born to one or more foreign parent, they averaged 30 percent.

The environment of the time was one that encouraged the ideal of the "melting pot," and there was considerable pressure to become Americanized and Texanized. Some groups, such as the Japanese and Germans, made major efforts to assimilate; others, such as the Greeks, attempted to become American while retaining their ethnic heritage. Houston's popular culture also reflected comparatively little of an international flavor, although the well-to-do were traveling abroad more and had begun to collect art and artifacts from overseas. Our restaurants were mainly steak, "Texican," and barbeque with little identifiable foreign influence, and the general populace was not much affected by international trends in clothes, culture, or ideas. At the same time this was not the cultural wasteland pictured in the northern press. We were developing a firm foundation in the fine and performing arts. The Rice Institute brought prominent European scholars to speak and teach in Houston, and our municipal leadership was not all that parochial. In fact, in 1956 only one member of the Chamber of Commerce was a native Houstonian and only twelve were native Texans, out of a total of twenty-nine.

The postwar years led to a dramatic change in both the character of Houston and how it was perceived in the rest of the country and the world. Houston is now viewed as the "energy capital of the world," the fourth-largest city in the United States (soon to be third), with its port the largest in foreign tonnage in the country. Its high-technology industry and petrochemical expertise have attracted businesses from the capitals of the world, and its sons and daughters can be found from Singapore to Aberdeen and from Venezuela to Saudi Arabia. By 1980 the Chamber of Commerce could point to more than four hundred companies with one or more offices overseas, almost fifty consulates and five foreign trade offices, more than thirty foreign banks, and thousands of visiting and resident foreign businessmen. International travel is commonplace; Houston hosts offices of more than forty foreign airlines, and in its first two years of existence—from 1978 to 1980—the United States Passport Office in Houston provided more than a quarter of a million passports. Almost every shopping center seems to have a travel agency; in fact, there are more than five hundred agencies in the city. Tourists or business travelers who want to "speak like a native" can find instruction in one of twenty language schools. And the process is accelerating. Houstonians often point out that the first word spoken on the moon was "Houston."

In the last twenty or thirty years the international influences on the city's people and culture have also expanded. The growth of Houston has been accompanied by new stirrings of ethnic identity and self-awareness, heightened by the arrival of fifty to sixty thousand new Houstonians a year as recently as 1982. This influx of people has come not only from northern towns with a strong ethnic heritage, but also from a wide variety of foreign countries. We now see communities that were almost entirely absent from our city in the prewar years. Whereas there were fewer than two hundred residents of Asian ancestry in those days, we now have more than 130,000. Among them are approximately 50,000 Indochinese, a people who numbered fewer than one hundred early in 1975. While our black citizenry has maintained the same approximate percentage of the general population since the nineteenth century, the influx of Hispanics has been such that officials now estimate that the majority of children in the Houston Independent School District will be Hispanic by 1990. In addition, Houston has for the first time received large enclaves of temporary foreign residents, particularly Japanese, French, and Germans.

The influx of "yankees," temporary foreigners, and immigrants has led some to question the depth of internationalism in this city and the extent to which ethnicity plays a major role among its citizens. We can easily observe the more superficial signs of a growing internationalism. Driving through the city, we see individuals who simply look different from those who were here before. A trip to the Galleria is often like walking through the United Nations. A visit to the Texas Medical Center quickly shows the extent to which it has become a mecca for both foreign patients and staff. Certainly any gastronomic index of Houston's food habits would show that the old Texican and barbeque habits are giving way to something more exotic. Not only do our food stores regularly stock a wide variety of foreign foods, but by the early 1980s the city could also boast of more than sixty-five Chinese restaurants, an increasing number of Vietnamese establishments, and more than a dozen French, half a dozen German, about five dozen Mexican, eight Greek, more than ten Japanese and Korean, more than thirty Italian (not counting the ubiquitous pizza parlor), as well as Swiss, Russian, Lebanese, Jewish, Thai, Indonesian, Argentinian, Spanish, Scandinavian, Indian, and Filipino restaurants. Even our shopping habits are changing; it is now possible to visit a Scottish specialty shop in the Memorial area, an English one in the University Village, a Vietnamese store on Main Street, Chinese on Chartres Street, French on Westheimer, and on and on. We are now a regular stop for major figures in the performing arts and prominent exhibits of the fine arts. Our art galleries offer opportunities to purchase the best from throughout the world. And Houston has made its own contributions to world culture in opera, theater, symphonic music, and art. Without a doubt, the reality of "Houston the International City" has come up to the early claims of our city's leaders.

Once we look past these more superficial aspects, what can we say about Houston's ethnic portrait today? As our authors will illustrate in this volume, Houston's ethnic population falls into four basic types: the foreigner, the immigrant, the American ethnic, and the assimilated. Each of these could be subdivided, but these four categories roughly encompass Houston's population.

The Foreigners

In the last two decades an increasing number of foreigners have arrived in this city. Many are visitors, including Arab or German businessmen here to trade or invest, tourists off to see NASA (or hopefully to view a real live cowboy), South Americans on a buying trip in the Galleria, or the sizable number of patients at the medical center. Houston is becoming a regular stopover for the traveler who wishes to "see America," and its importance as a trading and technological center makes it an important locus of international business.

The other kind of foreigner is the temporary resident, including business people sent here for varying lengths of time as managers, technicians, students at our universities, many of the staff at the medical center, and consular officials. Some of these visitors have extended tours in Houston, bringing their families, establishing their own social clubs, and sending their children to special schools, often on Saturdays or in the afternoons. For example, most of the Japanese in Houston and many Germans and French are in this category. This is no longer the hardship post it once was for British consular officers, and the increasing international character of Houston offers temporary residents the opportunity to purchase national foods and interact socially with fellow countrymen while learning something of the exotic culture of Texas.

The Immigrant

Houston is increasingly the home of newcomers to the United States. Most of these people have been drawn to the city by the same economic motives that attracted the early immigrants. Their perception of Houston is of a rich, vital city with unlimited opportunities for wealth. Combined with new immigration laws and better global transportation, this view of the city has brought a far wider range of immigrants than arrived in the first decades of this century. For example, among the largest groups of newcomers are the Asians and Hispanics. A visit to the annual Asian Festival gives the opportunity to see performing arts or taste the delicacies of Thailand, Vietnam, India, China, Japan, Indonesia, Cambodia, and Laos, to name only some of the representatives of our Asian community. Or a trip to St. Joseph's Church at its festival will provide a similar taste of Latin American and Eastern European influences.

An important distinction to be made within this category is between the immigrant who has voluntarily come to settle in the United States and the exile forced from his or her home. In the past Houston has been the home for many exiles, such as Jews, Hungarians, and Cubans. Most recently we have experienced a great influx of Indochinese and Central Americans. As the possibility of return wanes, the exile begins to consider himself an immigrant and finally decides on citizenship. This is often a very difficult decision, and the hope for return rarely dies completely. However, the transformation from immigrant to new American is almost a completed process for the European exiles and a continuing one for the newer Indochinese and Central Americans.

The American Ethnic

Other American cities have long been home to concentrations of ethnic groups who have maintained much of their traditional heritage. Communities such as Chinatown in San Francisco, the Polish sections of Milwaukee, and Puerto Rican neighborhoods in New York have not had their counterparts in Houston. Some neighborhoods here have had an overrepresentation of a particular ethnic community, especially around a church or synagogue, but generally Houstonians have been highly mobile. At the same time, some ethnic groups have maintained elements from the past to a greater extent than have others. These remnants may be language, customs, attitudes, or organizations. During the first half of this century, assimilationist pressures weakened these ethnic ties, but recent immigration and changing attitudes have led to a resurgence of the ethnic American in Houston.

Newer immigrants naturally retain more of their foreign heritage. In part the strength of their ethnicity may be self-chosen, but it is often the result of prejudice from the dominant community. The ethnic group is thus more isolated and seeks protection from people of the same background. In Houston today the more ethnically integrated communities include the Greeks and Southeast Asians, while the English and Germans have been more assimilated.

The Assimilated

Most Houstonians have been so assimilated that they have lost almost all their ties to the old country. While they may retain a few Christmas rituals or display artifacts from their ancestors, they do not speak the language, follow the customs, or belong to organizations related to their ethnic heritage. This is particularly true of third- and fourth-generation Houstonians of European ancestry who were able to blend easily into the local culture. Even those of Cajun origin in Houston, a population perceived as having a strong ethnic base, have lost most of the elements that set them apart from others. We know comparatively little about the levels of ethnic identity within these groups, since most researchers have been more interested in the ethnically oriented elements of society. The assimilated groups do not attend ethnic associations and gatherings and are not identified with ethnic political causes, so their national background is not obtrusive.

Finally, we can turn to the general ethnic environment of Houston today. Three obvious characteristics dominate the picture: diversity, an increased intensity of ethnicity, and a commitment to maintaining elements of tradition within an American value system.

Diversity

Texans are often themselves surprised at the ethnic diversity of their state, although a visit to the Institute of Texan Cultures would soon enlighten them. When asked to define their ancestry in the 1980 census, Texans showed their rich ethnic heritage. The state ranked in the top twelve in terms of population for twenty-three ethnic groups and was in the top six for Colombians, Czechs (second), French, Iranians, English (second), Irish, Scottish (second), and Welsh. In 1983 a survey was taken by the Houston Independent School District to assess the number and type of languages spoken by children who exhibited limited proficiency in English. Many observers expected to find a relatively high percentage speaking Spanish, and they were not mistaken, although these included children from the United States as well as Mexico, El Salvador, and other Latin countries. The surprising result was the variety of languages to be found in the homes of Houston. Altogether, the students who had limited proficiency in English came from seventy-two countries, with the largest numbers coming (in order) from the United States, Mexico, Vietnam, El Salvador, Cambodia, Laos, India, China, Colombia, and Guatemala. These figures were from but one school district and did not include students who spoke English fluently or adults from a foreign background.

This diversity is an important attribute of the new ethnic character of Houston. It gives a richness to our culture, food, and politics heretofore missing. It is reflected in many ways, including the variety of our restaurants, church services in a multitude of languages, the existence of local publications for the Chinese, Vietnamese, Hispanic, Jewish, Arab, and black communities, radio programs intended for Vietnamese, Indian, Spanish, black, and various European audiences, and an increasing number of schools teaching foreign languages to children and adults. Even local merchants are finding it useful to have signs or sales personnel to aid the international visitor or resident. Finally, our politicians are seeing the desirability of catering to these new communities, and some of the more astute members of Houston's ethnic groups are learning how to employ the democratic process for the betterment of their people.

Increased Intensity

A second ethnic characteristic of the new Houston is an increasing intensity of ethnic identity. Ethnic groups are becoming more aware of their heritage and more interested in retaining and refining it. Several factors are responsible for this pattern. The United States is changing its view of itself from the melting pot ideal to the acceptance of ethnic pluralism. Being a homogenized American is no longer a national goal, and looking to one's "roots" with pride is allowed and even welcomed. In Houston itself the heavy in-migration of northerners and immigrants has not only provided new foundations for ethnic identity, but has also stirred the ethnic memories of older Houstonians. Meanwhile, certain communities have long given considerable attention to their ethnic backgrounds, the most obvious being the Mexican-Americans. The church, special holidays, festivities, social organizations, and political causes have tended to integrate each community in at least an ethnic sense.

At the same time it would be a mistake to underestimate the attraction that American culture holds for the ethnic youth. A constant complaint of many ethnically oriented parents is that their children are losing their language and culture. For example, the Indochinese see the "McDonald's generation" as seditiously influenced by television, fast foods, rock music, and American slang, to the point where they forget not only their culture, but also the traditional relationships between parent and child. The intensity of this pressure in a city without the reinforcing presence of ethnic neighborhoods may mean a serious diluting of ethnicity in future generations. At present, these "insidious" attractions are cause for considerable tension within many immigrant families.

Pluralism

Finally, Houston ethnics have consciously attempted to balance a desire to retain their ethnic heritage with a recognition of the need to develop within a peculiarly American environment. They generally seek a plural society, basically American in its values, but accepting and sustaining cultural heterogeneity. Contemporary Houston, differing from its more parochial years, can allow and even foster this sense of pluralism. The high mobility of its population and newfound internationalism are both conducive to this pluralistic goal.

Following this introduction, the eleven chapters of this book review the history, achievements, and problems of Houston's blacks, Chinese, French, Germans, Greeks, Indochinese, Japanese, Jews, Mexicans, and Scandinavians. Each author has attempted to emphasize six aspects of that community's life: its history; why its members came and stayed in Houston; attitudes toward Houston and other ethnic groups in the city; differences within the community itself; the degree to which ethnic identity has been retained; and important values within the community and how they have changed over time.

We must emphasize that these ten groups are but a part of a colorful ethnic mosaic that is now Houston. Another volume could easily be designed to include the English, Irish, and Czech populations that have lived in this city since the nineteenth century, or newer residents such as the Indians, Koreans, and non-Mexican Hispanics. We are all the richer for this real internationalization of Houston.

Blacks

Cary D. Wintz

John T. Biggers, who came to Houston in 1949 to serve as head of the Art Department at the newly founded Texas Southern University, is one of the nation's foremost artists. This photograph, taken during the summer of 1983, shows Dr. Biggers being interviewed by students while he was working on a mural in Adair Park south of Houston. Photograph by the author.

ooking at the modern skyscrapers and shopping centers of Houston, we sometimes find it difficult to believe that the history of this area goes back several hundred years. Blacks have been a part of this history from the beginning. Today the city of Houston is approaching its 150th birthday. The first Europeans to explore what is now known as Texas, however, arrived more than three hundred years before the founding of Houston. In the fall of 1528, a ship under the command of Cabeza de Vaca was caught in a Gulf storm and ran aground at Galveston Island. Among the crew members who waded ashore were several African slaves. Only de Vaca and three of his men survived the hardships that awaited them on the Texas coast. They lived eight years among the Indians, first as prisoners and slaves, then as medicine men and traders. One of the four survivors was an African named Esteban. Esteban's linguistic skills enabled de Vaca to communicate with his captors and contributed significantly to the group's survival. After eight years in Texas, de Vaca, Esteban, and two others made their way across almost eight hundred miles of desert and mountains to a Spanish outpost in northwestern Mexico. Esteban and his comrades had become the first explorers to cross Texas and the American Southwest.

Esteban's prominent role in the early exploration of Texas was not unique. Blacks accompanied most Spanish expeditions, including that of Francisco Coronado, who explored New Mexico and parts of northern Texas in 1540 and 1541. When the Spanish established permanent settlements in Texas, blacks were there also. Most Spanish settlements and garrisons in eighteenth-century Texas counted blacks among their inhabitants. Although accurate records were not kept, it is estimated that between 15 and 25 percent of the population of Spanish Texas was black. For example, in the San Antonio area in 1778, 151 of 759 men were black or mulatto, and only 4 of these were slaves. Although the Spanish introduced slavery to Texas, free blacks were common in the province, and they faced few, if any, restrictions on their freedom. They were accepted socially and followed whatever trade or profession they chose. Blacks worked as farmers, merchants, teachers, shoemakers, carpenters, teamsters, priests, laborers, and domestic servants. Several owned land and cattle.

Most of the free blacks who resided in Spanish Texas were born there or even farther south in what is present-day Mexico. However, beginning in the early 1800s, an increasing number came from the nearly twenty states that formed the United States. This migration continued after 1821, when Mexico won its independence from Spain. Free blacks came to Texas because there was greater economic opportunity for them and much less racial prejudice under Spanish and Mexican governments than in the United States. Texas also attracted its share of runaway slaves, especially from neighboring Louisiana.

Several blacks prospered and even rose to positions of prominence in early Texas. For example, William Goyens, a free black from North Carolina, settled in Nacogdoches in 1820. There he ran a boarding house and a variety of businesses. He was at times a blacksmith, gunsmith, wagon manufacturer, freight hauler, mill owner, land speculator, and planter. Along with several other Texas blacks, Goyens owned, bought, and sold slaves as part of his business activities. In 1832, he married a white woman from Georgia. Goyens associated with the most important men in Texas, including Thomas Rusk and Sam Houston; and during the years around the Texas Revolution he served the Texas government as an envoy to the Cherokee Indians. Even though Texas became much less tolerant of blacks following its separation from Mexico, Goyens continued to prosper. At the time of his death in 1856, he owned more than 12,000 acres of land and was a wealthy man. While Goyens' achievements were unusual, political and social conditions in Texas were good enough under Mexican rule for abolitionist Benjamin Lundy to seek official permission to establish a colony of free American blacks there in the early 1830s. The Mexican government approved the proposal, but the project was dropped after the Texas Revolution.

During the period of Spanish rule, most blacks in Texas were free. This situation changed dramatically when the Mexican government opened Texas' borders to colonists from the United States. When Moses Austin rode into San Antonio in 1820 seeking permission to establish a colony in Texas, he brought a black servant with him. Nearly all of the settlers who migrated to the Austin colony either brought slaves with them or strongly supported the institution of slavery. Even though Mexican law prohibited slavery, this law was never effectively enforced, and slavery became common in Texas. Not all of these early settlers owned slaves; in 1825, for example, only 69 of the 1,347 residents of the Austin colony were slaveholders. Still, the slave population grew rapidly as more Americans migrated to Texas, and by the late 1820s slaves far outnumbered free blacks. The number of slaves in the Austin colony grew from 443 in 1825 to approximately one thousand in 1835; in the latter year there were about five thousand slaves in all of Texas. After independence the slave population increased from 11,323 in 1840 to 58,161 in 1850, and then to 182,556 in 1860. On the eve of the Civil War, nearly one Texas family in four owned slaves, but only 2,163 families owned 20 or more. There were only 54 Texas families who had more than 100 slaves.

Pre–Civil War Houston

While the typical Texas slave worked on a plantation or farm and lived in a rural area along the coast or in the river valleys of Central and East Texas, urban slavery also became common as Texas towns grew. By 1860 both Houston and San Antonio were home to more than a thousand slaves, and many smaller communities had more than a hundred. The first blacks who lived in the Houston area were slaves who arrived a number of years before the city was founded. Between 1816 and 1821, first Louis de Aury and later the pirate Jean Lafitte used Galveston Island and the bayous around Galveston Bay to warehouse slaves prior to smuggling them into the United States. In 1819 and 1820, several blacks accompanied Dr. James Long on his ill-fated filibustering expeditions to Texas. When Jane Long followed her husband into Texas she brought with her Kiamata, a young slave girl, as a companion for her five-year-old daughter. Mrs. Long and the two girls survived two years of severe weather and hostile Indians on Bolivar Point as they waited in vain for Dr. Long's return. He, however, had been captured and killed in Mexico. Finally, the trio was rescued by settlers on their way to Austin's colony. Mrs. Long, her daughter, and Kiamata joined the colony. They lived first in what is now Harris County, then in what is now Brazoria County, where Kiamata helped Mrs. Long run a boarding house, and finally in the area

now known as Richmond, where the two women ran a prosperous plantation. Kiamata married and had four children. One of her sons became an overseer on the Long plantation, and one of her grandsons, Henry C. Breed, became a Houston police officer.

In the city of Houston, many of the initial settlers brought slaves with them. Early accounts mention that blacks and Mexican prisoners-of-war cleared the land for the original townsite in the summer of 1836. From the beginning, slaves made up a significant portion of the population. In the censuses of 1850 and 1860, slaves composed 22 percent of the city's population. Slavery was even more widespread in the plantation areas that surrounded Houston. In Harris County and the other counties that constitute the metropolitan area today, slaves accounted for 49 percent of the population in 1860.

Many of the slaves in the Houston area raised cotton and sugar cane on the plantations situated south and southwest of the city along the Brazos River. While life on these plantations varied greatly from place to place, the Peach Point Plantation, owned by James Perry in Brazoria County about forty miles south of Houston, provides an interesting picture of the conditions that at least some slaves in the area experienced. In the 1830s and 1840s, this plantation produced cotton as well as corn and other foodstuffs to supply its own needs. In the 1850s, sugar cane replaced cotton as the principal cash crop.

Plantation records for Peach Point in 1848 and 1849 illustrate the work regimen of the field hands. In early February, slaves began to prepare the fields for planting. Planting started on March 1 and was followed by the first plowing, which began on March 31 and lasted almost two weeks. The second plowing and regular hoeing commenced on May 1. Between February and the end of June, slaves worked every day in the fields, planting, weeding, plowing, and hoeing. From June 20 through the end of July, field work eased, and slaves spent most of their time on general plantation maintenance as they waited for harvest time. In 1848 the harvest started on July 31; twenty slaves had picked almost 155,000 pounds of cotton by October 11. From October until early February the slaves baled the cotton; then the cycle began again. In addition to tending cotton that year, Peach Point's slaves grew corn, potatoes, and a little tobacco;

they split rails, cut board timber and basket timber, tore down and rebuilt fences, hauled wood, shelled corn, slaughtered hogs and beef, and kept birds out of the corn fields. In addition, they worked on the roads, cleaned out drainage ditches, built a chimney, and cared for a brood of sows and piglets. Slaves worked from sunrise to sunset, with time off on Saturday afternoons and all day on Sundays. Perry allowed his slaves to work small plots of land for themselves, on which they raised cotton, corn, and vegetables. They sold these crops for cash, which they used to purchase extra shoes, clothing, and tobacco and other merchandise from the plantation store. In the 1850s, when sugar cane became the principal cash crop at Peach Point and slaves had to work seven days a week during the sugar-refining season, Perry paid his slaves a small wage for their overtime.

Slave life in the city differed greatly from that on the plantations. City slaves generally had more freedom and a somewhat easier, more rewarding life than their counterparts on the plantations. Many slaves in Houston worked as house servants. Others worked on farms and plantations on the edge of town, as cooks and waiters in hotels, as teamsters, or as laborers on the docks and in warehouses. Black labor helped build the plank roads and railroads that were vital to the city's prosperity, and helped construct many of the city's buildings. While most slaves performed unskilled labor, there were enough black craftsmen and skilled workers in the city to alarm white workers. One objective of the early workingmen's associations and trade unions in Houston was to limit the employment of black craftsmen.

Houston and Galveston were the most important centers for slave trade in Texas. On his visit to Houston in 1854, Frederick Law Olmsted reported observing a prominent slave market that contained a large number of slaves awaiting auction. While only one person operated a business devoted exclusively to the slave trade, many successful merchants sold slaves as one phase of their activities. For example, Augustus C. Allen and John Allen, the city's founders, imported a large number of slaves into Houston for sale. In the late 1830s, G. Everett sold slaves along with horses, mules, and carriages at his auction yard. In the 1840s

and 1850s, F. Scranton operated a similar business. He was joined in the late 1850s by men like Edward Riordan, who advertised himself as a "Negro and Real Estate Broker" selling slaves from his office on Congress at La Branch. Colonel John B. Snydor operated a slave market on Congress between Main and Fannin. Scott and Lubbock are the surnames of one partnership that sold blacks on consignment from an office in the Mansion House on Fannin Street.

While most of the white residents of Houston supported the institution of slavery, some expressed concern about the presence and demeanor of the city's sizable black population. Newspapers frequently complained about the freedom of movement and the rowdy behavior of blacks in the city. Both the city and state passed laws that attempted to control the situation. Slaves were prohibited by law from gambling, carrying weapons, buying liquor, or selling anything without their masters' permission. They were required to treat whites with respect, were subject to a curfew, and could not appear on the streets without a written pass from their owners. Slaves were not allowed to hire out their own time, nor to live in a dwelling not adjacent to that of their owners. They could not gather in groups of more than four, unless their owner or another responsible citizen was present. Finally, slaves who were convicted of crimes received harsher punishment than whites convicted of similar acts. In addition to the controls placed on slaves, legal restrictions also limited the freedom of free blacks. State law, in fact, attempted to prevent the migration and permanent residence of free blacks in Texas, while the Houston City Council passed an ordinance in 1839 requiring all free blacks to leave the city within thirty days.

There is some question about how effectively these laws were enforced. Though it was illegal, many owners hired out their slaves to other employers, and some even allowed slaves to hire out their own time. Slaves who "hired out" often lived away from their owners and consequently were not closely supervised. Laws attempting to restrict the movement of slaves and slave gatherings, drinking, and gambling also were rarely enforced. Visitors to the city noted that blacks were always visible on the streets; newspapers confirmed this, complaining that blacks went wherever they pleased without supervision or passes and frequently congregated in the evenings at unruly parties and gatherings. Much of the hostility toward free blacks developed because of the difficulty their relative freedom presented in controlling the activities of the city's slave population. A grand jury in 1839 accused the free black population of corrupting slaves by presenting an example of laziness and by introducing them to vice and petty crime. For a time following that accusation, the laws against free blacks were enforced somewhat more stringently; some free blacks left Houston. In 1839 there were approximately twenty free blacks in the city; the census of 1860 counted only eight, seven of whom were women who worked as laundresses, seamstresses, or housekeepers and who enjoyed the support of a number of prominent citizens. Some free blacks apparently ignored the restrictions placed on them: Peter Allen, a barber, moved to Houston in 1846 but did not seek legal permission to reside in Texas until 1863. It seems that others did likewise and lived in the city and state for years in spite of laws prohibiting this.

Free blacks occupied a curious legal status in Houston. They could not become citizens, and, like slaves, they faced restrictions on their freedoms. One law discouraged them from gathering in saloons; they had to obtain permission from the mayor before they could legally hold dances; and in 1855, a local ordinance required them to post bond and receive permission from the city council before they could rent a house within the city limits. On the other hand, free blacks were guaranteed a trial by jury; and in most cases, if they were convicted of a crime, their punishment would be the same as if they were white.

The great advantage that the urban slave experienced was the relative freedom of city life. While many slaves in Houston worked directly under the supervision of their masters, the widespread practice of hiring out allowed others to avoid such close control. This system, although technically illegal, was both common and popular, because it enabled the slaveowner to receive significant profit on the labor of his bondsmen, especially in the 1850s when the rapidly rising cost of

slaves pushed wages upward. The system also allowed slaveowners to transfer part of the cost of a slave's upkeep to the party who contracted for the slave's labor. Some owners allowed their bondsmen to hire their own time. Under this system slaves found their own employment, gave their masters a specified sum each month, and kept the rest of their wages for their own use and support. These slaves enjoyed a great deal of freedom, particularly if they rented housing away from their masters' dwellings.

As a consequence of the hiring-out system and the presence of free blacks, Houston had a significant number of black residents who seemed fairly prosperous and who did not appear to be under anyone's supervision. One visitor to the city recorded that he saw numerous well-dressed blacks, some of whom had the privilege of using their masters' carriages for pleasure drives. Another visitor in 1849 reported that he met a free Negro man and woman who dressed in the latest Parisian fashions and ran a dancing school for wealthy whites in Houston and Galveston. This visitor also noted the presence of a black-owned restaurant that seemed to be doing an excellent business providing both food and entertainment for the city's black population.

Slaves clearly recognized the advantages of urban life, and most resisted any attempt to transfer them to a plantation. In turn, plantation owners were reluctant to buy urban slaves, whom they considered to have been spoiled by city life. Usually before a planter would purchase a city slave he demanded a trial period to determine whether the slave could adjust to plantation life; in most cases, slaves failed this trial and were returned to their city owners. Few slaves wanted to surrender the advantages of urban life for the regimen of the plantation, and many took extreme measures to avoid it. A slave known only as "Dave," who belonged to William Ballinger, a Galveston and Houston attorney, clearly demonstrated this attitude. During the Civil War, Ballinger tried to hire Dave out to work on Aaron Coffee's plantation. The effort failed. As Coffee observed, Dave was deeply attracted to urban life and "has sworned not to work on any plantation and says he will not live out of a city or town."

Dave never reconciled himself to life outside of the city. After eight months he escaped and returned to the Ballinger household in Houston. Every time that he was returned to Coffee, he ran away again. Dave did not seek complete freedom, but he made it clear that he would accept slavery only in an urban setting. Ultimately his efforts prevailed. After spending less than a year with Coffee, he was allowed to return to Houston, where he worked as a domestic for the Ballingers and occasionally hired out as a day laborer.

One of the advantages of urban life was that it gave blacks the opportunity to establish the rudiments of their own community and social life relatively free from outside interference. By 1849, blacks in Houston had a church—a small, somewhat shabby house that stood behind the white churches—where slaves and free blacks had their own services (probably under the direction of a white minister). These church services and occasional dances were tolerated by the city. Other social gatherings created more concern. Newspapers worried about the eating, drinking, singing, dancing, and card-playing that commonly occurred at the frequent illicit black gatherings in town. On the other hand, slaves were a vital element of the work force and made a significant contribution to the development of the city. For example, nearly everyone praised the role that blacks played during the Civil War when, due to the manpower shortage, they took over and operated the fire department. Years later one Houstonian recalled that they were "splendid firemen" who "threw their whole souls into the work."

Post–Civil War Houston

The End of Slavery

In the late spring of 1865, a cloud of uncertainty descended upon the city. In nearly every issue, newspapers reported rumors, still unconfirmed, that the South had suffered major military setbacks. However the war went, it would affect Houston's blacks. If the war continued, Houston newspapers estimated that 200,000 black troops would be used by the Confederate Army that summer. Instead, the war ended. On June 19, 1865, General Gordon Granger landed with the first Union soldiers at Galveston and immediately announced that all slaves in Texas were free. Houston officials expressed concern about the effect that this change in status would have on the city's blacks. Specifically, they worried about idleness and vagrancy among the black population and urged strict enforcement of the municipal vagrancy law.

City officials did not anticipate the sudden increase in the black population that was to come within days after emancipation. As news spread and slavery collapsed, hundreds of freed slaves poured into Houston from Peach Point and other plantations in Brazoria, Fort Bend, and neighboring counties. A witness to this migration described it vividly: "They travel mostly on foot, bearing heavy burdens of clothing, blankets, etc., on their heads—a long and weary journey, they arrive tired, foot sore, and hungry." Most came to Houston hoping to make a better life for themselves. They expected to receive assistance and protection from federal officials in the city. Some apparently had heard rumors that the Union Army would provide them with food, housing, and jobs; others believed that they would not have to work. Reality, of course, was different. Federal officials were overwhelmed by the number of refugees. Colonel Clarke, the commander of Union troops in Houston, put blacks to work repairing streets and cleaning out ditches in the city, and provided food and shelter; but the government could not accommodate all of the newcomers. Local newspapers urged blacks to remain on the plantations for their own good.

This flood of blacks into the city was not welcomed by city officials or the majority of the citizens. Many problems, some imagined and some real, were associated with this migration. Some feared that the city could not absorb the influx and worried about the expected rise in vagrancy and especially crime. By July 1865 almost every issue of the *Houston Tri-Weekly Telegraph* noted the growing number of robberies and petty crimes attributed to black vagrants in the city. A more serious problem was the shortage of available housing for blacks and the overcrowding and public health crisis that resulted. With more and more blacks crowding into old, dilapidated, vacant buildings, especially warehouses and stables, officials grew concerned about the danger of fire, disease, and poor sanitation. Some observers worried that much of the housing was not fit for human occupation, and they wondered how blacks would manage when winter came. White workers also were apprehensive that blacks might take their jobs. In July 1865 the white mechanics of the city officially protested the hiring of black mechanics, while other white workers tried to block the employment of blacks as wagon and omnibus drivers. The editors of the *Tri-Weekly Telegraph* and other business leaders suggested that European immigrants be recruited to replace blacks as the city's labor force, and recommended again and again that blacks should leave Houston and return to the "comfortable homes" that they had left behind. But not all reports about blacks were negative. The newspaper acknowledged that many blacks had taken jobs to pay for the food they were buying from the army, and that the newcomers who were working on the streets and ditches had made great strides in cleaning up the city. And, of course, blacks continued to come. The migration to Houston that began in the summer of 1865 has continued ever since.

There is no accurate count of the number of blacks who came to Houston at the end of the Civil War, remained briefly, and then returned "home" as they were urged to do. Houston could not immediately absorb all who came to the city, and there was a strong demand for labor on the old plantations. However, many came and stayed. The black population grew from 1,077 in 1860 to 3,691 in 1870, while the proportion of blacks in the Houston population increased to 39.3 percent. Those who remained would face and gradually solve most of the problems they encountered there. In the process, they would lay the foundations for the black community in Houston.

Union troops arrived in Houston on June 20, 1865, and initially the provost marshal's office assisted blacks who moved to the city. But since the city remained orderly, the provost marshal's office closed the following November. At that point, the Freedmen's Bureau took over the responsibility of assisting Houston's blacks. In the summer of 1865 the provost marshal's office concentrated on providing food and shelter to destitute blacks and put some of them to work, under city supervision, on the roads and ditches. Due to limited federal resources, however, most blacks had to fend for themselves when they arrived in the city. When Freedmen's Bureau officials reached Houston in the fall, they focused on providing legal protection for blacks, helping them negotiate labor contracts, and opening schools to educate the largely illiterate black population. For a time many blacks believed rumors that the federal government would present land to all of the freedmen on Christmas Day, 1965. Despite firm denials by the government, belief in the rumor persisted until after Christmas.

In spite of the government's efforts, federal authorities did not have sufficient resources to care for the freedmen, and most of the blacks who came to Houston had to rely on themselves. Housing was a major and immediate problem. Many sought shelter in empty warehouses, like the "Hotel d'Afrique," a rundown building where a large number of homeless blacks slept each night; others camped on the outskirts of town. The housing problem could not be solved overnight. In the summer and fall of 1865, blacks in the city held "colored fairs" in several parts of town to raise money to help the newcomers. Black churches also provided assistance when they could, while others organized a Freedmen's Aid Society. Free blacks and the former urban slaves provided most of the aid, helped many of the new arrivals find jobs and shelter, and set up many of the early organizations and institutions in the black community.

Social and Economic Changes

In the years following the Civil War, blacks lived in each of the city's wards, usually at the edge of town. The largest numbers lived in the Third Ward, in Freedmantown and similar neighborhoods on the outskirts of the Fourth Ward, and in the Frosttown area of the Second Ward. Surprisingly, some blacks quickly acquired title to land and built their own homes. As early

In the 1920s Houston was known as the Black Fraternal Capital of Texas. Colonel William Wyndon, a cabinetmaker, was an officer in the Odd Fellows.

as the fall of 1865, several blacks had bought property in Freedmantown, and the number grew rapidly during the next two years. By the early 1880s approximately 25 percent of the black households in the Fourth Ward were owner-occupied. In the Third Ward, the percentage was about the same. It is not clear exactly how blacks acquired property so quickly. Many whites seem to have been willing to sell land to blacks on credit, and immediately following the war land on the edge of the city was cheap. Several businessmen did quite well subdividing farms just outside the city to provide building lots and rent houses for the rapidly growing population. Most of those who acquired their own houses were skilled workers, shopkeepers and owners of small businesses, teachers, and ministers. None of the areas where blacks lived was totally segregated. In some areas like Vinegar Hill, a vice-filled slum area on the north bank of Buffalo Bayou, the races mixed without restraint. Elsewhere, whites (often German and Italian immigrants) and blacks lived in the same neighborhoods, occasionally even on the same block or across the street from each other.

Jobs were the second major need of the freedman. In the summer of 1865 many whites were concerned about vagrancy among blacks, while white workers worried about job competition. During slavery, black labor had been very important to the city, and the city continued to need their contribution as part of the work force. The former "hired-out" slaves were most feared by white workers who had even objected to their employment as skilled labor before the Civil War. Some blacks took advantage of freedom to open their own businesses. As early as July 1865, blacks operated blacksmith shops, shoemaking establishments, and several other small enterprises. Finding a job was a greater problem for the newcomers to the city who, as former plantation slaves, usually had few salable skills. Many whites in Houston advocated a contract labor system for these blacks. Under this system, which in many respects was similar to hiring out, blacks surrendered much of their freedom to their employers. This system was often abused until the Freedmen's Bureau stepped in to police it. While some blacks achieved economic success, most ended up as low-paid, un-

skilled workers. As of 1870, 82 percent of the city blacks still worked as domestic, unskilled, or semi-skilled labor.

At the center of the emerging black community was the church. Black churches predated the Civil War. As early as 1849, black Methodists had their own church building, behind the white church, presided over by a white minister. After the war black Methodists, led by minister Elias Dibble, purchased their own lot at Travis and Bell streets and established Trinity Methodist Episcopal Church. If Trinity Methodist was the first black church, Antioch Baptist was by far the most prestigious. The Reverend William C. Crane, a white missionary, organized Antioch in January 1866. Initially the congregation met in white Baptist facilities; then it moved to the banks of Buffalo Bayou under the direction of the Reverend I. S. Campbell. The church did not begin to flourish until 1868, when it selected its first pastor, John Henry Yates. Under his leadership, Antioch built its own quarters in the Fourth Ward and began a long period of growth. Along with churches, black Houstonians established fraternal and other social organizations during the early years of Reconstruction. The most significant of these was the Young Men's Benevolent Club, founded in 1867 to raise money for black charities.

One of the most important developments among blacks following the Civil War was the reinforcement of the black family and the major role that this institution would play in the black community. Even though slave marriages had no legal status, many families survived the pressures of slavery intact. Immediately following the war, hundreds of former slaves crowded the courthouse in Houston to obtain marriage licenses to legalize their existing marriages. The family then became the basic unit in the community, one that played a major role in helping blacks adjust to life in Houston. Families provided food and shelter to newly arrived relatives and helped ease the transition to city life.

To a large degree, then, blacks took care of their own basic needs, especially in the areas of housing, employment, and spiritual sustenance. In the area of education, however, they depended more on government assistance. Although a few blacks were educated in the churches before the Civil War, the real beginning of black education in Houston came when the Freedmen's Bureau and the American Missionary Association opened schools in black churches during Reconstruction. The Freedmen's Bureau funded and operated the schools, while the American Missionary Association staffed them with northern white missionaries. They concentrated their efforts on providing adult blacks with basic literacy and arithmetic skills. Their success persuaded the Texas legislature in 1870 to create public schools for blacks in the cities. That year the Gregory Institute opened in the Fourth Ward under the supervision of a group of Houston's leading black citizens, including Richard Allen (a businessman and Republican politician), the Reverend Elias Dibble, and Sandy Parker. When the Freedmen's Bureau schools closed in 1872, most of the students and teachers transferred to Gregory. From the beginning, black education in Houston was segregated. In the early 1870s, after several public complaints, black teachers replaced white teachers at the school. When the city of Houston established its school system in the 1870s, black teachers taught black students in black schools.

Early Black Political Involvement

Black Houstonians played a surprisingly active role in local politics in the years following the Civil War. Immediately after emancipation, the state passed laws prohibiting black suffrage; but emboldened by Congressional passage of the Fourteenth Amendment, the city's blacks began to take a greater interest in politics. Initially, blacks directed their political efforts toward the Democratic Party. In early 1868, a group of blacks founded the Colored Executive Committee to mobilize black votes in the city. That summer, Henry Love and Calvin Bannister established the Colored Democratic Club. Meanwhile, Republicans launched a campaign in the city to involve blacks in their political organizations and win the black vote. In March 1869 blacks participated in the organization of the biracial Harris County Republican Club. This was one of the

few truly integrated groups in the city at this time. Blacks served as vice-president and secretary of the organization and held two of the five seats on the executive committee. The club held several of its early meetings at Antioch Baptist Church.

The political strength of Republicans in Texas and Houston centered on registering all eligible blacks and ensuring that they voted. Reflecting this, when a Republican-dominated government took over Texas in 1869, it appointed a radical Republican, Thomas H. Scanlan, as mayor of Houston and named several blacks to the city council. This council named a black, James Snowball, as street commissioner and hired several blacks in the police department. By 1870, due to restrictions that prevented a number of former Confederates from voting, black voters outnumbered whites in Houston. In 1872 Scanlan and three black city councilmen won reelection, largely because of the black vote. However, despite their visible role in city government, black leaders were becoming increasingly dissatisfied with their position in the Republican Party. In 1871 black leaders denounced white Republicans for blocking their efforts to nominate a black candidate for the legislature, and in 1873, though they held three of ten city council seats, they received only five of the twenty-five appointments to standing committees. Blacks did not hold on even to these elected positions in municipal government for very long. The victory of the Democrats in the 1874 city election led to the collapse of Republican-black control. For the next twenty years, blacks would continue to vote and play an important role in the local Republican Party, but their fairly even distribution among the city's wards would prevent them from electing any of their own to be city officials.

The Emergence of Segregation

In the late 1860s and early 1870s, blacks created the institutions that would become the basis of the black community in Houston. For the next seventy years, black Houstonians would build this community in a segregated environment. Segregation, which was per-

haps overlooked in the euphoria that followed emancipation, had become well entrenched in the city by
the mid-1870s. More than any other single factor, this
determined the nature of black Houston. Segregation
developed in a somewhat haphazard manner, partly
by law and partly by custom. Although Houston never
enacted a complete code of laws to regulate black behavior, from time to time state laws and city ordinances contributed to the growing policy of racial segregation. School segregation was legally imposed by
the state's Constitution in 1876; state laws segregated
railroads in 1891, while a city ordinance separated the
races on Houston streetcars in 1903. In 1907 the city
council enacted a law that authorized segregation in
hotels, restaurants, theaters, and other public facilities;
and in 1922 a new city code of ordinances segregated
parks and outlawed biracial cohabitation. On the other
hand, custom segregated blacks and whites in the city
jail and the city hospital. Blacks had no library facilities
until a "colored branch" of the Houston Public Library
opened in 1913. Public swimming pools, restrooms,
and drinking fountains were also segregated. In 1928,
at the Democratic National Convention, black specta-
tors were seated in a small area in the gallery that was
fenced off by chicken wire. In 1933 city officials re-
jected plans for a new Southern Pacific Railroad station
because blacks and whites would have had to use the
same ramps to board the train.

Houston had no ordinance segregating residential
areas. Blacks who entered the city following the Civil
War tended to congregate in specific areas, gradually
leading to the emergence of fairly well-defined black
neighborhoods. While blacks continued to live in each
of the city's wards, the largest black enclaves developed in the Fourth Ward, southwest of downtown
around the old Freedmantown neighborhood; in the
Third Ward, southeast of downtown; and in the Fifth
Ward, northeast of the business district. In spite of the
existence of sizable black enclaves, the majority of
the population of each of these wards remained white.
As late as the early 1920s, blacks lived in several distinctive neighborhoods within these wards but constituted no more than about 30 percent of the total population of each.

Table 1
Black Population in Houston, 1850–1980

	Total Population	Black Population	Percentage Black
1850	2,396	533	22.2
1860	4,845	1,077	22.2
1870	9,382	3,691	39.3
1880	16,513	6,479	39.2
1890	27,557	10,379	37.7
1900	44,633	14,608	32.7
1910	78,800	23,929	30.4
1920	138,276	33,960	24.6
1930	292,352	63,337	21.7
1940	384,514	86,302	22.4
1950	596,163	125,400	21.0
1960	938,219	215,037	22.9
1970	1,232,802	316,551	25.7
1980	1,594,086	440,257	27.6

Source: United States Census data

The influx of blacks that began with emancipation
continued unabated in the years that followed. Black
population increased from 3,691 in 1870, to 10,379 in
1910, and 86,320 in 1940. Most of the blacks who
moved to Houston during this period came from
nearby rural areas in Texas and Louisiana, and they
usually moved to Houston to attend high school or to
get a job. When they arrived, they often lived for a time
with relatives or friends and relied on these contacts
to help them find jobs and adjust to life in the city.
Even though Houston was growing rapidly, the family
ties that stretched from city to country and the fact that
blacks were not concentrated in a single ghetto meant
that black neighborhoods retained many of the qualities of small towns well into the twentieth century.
Many blacks recalled the small-town atmosphere of
black neighborhoods in the three wards as late as the
1930s and early 1940s. Also, despite the prevalence of
segregation, a few white families still lived in black
areas. Most blacks remembered one or two white
families who lived nearby. Since residential segregation was a matter of custom rather than law, there was

never absolute separation of the races. Usually the whites who lived in these areas were either poor or immigrants or had a business in the neighborhood. Many Germans, Jews, Greeks, and Italians owned shops in these older neighborhoods and often lived next door to or above their stores.

As the black population of the city grew, new enclaves developed in the wards and beyond their boundaries. For example, Independence Heights, initially a separate black-governed suburb northwest of the city, was annexed in 1927. Even more interesting was Frenchtown, a Fifth Ward neighborhood of approximately five hundred Louisiana blacks of French descent who imported their Creole culture in the early 1920s. The blacks of Frenchtown were French-speaking Catholics, and most worked as skilled or semiskilled labor for the Southern Pacific Railroad. With their distinctive language, religion, cuisine, and music, they maintained their cultural integrity within the black community. Finally, as the black population expanded in the 1920s, realtors developed subdivisions that offered the black middle class homes comparable to those being built for whites at this time. These black subdivisions were generally built on the fringes of existing black enclaves but offered sidewalks, paved streets, and other amenities not usually found in older black neighborhoods.

Most blacks during this period occupied poor housing in a neighborhood that received less than its share of city services. While a significant number of blacks owned their homes (the percentage rose from 20.1 percent in 1910 to 31.4 percent in 1930, before the depression reduced the number to 21.7 percent in 1940), and while many of these homes were substantial dwellings, the typical black family lived in substandard housing. For example, as late as 1940, 23.3 percent of black-occupied housing units did not have running water, while only 5.3 percent of nonblack units lacked this convenience. Black dwellings were also more crowded. According to 1940 census data, 30.6 percent of black-occupied housing units contained more than one person per room, but only 19.7 percent of nonblack homes were this crowded. Black neighborhoods often did not have paved streets, street

lights, or sidewalks, and typically they suffered from poor drainage that regularly made thrm inaccessible after heavy rains.

Efforts to improve the quality of black neighborhoods were only partly successful. Some work was done on a volunteer basis. Black newspapers urged their readers to clean up their yards, and they exposed residents who were particularly negligent in this duty. The desire to receive improved city services led to the formation of the first black community and civic associations. These organizations avoided confrontation but worked with some success through personal contacts within the city's power structure. While some improvements occurred in the 1920s, especially in the area of street repair, on the whole black neighborhoods continued to suffer from a lack of basic city services.

The most dramatic change in housing came in the late 1930s and early 1940s when the city established the Houston Housing Authority in order to participate in the development of federally funded low-income housing projects. Initial black fears that the city would overlook their housing needs were unfounded. In fact, the housing authority targeted the first two Houston projects, Cuney Homes in the Third Ward and Kelly Courts in the Fifth Ward, for blacks. By 1945 the city had provided low-income housing for 3,868 black Houstonians. While the black community benefitted from these two projects, they suffered from other actions of the housing authority. In 1938 the city announced plans to clear a large section of the Fourth Ward north of Dallas Street to construct San Felipe Courts, a 1,000-unit housing project for low-income whites. In spite of protests to both city hall and the federal government that this project would dislocate hundreds of poor blacks from one the of the city's first black neighborhoods and destroy many of the black community's oldest churches, schools, and other institutions, the government went ahead with its plans.

Blacks not only faced inferior housing in Houston, but throughout the period of segregation they also held the poorest jobs in the community. In 1880, for example, 84 percent of the city's black workers were employed as domestic, unskilled, or semiskilled labor,

Table 2
Houston's Black Population by Ward, 1870–1910

Ward	Total Population	Black Population	Percentage Black	Percentage of Total Black Population
		1870		
1	738	250	33.9	6.8
2	1,638	474	28.9	12.8
3	2,812	1,075	38.2	29.1
4	3,055	1,314	43.0	35.6
5	1,139	578	50.7	15.7
Total	9,382	3,691		
		1890		
1	1,980	777	39.2	7.5
2	3,341	1,261	37.8	12.2
3	7,366	2,661	36.1	25.6
4	8,761	3,682	42.0	35.5
5	6,109	1,997	32.7	19.2
Total	27,557	10,379		
		1910		
1	6,954	1,390	20.0	5.8
2	7,572	2,335	30.8	9.8
3	24,705	7,662	31.0	32.0
4	16,772	6,366	38.0	26.6
5	16,854	4,967	29.5	20.8
6	5,943	1,209	20.3	5.1
Total	78,800	23,929		

while only 9.1 percent held skilled jobs and only 1 percent were professionals. Most of those classified as skilled laborers at that time were bakers and other service workers. In the decades after the Civil War, only a few blacks successfully engaged in trades like carpentry or blacksmithing. Also, the vast majority of women and children who worked in Houston in 1880 were black. In general, during the late nineteenth century black Houstonians faced job conditions that were significantly worse than those faced by the average white. When blacks could enter the skilled trades, they usually received lower wages and performed work that was physically more demanding than that of white workers. Also, black women and children entered the work force more often than their white counterparts, although this situation improved somewhat near the end of the century.

The job situation for blacks did not change substantially during the next sixty years. In 1940, 75.1 percent of black workers in the city still worked in the three lowest job categories (domestic, service worker, and common laborer), and only 2.9 percent were classified as professional or semiprofessional workers. In contrast, 10 percent of white workers were professionals, while only 14.4 percent fell into the three lowest job categories. Although relatively few black children worked in 1940, black women still outnumbered white women in the work force. In that year 53.7 percent of the black women worked, but only 29.2 percent of the white women did. While the strength of Houston's economy during this period provided a sufficient number of jobs for blacks and whites, during periods of economic distress blacks suffered more than whites. In 1940, for example, 11 percent of the black work force was unemployed, compared with only 7.1 percent of white workers.

A major factor that contributed to the low status of black Houstonians was the relationship between black workers and local unions. As we have seen, even before the Civil War unions attempted to prevent the employment of blacks in skilled jobs. After emancipation this hostile relationship between black and white labor persisted, and early unions were segregated. In the early 1870s local blacks helped organize the Texas branch of the National Labor Union (Colored), and for two years this union operated in the city. The most significant union in the 1880s, the Knights of Labor, theoretically opened its doors to workers of all races; but in Houston blacks could participate only in separate assemblies. By 1885 two black assemblies existed in the city. There was very little contact between black and white members of the Knights of Labor; all social functions, picnics, and even Labor Day celebrations were segregated.

In the 1890s, trade unions had replaced the defunct Knights of Labor as the principal voice for labor in the city. Blacks played only a minor role in the trade union movement because most blacks were unskilled workers, while the few who were skilled were excluded from membership. The American Federation of Labor finally set up segregated trade unions for blacks shortly after the turn of the century. Generally, the black labor movement in Houston was weak and isolated, receiving little assistance or sympathy from white unions. A major exception to this situation existed on the city docks. Ever since the Civil War, black dockworkers had been a major force on the wharves of both Houston and Galveston, largely because of the influence of Norris Wright Cuney, the prominent black Republican who served for a time as port collector in Galveston, and his associate, Richard Allen, who served for a time as port collector in Houston. When the Houston ship channel opened in 1914, black and white longshoremen organized separate unions and split the work on a fifty-fifty basis.

Not all blacks held unskilled or semiskilled jobs. There were black businessmen and professionals in the city, although their numbers were relatively small. To a large degree these blacks benefitted from the racial situation in the city, because their businesses served the black communities that emerged out of segregation. Most black professionals were ministers and teachers; a 1915 survey identified only seven black attorneys, eight physicians, five druggists, and two dentists. These professionals, plus the ministers and teachers, served an exclusively black clientele. Of the nearly 400 black establishments listed in 1915, most were barbershops, groceries and meat markets, restaurants and cafes, and delivery services. By the turn of the century, blacks in Houston could obtain most items and services within their communities. Most of the establishments that operated there, however, were small, principally because black businessmen lacked sufficient capital or credit to expand, and because they faced stiff competition from white businesses that operated both in black neighborhoods and downtown. Some black entrepreneurs nevertheless became quite prosperous. J. H. Harmon, for example, opened a thriving dry goods store in the city in 1903. Five years later, the Reverend N. P. Pullum spoke of his business successes at the convention of the National Negro Business League in Baltimore. Pullum noted how he had used his income as a minister to finance a brickyard, a shoe store, and two drug stores.

In the mid-1920s several community leaders attempted to promote black business in the city. Clifton F.

During the nineteenth and early twentieth centuries many blacks who lived in the Houston area worked as agricultural laborers on farms outside of the city. The workers in this photograph are loading potatoes on wagons for shipment to market. Photograph from the Bank of the Southwest/Frank J. Schlueter Collection, Houston Public Library Metropolitan Research Center.

Richardson, publisher of the black weekly newspaper called the *Houston Informer,* took the lead in these efforts. Richardson urged his readers to patronize black-owned establishments; in 1923 he established the first of several businessmen's organizations, each of which enjoyed a brief flurry of success before fading from the scene. Even the Houston Negro Chamber of Commerce, chartered amid great fanfare in the mid-1930s, had little real impact on the growth of black business and eventually became essentially a social organization. On the whole, black-owned businesses and black business leadership have not had a major impact in Houston, dominated as they have been by service establishments oriented toward the black community. In 1929, for example, 71.8 percent of black businesses were either dining establishments or food markets; and even in these areas, black businessmen faced competition within their neighborhoods. Greeks, Italians, Germans, Jews, and Chinese operated similar establishments in the black enclaves. Also, a large number of the people preferred to patronize white businesses, where they believed that they received better products, service, and prices. Only businesses that offered services specifically oriented

Black dock workers have worked at the turning basin since the day it opened. Photograph from the Bank of the Southwest/Frank J. Schlueter Collection, Houston Public Library Metropolitan Research Center.

toward black needs—barber shops, beauty salons, photographers, and funeral homes—encountered little outside competition. Despite these shortcomings, Houston's black businesses compared very favorably with those in other American cities. In 1929 Houston's black population was the thirteenth largest in the nation, but it ranked tenth in the number of black-owned businesses, and seventh in average amount of sales per black business.

The Development of Black Institutions

During the period of segregation, black churches and black schools were the most significant and influential institutions in the black community. Almost every black Houstonian was an active member of a black church during the period before World War II. Divisions between churches usually reflected divisions in the black community. The largest black denominations in Houston were Baptists and Methodists, although there were a significant number of Catholics, especially in the Fifth Ward, and a large number of small evangelical congregations and storefront churches. Antioch Baptist remained the most prestigious black church. In the 1920s, under the leadership of the Reverend Earl L. Harrison, Antioch purchased a site at West Dallas and Frederick Streets in the Fourth Ward and planned the construction of a new building at a cost of more than $250,000. However, financial difficulties prevented ground from ever being broken for this project. Instead the original building on Robin Street, renovated and with a new facade, continues to serve the congregation. Another prominent Baptist church was St. John Baptist Church on Dowling Street, which in 1941 boasted the largest congregation in the city. By the early 1930s, the 180 Baptist congregations claimed 80 percent of black Houstonians as their members. Several divisions of the Methodist church operated in Houston's black communities as well. The oldest black church in the city, Trinity Methodist Episcopal, continued to exert a significant influence in the city. In addition to Methodist Episcopals, the city contained active congregations of African Methodist Episcopals and Christian Methodist Episcopals. The first black Catholic church, St. Nicholas, was organized in the Fifth Ward in the 1880s. By 1945 St. Nicholas had approximately 3,000 members, while a second black Catholic church, Our Mother of Mercy, located near Frenchtown, had 800 parishioners. Both Catholic and Protestant churches were social and civic centers as well as houses of worship, and black ministers provided much of the leadership for the community.

During this period the fraternal orders, mutual aid societies, and social and civic clubs that emerged in the late nineteenth century continued to play an important role in the community. The most visible were the fraternal lodges, which demonstrated their strength by erecting imposing structures during the 1920s. The most prominent lodge, the Grand United Order of Odd Fellows, established in 1881, occupied the most impressive lodge building. By the late 1920s there were so many active lodges in the city that the *Houston Informer* called Houston the black fraternal headquarters of Texas. In addition to the social functions that they sponsored, these fraternal orders provided their members with death and burial benefits—

often the only insurance that many blacks possessed. Mutual aid societies provided similar services; but these organizations were usually not as financially secure as the fraternal lodges, and consequently they did not have a very good survival rate. However, during the depression, many of the fraternal lodges discovered that they had placed too many of their resources in their buildings. Several were unable to meet their obligations. Most of the social clubs focused their energies on entertainment and recreational activities, although several also funded scholarships. The civic associations, on the other hand, were interested principally in upgrading black neighborhoods, particularly by obtaining more city services for these areas.

Next to churches, schools were the most important institutions in the black community. From its inception the Houston Independent School District was segregated, and as early as 1871 a separate facility existed for black children in each ward. Throughout the period of segregation black schools suffered from overcrowding and inadequate funding. In the 1880s, for example, black male teachers were paid only 58 percent as much as white male teachers; and in 1918 the state provided $9.06 for the education of each white student, but only $6.90 for each black. By the early 1920s most black schools were in dilapidated condition and were severely overcrowded. Because of poor drainage, the Gregory Institute sat in a lake every time it rained; and in 1923 Colored High School had only five hundred seats for an enrollment of more than a thousand students.

Although inequality in educational facilities continued to exist, blacks did benefit from a massive program of school construction in the city during the mid-1920s. In 1921 there were sixteen black elementary schools and one black high school; by 1940 the number had increased by twenty-four elementary schools, three junior high schools, and three high schools. In addition to the construction of new schools, many older black schools received new buildings. The most significant development in black education occurred in 1927, when the school district established Houston Colored Junior College. This institution grew out of extension classes begun in the city by Wiley Col-

Houston College was a black institution founded in 1885 by the Baptist Missionary and Educational Association of Texas. It offered high-school and some college-level courses at its campus on West Dallas Street in the Fourth Ward. This 1914 photograph shows the school's football team with campus buildings in the background. That year the school had 109 students and 9 faculty members. Photograph from the Bank of the Southwest/Frank J. Schlueter Collection, Houston Public Library Metropolitan Research Center.

lege of Marshall, Texas, in 1925 for the purpose of certifying and upgrading the quality of black school teachers. In 1934 the institution became a four-year college, and in 1947 it became a state university, Texas Southern University.

The segregation of various kinds of facilities led to the development of a self-contained black community in Houston. Most blacks responded to segregation by turning inward, relying on their own families and communities, creating their own institutions, and avoiding, as much as possible, contact with the outside (white) world. Blacks in Houston had their own schools, newspapers, parks, baseball teams, and amusement facilities. There were black restaurants, saloons, theaters,

and movie houses. Blacks celebrated their own holiday, Juneteenth; and around the turn of the century they established their own fall festival, De-Ro-Loc, a black version of the historic No-Tsu-Oh Carnival. (*No-Tsu-Oh* is *Houston* spelled backward.) In one sense segregation stimulated the black community. Many black businesses existed primarily to serve the black population; segregated schools provided employment for black teachers and administrators. The price of segregation, however, was very high. Blacks often lived in inferior housing and worked at low-paying jobs; black schools were poorly funded, and black neighborhoods did not receive their share of city services.

The price of segregation must be measured in more

The Fourth Ward, one of the oldest black neighborhoods in the city and once the economic and cultural center of black Houston, today faces an uncertain future as developers and investors eye its proximity to downtown. Photograph by the author.

than just economic terms. For most blacks, it was a humiliating experience. Custom dictated that blacks address whites with respect and enter many white-owned homes and businesses only through the rear door. In some stores blacks could obtain services only by remaining in a separate section of the shop, and only after all white customers had been waited on. In most dress shops, black women were not allowed to try on clothing; if they were interested in purchasing a hat, a white woman had to model it for them. If white movie theaters admitted blacks at all, it was through the side door; there was either a special showing, or else blacks had to be seated in a special section of the balcony. Blacks were also subjected to verbal and oc-

casionally physical abuse, especially if whites judged their demeanor to be "out of line." Newspapers often referred to blacks in insulting terms, and whites usually addressed blacks as "boy," "uncle," or "Sal." Perhaps the most destructive aspect of segregation was the feeling, voiced by a black mother, that her children were cut off from most of the world, and that they would never have the opportunities and experiences for growth that were available to white children. Nevertheless, by the early twentieth century segregation was so well entrenched that most blacks chose not to confront it and knew nothing else; some even seemed to endorse it. In 1915 the editors of the *Red Book of Houston*, a black publication describing the

Texas Southern University, founded in 1947, today serves approximately nine thousand students. Its location in Houston's Third Ward has helped make that neighborhood the center of black culture in the city. Photograph by the author.

leaders and institutions of the black community, advised their readers, "A worthy man in his race, whatever it is, loses that worthiness when he attempts to obliterate social and racial barriers imposed by a benevolent Jehovah. He must stay in his own to prove the worthiness of his life."

The Struggle Against Segregation

Not all blacks quietly accepted this denial of their civil rights. Many protested various aspects of segregation, sometimes subtly, sometimes directly. Much of this protest was focused on the effort to regain political

rights. In the years following Reconstruction, local blacks continued to play an active, although diminishing, role in the Republican Party. For example, between 1876 and 1912, three black Houstonians—Richard Allen, John M. Adkins, and M. H. Broyles—served as delegates to the National Republican Convention. Allen also served on the Rules Committee at the 1876 and 1884 conventions. However, by 1908 the conservative, "lily-white" faction had gained control of the Republican Party in Texas and eliminated blacks from positions of influence in the state Republican organization.

Unlike the southern states, Texas never completely prohibited blacks from voting. However, the implementation of the white primary on the local and state levels severely restricted the political impact of blacks. Although they could and often did vote in general elections, their exclusion from the primary in a one-party state effectively negated their political power. In the 1920s, when these restrictions were completely in place, blacks in Houston devoted much of their energy and resources to the struggle against the white primary. In January 1921 the City Democratic Executive Committee of Houston passed a resolution expressly prohibiting blacks from voting in the next primary election. C. F. Richardson, editor of the *Informer,* condemned the decision as a direct violation of constitutional rights, while C. V. Love, editor of the *Texas Freeman,* and a group of local black leaders filed suit against the chairman of the Harris County Democratic Party. This suit was the first step in a legal battle that would last almost a quarter of a century and that would involve the city's black newspapers, much of its black legal talent, and many of its black civic leaders. Many black Houstonians blamed their early setbacks on the failure of the national office of the National Association for the Advancement of Colored People (NAACP) to cooperate with local black leaders in pursuing these cases to the level of the Supreme Court. In 1940, however, after raising sufficient funds from local branches of the NAACP and obtaining the full cooperation of the national office (including the services of attorney Thurgood Marshall), Houston blacks launched their final assault on the white primary. On November 15 Marshall filed suit in federal court on behalf of Dr. Lonnie Smith, a local dentist and NAACP member, against the election judges in the Fifth Ward Precinct where Dr. Smith had tried to vote without success. On April 3, 1944, the Supreme Court ruled in the case of *Smith* v. *Allwright* that any effort to exclude blacks from voting in a primary election was a violation of the Fifteenth Amendment of the United States Constitution. That summer, for the first time in many years, black Houstonians went to the polls and voted in a primary election without experiencing any major problems.

The victory in *Smith* v. *Allwright* did not bring about an immediate change in black political behavior. Sev-

eral blacks were elected as precinct judges in those areas that had a predominately black population; but for the next twenty years, blacks would win election to major posts only on rare occasions. Between 1948 and 1965, blacks competed in eighteen races but won only three. The first black in the twentieth century to be elected to a major position was Hattie Mae White, elected to the school board in 1958. For the most part, however, blacks did not take advantage of the right to vote; for many years, the majority of blacks in the city remained politically apathetic. Only a few middle- and upper-class blacks paid the poll tax and registered to vote. It would not be until the mid-1960s that black voting strength was sufficient to elect black candidates or affect the election of whites.

Two developments increased black political influence in Houston in the post–World War II period. First, the NAACP conducted a series of voter registration drives in an effort to increase black voting in the city. The most successful of these drives, following the 1965 Voting Rights Act and the division of the state into single-member legislative districts, achieved measurable results. The following year Barbara Jordan was elected to the Texas Senate and Curtis Graves won a seat in the state House of Representatives. By the mid-1970s five black Houstonians were serving in the state legislature, one was serving in the United States Congress, and a large number held other elected and appointed positions in local government. In 1971 Judson Robinson became the first black in almost one hundred years to be elected to the Houston City Council.

The second development that increased black political influence in Houston was the creation of several black political pressure groups. The first of these, the Harris County Council of Organizations (HCCO), was formed in 1949 to conduct voter-registration drives and voter-education programs. It achieved its greatest success through a candidate-endorsement program. As black voting strength grew, more and more candidates, both black and white, sought the endorsement of the HCCO and of similar black political organizations. By the mid-1970s the endorsement of these organizations would become a means of winning the

Black construction workers have been active in Houston since the days of slavery. Photograph from the Bank of the Southwest/Frank J. Schlueter Collection, Houston Public Library Metropolitan Research Center.

black vote, a factor that would often determine the outcome of city-wide elections.

During the 1920s and 1930s, Houston blacks also attempted to mitigate some of the effects of educational segregation. Community leaders focused their efforts on the discrepancies in teacher salaries. While black teachers and administrators were usually reluctant to complain about their pay, as early as 1919 the black press and several prominent blacks protested the wage scale that paid black teachers only about 60 percent as much as whites, even though they taught the same curricula and performed the same duties. During the 1930s the *Houston Informer,* the local chapter of the NAACP, and the Houston Negro Chamber of Commerce tried unsuccessfully to correct this inequity. No effective change occurred until the early 1940s, when a group of elementary school teachers finally joined in the demand for salary equalization. In 1943 the school board, threatened with a law suit that they did not think they could win, gave in to the black teachers' demands and raised their salaries to the level of their white counterparts.

Most blacks avoided confrontation during this period of segregation, but this was not always possible. One continuing problem was the relationship between the black community and the police. Blacks in the city complained that they faced regular harassment and verbal abuse from policemen, and that occasionally they were the victims of physical brutality. Black newspapers frequently publicized these incidents and

Table 3
Major Occupational Divisions Among Blacks
and Whites in Houston, 1940

Occupational Category	Number of Blacks	Percentage of Blacks	Number of Whites	Percentage of Whites
Professional and semiprofessional workers	1,178	2.9	12,097	10.0
Proprietors, managers, and officials	756	1.8	16,519	13.7
Clerical, sales, and kindred workers	855	2.1	37,650	31.2
Skilled and semiskilled workers	7,403	18.1	37,062	30.7
Domestic, service, and unskilled workers	30,698	75.1	17,389	14.4
Total	40,890		120,717	

blamed them on the caliber of men hired for the city's police force. In 1938 the *Houston Informer* charged that the police force consisted mainly of "ex-convicts, discarded police officers from other towns, rough-necks, and a few earnest men, green and untrained in the duties of a police." Black leaders hoped to combat police brutality by pushing for the prosecution of guilty officers and by adding black officers to the force to patrol black neighborhoods.

Police brutality was related to the worst example of racial violence in the city's history: the 1917 riots. Trouble began when northern black soldiers stationed at Camp Logan, just west of downtown Houston where Memorial Park is today, encountered the local segregation. Tensions increased for several weeks. The riot occurred when rumors circulated that a Houston policeman had killed a black soldier in the Fourth Ward. Although this rumor was false, the reputation of the city's police force made it believable. Approximately one hundred armed black soldiers marched into the city seeking vengeance. Before the army restored order, thirty-five whites, four blacks, and one Mexican-American lost their lives. In the series of court martials that followed, nineteen black soldiers were executed, and sixty-three were sentenced to life in prison. Although no black Houstonians were involved in the riot, they were affected by it. Shortly after the riot, Houston police conducted a house-to-house search of

black neighborhoods and temporarily confiscated all firearms owned by blacks.

The racial tensions generated by the riot continued into the early 1920s and contributed to a revival of the Ku Klux Klan in the city. In March 1921 a Klan mob brutalized a black dentist, and four years later they tarred and feathered a local black doctor. The Klan also threatened outspoken black leaders who criticized their actions, including *Houston Informer* editor C. F. Richardson. In June 1928, several years after Klan influence had diminished, Houston recorded its only documented lynching. The victim was Robert Powell, who had killed a white policeman in a Fourth Ward shootout. A white mob took Powell from Jefferson Davis Hospital, where he was recovering from wounds, and hanged him from a bridge that crossed a gulley on Post Oak Road. Both black and white Houstonians expressed shock and outrage over this incident. The city appropriated funds for an investigation, while the governor and several groups of citizens offered rewards for the apprehension of the guilty parties. Although the county ultimately indicted seven men for the crime, only two came to trial, and they were acquitted. In spite of events such as these, Houston was relatively free of racial violence during the period of segregation. Even the outspoken *Houston Informer* observed in 1930 that blacks were fortunate to live in a city like Houston where "the mob spirit" was not rampant.

Antioch Baptist Church, one of Houston's oldest and most important black churches, sits today surrounded by the office buildings that have already replaced the homes and businesses in the eastern half of the city's old Fourth Ward. Antioch Baptist was founded shortly after the Civil War, in 1866. It moved into its present home on Robin Street in 1879. Photograph by the author.

The Black Community Today

The two most significant developments that have occurred in the black community during the past thirty years are the breakdown of segregation and the rapid growth of the black population. Desegregation in Houston began in 1950, when five blacks filed suit to gain access to the municipal golf course. Three years later the public library integrated its facilities, and in 1954 segregation on city buses was abolished. School desegregation took much longer. Following the 1954 Supreme Court ruling, several blacks tried, without success, to register at all-white schools. In December 1956 the NAACP backed a law suit by Dolores Ross and Beneva Williams to end school segregation. Endless delays by the conservative school board finally prompted Federal District Judge Ben C. Connally to order the desegregation of all first grades in September 1960, and then to proceed at the rate of one grade per year. However, the school board placed such severe restrictions on transfer eligibility that only twelve black students met the requirements to attend white schools. This and similar delaying tactics caused the federal courts to intervene again, and in 1966 all schools were ordered to desegregate. While no schools are totally segregated today, most black students attend predominately black schools. Nevertheless, in 1980 the Houston Independent School District was found to have complied substantially with the desegregation order. Most black parents are more concerned about the quality of the education that their children receive today than about continuing pockets of segregation.

The desegregation of restaurants, lunch counters, and other public facilities began in the spring of 1960, when students from Texas Southern University staged the first sit-in demonstration in the state at the lunch counter of the Weingarten's grocery store in the Third Ward. Within a few days, the sit-in movement had spread to downtown lunch counters and to the City Hall cafeteria. Officials at Foley's department store, anxious to avoid the negative publicity that civil-rights demonstrations were bringing to other southern cities, convinced other Houston store managers to cooperate with black organizations so that downtown dining facilities could be desegregated as quietly as possible. Consequently some racial barriers began to disappear as city leaders adjusted to new realities. By 1963, city and county parks, beaches, and swimming pools were integrated. The only violence during this period occurred in two confrontations on the Texas Southern University campus in 1965 and 1967 as students clashed with police. The second incident, the more serious of the two, ended when police opened fire on a dormitory and then arrested 488 students. One policeman died in the disturbance (some think from a ricocheting police bullet), and students accused the police of wrecking the dormitory and destroying personal property. However, most changes came peacefully, and by the early 1970s most of the old barriers of segregation no longer existed. While not all traces of discrimination have disappeared, those that remain are more subtle and more likely to be based on economics rather than race.

Equally dramatic was the growth in the black population. Between 1940 and 1980 the number of blacks in the city grew from 86,302 to 440,257, an increase of more than five hundred percent. The need to absorb this growth had a tremendous impact on the black community. The most visible change has been the expansion of black neighborhoods. While the traditional enclaves in the Third, Fourth, and Fifth Wards absorbed some of the newcomers, most of the growth occurred outside of these neighborhoods. New black subdivisions opened northeast, east, and southeast of Houston, while blacks from the Third Ward spread south into the previously all-white Riverside area. Also, in the 1970s residential segregation began to break down as some blacks moved into racially mixed neighborhoods and apartment complexes, especially in the west and southwest sections of the city. Housing desegregation was facilitated by a fair-housing ordinance that outlawed discrimination in the sale or rental of housing. In spite of these changes, in 1970 almost 10 percent of the city's census tracts were more than 90 percent black, and in the mid-1970s three-fourths of the black population still lived in areas that were at least 70 percent black.

Some blacks expressed concern that residential desegregation would weaken the traditional black neigh-

Table 4
Comparison of Black Neighborhoods, 1970 and 1980

Neighborhoods	Total Black Population	Percentage of Population that is Black	Percentage of Blacks who are High-School Graduates	Median Income of Black Families	Percentage of Black Families Below the Poverty Level	Percentage of Black Homes that are Owner-Occupied
			1970			
Third Ward	46,777	91.1	39.0	$ 5,637	27.4	20.2
Fourth Ward	6,347	69.4	15.0	3,385	50.7	3.5
Fifth Ward	33,656	69.6	24.8	4,859	36.1	23.5
Sunnyside; Scottcrest	27,204	97.2	37.4	7,409	17.7	73.4
Southpark; MacGregor	48,687	66.1	44.6	7,603	18.0	68.4
Pleasantville	10,619	88.6	32.9	8,086	16.6	72.3
Total: Wards	88,780	79.8	31.7	5,172	32.5	20.3
Total: New Neighborhoods	86,510	76.1	40.7	7,601	17.7	70.5
Total: Entire Population of City	316,551	25.7	51.8	9,876	10.7	48.4
			1980			
Third Ward	34,652	92.7	48.1	$11,566	29.6	23.2
Fourth Ward	4,361	63.4	29.2	6,350	48.6	5.0
Fifth Ward	23,957	73.9	37.1	9,126	36.9	27.2
Sunnyside; Scottcrest	25,033	96.9	49.7	16,542	19.5	70.4
Southpark; MacGregor	71,391	94.2	59.0	16,190	17.6	59.3
Pleasantville	7,536	86.7	45.1	19,838	11.2	76.8
Total: Wards	62,970	82.1	42.6	10,307	33.7	23.5
Total: New Neighborhoods	103,960	94.3	55.4	16,549	17.6	63.4
Total: Entire Population of City	440,257	27.6	68.3	21,817	10.1	48.0

The Julia C. Hester House was founded in 1943 as a settlement house and community center to serve the growing black population in Houston's Fifth Ward. Hester House continues to offer a variety of programs for its clients. This photograph, taken in the summer of 1983, shows a quilt-making group. When completed, the quilts are auctioned off to raise money for other senior citizens' activities. Photograph by the author.

borhoods by draining away middle- and upper-class blacks. In other words, all who could afford to move from the older areas would do so, leaving behind only the poorest members of the neighborhoods. There has been a tendency for this to happen, especially among younger blacks, and especially in the Fourth and Fifth Wards. Desegregation has also had a negative impact on many black businesses; more and more blacks patronize businesses outside of their immediate neighborhoods. The self-contained black communities with their small-town atmosphere that were common fifty years ago no longer exist.

A major effect of these changing residential patterns was to alter the traditional geographical alignment of black Houston. Until the mid-1930s, the Fourth Ward was the economic center of black Houston. West Dallas and nearby streets were the home of more than 95 percent of the city's black-owned businesses. By the early 1950s the Fifth Ward had gained the largest share of the black population in Houston, and Lyons Avenue and Jensen Drive had replaced West Dallas as the main streets of black enterprise. The Fifth Ward's dominance did not last long, however. The city's rapid population growth led to the development of new, more attractive black neighborhoods, especially in the southern parts of town. In the meantime, black businesses lost an increasing number of their customers to their white-owned competitors.

The Third Ward, on the other hand, prospered during this period. By the mid-1960s, although the three inner-city wards no longer contained the bulk of Houston's black population, the Third Ward had supplanted the Fifth Ward as the center of black business in the city. Even though only about 7 percent of the city's blacks lived in the Third Ward in 1970, almost 10 percent of the black-owned businesses were concentrated in the four census tracts that made up that neighborhood. More significantly, the Third Ward was the home of Riverside National Bank, Houston's largest and oldest black bank, as well as Standard Savings Association, the state's only black-owned savings and loan association, and the Houston Citizens Chamber of Commerce, the principal black business organization in the city.

During the last thirty years, the Third Ward has also become the cultural center of black Houston. To a large degree the Third Ward's preeminence as a cultural center was based on the emergence of Texas Southern University as a major educational institution. The original mission of the university was to provide black Texans with "educational opportunities equal to and comparable with those offered by other [state-supported] institutions." As higher education in Texas became desegregated, TSU's focus shifted to the problems and issues that confronted the urban environment and inner-city residents. Today, with an enrollment of nearly 9,000 students, Texas Southern is the third largest "historically black" university in the United States. Although it no longer serves an exclusively black clientele, Texas Southern has remained a predominantly black institution and a center of black education. In addition, with its FM radio station, library, art gallery, and active programs of music, art, and theater, it is a center for black culture in Houston. Furthermore, the presence of Texas Southern in the heart of the Third Ward has stimulated cultural development in the surrounding area: today the Third Ward is the home of the city's two leading black newspapers, its black-owned radio stations, and black theater, art galleries, and bookstores.

While the Third Ward has emerged as the center of black business and culture in Houston, the overall impact of changing residential patterns on the older neighborhoods has been negative. Even though the black population grew by more than 120,000 during the 1970s, the number of black residents in the wards declined slightly. In addition, the more affluent elements in the black community have tended to move out of the wards. As a result, by 1970 residents of the older black areas were generally more poorly educated, had lower incomes, were more likely to fall below the poverty level, and were less likely to own their own homes than were the residents of the newer black neighborhoods. These trends accelerated between 1970 and 1980. Furthermore, if the relatively prosperous and well-educated neighborhoods near Texas Southern University are eliminated, the differences between these older and newer black areas are even more pronounced.

The major problems that confront the black community in Houston today include poor employment and economic status, a high crime rate, and substandard health care. Although blacks do not enjoy the same economic position as whites, their status has improved significantly since the 1940s as blacks have shared in the city's economic strength. For example, black unemployment in Houston through the 1970s was about half of the national average, even though it was still higher than that of white Houstonians. Black income still lags behind white income, although the gap is narrowing. The median income of black families in the city was 54 percent of that for white families in 1950, 65 percent in 1970, and 70 percent in 1980. Improvements have also occurred in the employment status of blacks. In 1970, 10 percent of the city's blacks were classified as professionals, semiprofessionals, proprietors, or managers, while 45.9 percent of black workers were employed as domestics, service workers, or unskilled laborers. By 1980 the percentage of black professionals and managers had risen to 12.9 and the number of domestics, unskilled, and service workers had dropped to 32.4 percent. These figures represent a significant improvement over black employment status in 1940. (See Table 3.) Reflecting this, between 1940 and 1970 the proportion of black homes that were owner-occupied rose from 21.7 percent to 44.7 percent. Even with rapidly escalating housing costs and interest rates and the addition of more than 120,000 blacks to the city's population, the number of black homeowners had dropped only slightly to 43.4 percent by 1980. In spite of these gains blacks still occupy the lowest rungs of the economic ladder, and unemployment is a major problem among inner-city black youth. However, most of the middle-class blacks who responded to a 1981 survey indicated their confidence in Houston's economic vitality and agreed with the statement that people who are willing to work hard can make a good life for themselves and their families. Many did argue, though, that blacks have to work harder for success than do whites.

Most of the problems that the black community faces in the areas of crime and health care are related to its economic status. Economic pressures and a relatively high level of unemployment have contributed to high crime rates in the black community. Crime affects black Houstonians in two ways. First, blacks are more likely to be arrested, especially for serious offenses, than whites are. Although blacks constituted only 25.7 percent of the city's population in 1970, they accounted for 39.6 percent of the total number of arrests and 52.4 percent of those arrested for violent crimes (murder, rape, robbery, and assault). Second, since most crime is intraracial in nature, blacks run a higher risk than whites of being victims of crime.

Although the problem of inadequate law enforcement is a city-wide issue, it particularly affects the black community. Most black Houstonians believe that their communities are insufficiently protected by the police. Many also feel that they are more likely than whites to be victimized by the excessive use of police force. Relations between the Houston Police Department and the black community have deteriorated in recent years, due largely to the continuing perception (especially among black youth) of racial discrimination in the police department and of widespread police brutality directed toward the black community.

One of the unfortunate results of this perception is the reluctance of qualified blacks to join the police department. The appointment of a black chief of police in 1982 seems to have led to a more positive relationship between the police department and the black community. Chief Lee Brown has been fairly successful in removing the police department from the center of controversy; and most significantly, he has improved the image of the police in the black community. Reflecting this, in 1983, for the first time in over a decade, the police department was not a major issue in the mayor's election.

The level of health care available to black Houstonians is even more clearly related to economic status. Today all health-care facilities are integrated. The black health-care system that developed during the period of segregation has all but disappeared. Of the four black hospitals still operating in the city in 1970, only two, Riverside General Hospital in the Third Ward and St. Elizabeth's Hospital in the Fifth Ward, were still open in 1982. Income level has become the principal determinant of the quality of health care available to blacks. Middle- and upper-income blacks generally patronize the same hospitals as others of their economic class, while low-income blacks rely on public health-care facilities. In response to the rapid growth of the black community, the Harris County Hospital District has expanded its services in low-income black neighborhoods. In spite of this, blacks suffer from a higher rate of infant mortality and a higher general death rate than do whites. Part of the health-care problem in the black community is related to the relatively low number of black doctors and dentists practicing in the city. In Harris County today there are approximately seventy black dentists and black doctors serving a population of nearly half a million.

Blacks have assumed a more visible and active political role in the city during the last forty years. More blacks hold public office, and black voters have a greater impact on elections than at any time in the city's history. Also, black political organization has become more sophisticated in recent years. In addition to pressure groups such as the Harris County Council of Organizations and Blacks Organized for Leadership

Black cowboys and black rodeos have always been a part of the black experience in Texas. This local weekend cowboy is getting ready for the bronco-riding event. Photograph by the author.

Development, other blacks work behind the scenes to influence the appointment of blacks to administrative posts in city government. In spite of this, most blacks feel today that they still do not have an adequate voice in city government, although almost all agree that the situation has improved dramatically during the last twenty-five years. Leadership in the black community has always tended to come from professionals, especially ministers, lawyers, physicians, and newspaper editors. Businessmen, on the other hand, generally have not sought positions of leadership. A survey of black leadership in Houston in the mid-1970s identified twenty-five community leaders, thirteen of whom held elected offices. Of the total only three were businessmen, while the majority, fifteen, were professionals.

The family is the most important social institution in the lives of black Houstonians. Most blacks feel that they have a stronger attachment to their family than whites do. According to the 1980 census, the typical black family in Houston consists of two parents and children, but it is more likely than a white family to contain extended relatives—usually brothers, sisters, cousins, nieces, or nephews who have just moved to the city to study or work. Within the black family, husbands are generally viewed as the primary breadwinner, although wives often work as well. The wife is the homemaker; even if she works outside the home, she has the principal responsibility for the housework, raising the children, and handling family finances. Major decisions are usually shared by both husband and wife. Black families do not differ that much from white families, except that black women are more likely to control family finances and extended relatives are more likely to live in the household. Also, a black family is more than twice as likely to have a woman as the head of household than is a white family.[1]

What does it mean to be black in Houston? Unlike many other ethnic minorities, blacks are clearly identifiable by skin color. This visible difference makes complete assimilation virtually impossible and affects the way in which blacks are perceived by the rest of the community. To most nonblacks, skin color is the most distinguishing characteristic of blacks. Blacks, however, do not see themselves in this way. For most blacks the most important factors defining their ethnic identity are having been relegated to a second-class status in life and having been the victims of prejudice and discrimination. Blacks do not feel that they are different from other groups in the population, but they feel that they are *treated* differently. They also believe that they have to struggle to overcome barriers that nonblacks do not face. Ironically, many blacks also feel that this struggle has had positive effects. Some feel that it has strengthened blacks; others feel that it has given them a special approach to life that makes them more generous and compassionate and enables them to make the most of bad situations; still others believe that it has reinforced their ties to family and friends. Blacks stress, however, that at the core they are not different, that they are Americans like everyone else, but Americans who have endured special hardships and who have a special relationship with each other, with their community, and with their families.

1. In 1980, 32.4 percent of black families were headed by a woman, whereas only 12.5 percent of white families had a female as head.

Mexicans

Margarita B. Melville

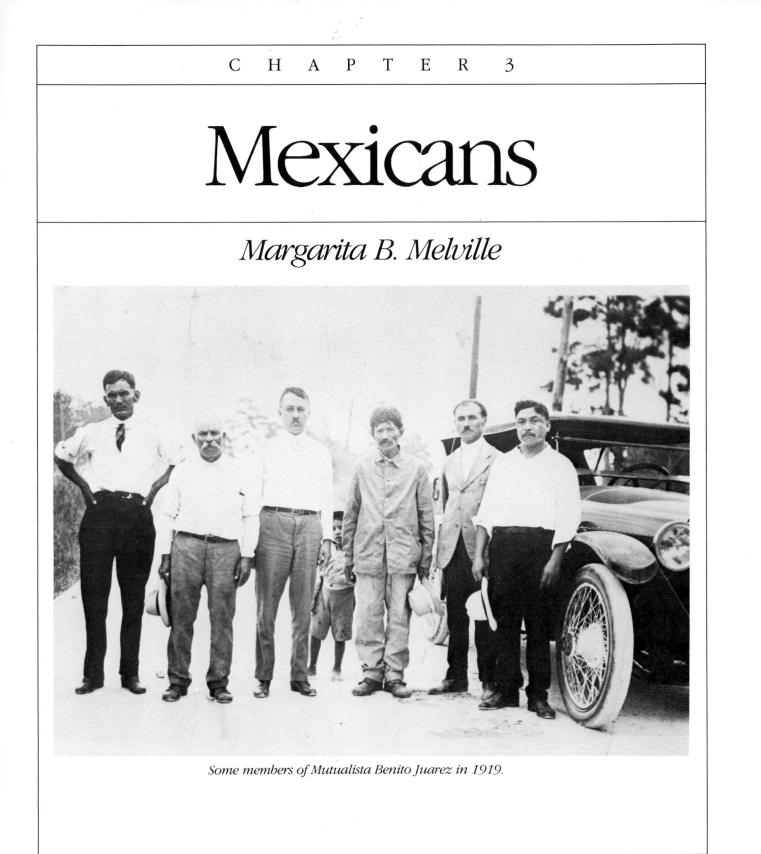

Some members of Mutualista Benito Juarez in 1919.

A clearly defined and active community of people of Mexican origin emerged in Houston in the 1910s and 1920s. Mexico was in the throes of a civil war that displaced many people: professionals, merchants, peasants, and workers. Houston was a growing young town in need of settlers who could contribute to the development of its port, its railroads, and new industries. Settlers from Mexico and Americans of Mexican descent from small Texas towns had been arriving since the 1890s, and there is even some evidence to indicate that there may have been some Mexicans who stayed behind as prisoners of war after the defeat of Santa Anna in 1836, at the birth of the Republic of Texas and the city of Houston itself. But there is no archival record of these early Mexican contributors to the first clearing and building that forged a city out of a swamp.

By 1900 approximately a thousand people of Mexican origin called Houston their home. Most of these people were Texas-born Americans of Mexican descent, but they were soon joined by friends, relatives, and newcomers from Mexico itself. A Mexican community, called a *colonia,* began to develop as people joined together to celebrate the traditional social and religious events. As they found housing close to work and to relatives and friends, they formed their *barrios,* or neighborhoods. These same barrios continue to be inhabited predominantly by Mexican-Americans today. El Crisol (now Denver Harbor) was close to the Southern Pacific railroad yards and derived its Spanish name from the pungent chemicals used to preserve railroad ties. The Second Ward extended along Buffalo Bayou from the center of town and was predominantly Mexican-American by the 1920s. Magnolia, southeast of the Second Ward, was located along the ship channel and became a Mexican-American barrio by 1915. Later the freeway system divided these barrios into several segments.

This beginning for Mexican-Americans in Houston contrasts markedly with Mexican-American communities in such Texas cities as El Paso, Nacogdoches, and San Antonio. Spanish explorers led the way for the friars who founded missions in 1659 at the base of a mountain trail pass called El Paso del Norte; Spanish explorers were also active in the eastern part of present-day Texas near Nacogdoches; and officials of the Spanish government established a community that has been in continuous existence since 1718 and is now located in downtown San Antonio. Following the missionaries came the merchants and settlers with major land grants—first from the Spanish crown and later, after Mexico's independence from Spain, from the government of Mexico. Some of the Indians were converted to Catholicism through the activities of these pioneering friars; they learned Spanish and settled near the missions, first farming the mission land and then becoming independent small landowners. There were some Mexican communities in South Texas that reached back more than fifty years before Texas gained its independence from Mexico in 1836, and Mexicans and Anglos had fought together against the government of Mexico in that war. The year 1836 is doubly significant in Houston's history, for the town was established that year as a new Anglo settlement by the Allen brothers, who had come from the northeastern seaboard of the United States with a land promotion plan.

Texas remained an independent republic for only nine years before it was annexed by the United States in December 1845. Four months later the United States declared war on Mexico. When the peace treaty was signed ending the war in 1848, the United States acquired vast territory extending from New Mexico to California that is called today—together with Texas and Oklahoma—"the Southwest." Thus, by February 2, 1848, all of the descendants of the early Mexican settlers in this southwestern land had become American citizens, and many continued to be called "Mexican-Americans."

The railroads, built in Texas after the 1850s, contributed decidedly to Houston's growth by bringing a great deal of commercial activity. Houston became a manufacturing and distribution center for Texas' cotton, timber, and oil products. Many workers were needed, and the railroad contractors found Mexican laborers to be hard, dependable workers. In 1908 at least 2,000 Mexicans were living in Houston, out of a population of approximately 75,000 people. A group of Mexican-American men gathered on March 2, 1908, to inaugurate a chapter of the Woodmen of the World, called "El Camp Laurel Lodge." Woodmen of the World was an international, mutual aid organization that offered its members fraternal companionship, recreation, and life insurance, and served as a support mechanism for Mexican-Americans in the unfamiliar surroundings of Houston. Within a few years, other mutual aid societies developed. Close by, the Rusk Settlement House (located in Houston at 2411 Canal Street) began to attend to the needs of Mexican immigrants, in addition to those of their Jewish clients. Some Mexican children attended the Rusk Elementary School, which soon became known as "the Mexican school."

The Catholic Church played an important role in those early days in organizing the social and religious activities of the Mexican-American community in Houston. The Oblate Fathers arrived in Houston in 1911 and established a modest residence in Magnolia Park, from which they extended their work into the various Mexican and Mexican-American barrios. After founding the Immaculate Conception church on Harrisburg, they proceeded to develop the parish of Our Lady of Guadalupe under very humble circumstances. The original structure was a simple frame building on Navigation, and the first Mass was celebrated there on August 18, 1912. Two years later, Father Esteban de Anta began the present structure and rectory, which was finally dedicated on September 2, 1923. Father de Anta also organized a group of catechists to help him with the work of teaching the faithful; he established sixteen catechetical centers throughout the city to instruct more than one thousand children. The Sisters of Divine Providence founded a parochial school about the same time as construction began on the new Guadalupe Church building. The impact of Our Lady of Guadalupe School cannot be overestimated in terms of the many Mexican-American and Mexican children who have been educated there.

One of the early Mexican families that made a large contribution to the development of the Mexican colonia in Houston was the Sarabia family, originally from Guanajuato, Mexico. The oldest son, Socorro, left Guanajuato at age fourteen to work for the railroads, and by 1914 he found himself in Houston. Four years later, he was a labor contractor for the Southern Pacific Railroad, making frequent trips to San Antonio, the first stop for people coming to Texas from Mexico. He is said to have brought eight trainloads of Mexican and Mexican-American laborers to Houston, each trainload containing hundreds of immigrants. In 1919 Socorro's father was killed in Mexico's revolution and his mother, three brothers, and young sister decided to join Socorro in Houston.

José Sarabia, one of Socorro's brothers, began by selling newspapers, then opened a small book and curio shop in the 400 block of Milam. In the 1920s he moved his store to a larger location at 1800 Congress. By the middle 1920s the area around Congress, Preston, Franklin, and Louisiana Streets became the hub of the Mexican-American commercial district. José Sarabia and a partner then opened the Azteca Mexican Theater, where they showed silent Mexican films and staged vaudeville shows. Dr. Angel Leyva, a medical doctor who had escaped the revolution, opened his office there, as did Dr. Estrella, a dentist. The area also embraced a Mexican drugstore, barbership, shoe-shine parlor, and restaurant. Nearby was the Farmers Market (later moved to Airline Avenue), where about one-third of the stalls were occupied by Mexican-American truck farmers from the Friendswood area selling their produce. Guadalupe Church was only a mile away on Navigation, and residents used the trolley, horses, and mules to go downtown. By 1929 Felipe Sarabia, another brother, had started his own store at 711 Preston where he sold groceries, magazines, and records to a predominantly Mexican-American clientele. Another well-known Mexican-American merchant at that time was Francisco Gabino Hernández, owner of Alamo Furniture. His huge store occupied an entire block downtown and had numerous employees and eight delivery trucks.

In Houston Heights, an area to the north of the downtown district that had a sizable Mexican-American community, the Mendozas, another family who came to Houston with the railroads, had a daughter, Lydia, born in 1916. She was later to become nationally known among people of Mexican descent as *la alondra de la frontera* (the meadowlark of the frontier), because of her deeply moving folk music. (For a more complete description of her career, see Chapter 12.)

Patricio Gutiérrez, born in San Antonio, became the first pianist of the fledgling Houston Symphony Orchestra in 1917. He had been sponsored by an Anglo group and had studied music in New York. He was the exception, however. Many Mexican-American artists such as Eloy Pérez and musical groups such as the Orchesta Típica de Magnolia performed exclusively for Mexican-American audiences. They found that the Houston colonia was very receptive to their artistic performances, so much so that music and dance halls proliferated. Their reception by the Houston Anglo community, however, was less enthusiastic. The members of the Orchesta Típica were denied rooms at a Galveston inn at one point, and the Club Mexico Bello often found that they could not rent appropriate accommodations to hold their dances.

These attitudes were decried in *La Gaceta Mexicana,* a magazine of literary essays and social news founded by José Sarabia and edited by Lorenzo Yañez in 1928. Four newspapers appeared regularly in the 1920s and circulated in the colonia, reinforcing Mexican values and ideals.

The celebration of the Fiestas Patrias stands out among the social activities of the Mexican colonia in Houston. The first recorded city-wide celebration was in 1917, when two Comités Patrioticos organized activities to commemorate Mexico's independence from Spain and to celebrate Mexican nationality. By 1925 this yearly celebration included a parade through downtown, baseball games, beauty contests, dances, and patriotic speeches about Mexican history. A dominant theme of these celebrations was the meaning of being a Mexican in the United States. Magnolia Park was one of the favorite locations for such celebrations of Mexican cultural heritage.

Cinco de Mayo (May 5) was celebrated in a less elaborate though no less enthusiastic fashion under the sponsorship of the Sociedad Benito Juárez. The Sociedad Benito Juárez was a mutual aid society that sponsored musical, social, and patriotic activities. Since its members were predominantly working class, they particularly favored this fiesta, which commemorates President Juárez's defeat of French intervention in Mexico and the promotion of Indian and working-class heritage in the 1860s. They built their own hall for social events in 1928.

The area just east of downtown Houston was known as the barrio El Crisol, and just south of this, across the railroad tracks and west of Lockwood, the barrio was called Las Lechusas, because of the abundance of night owls in a nearby wooded area. The nearest parish to these barrios was Our Lady of Guadalupe, about two miles away. Because there was no easy access to transportation, many people had to walk to church. Those who could not walk the distance did not attend church at all.

Several families from these barrios approached the Oblate Fathers at Our Lady of Guadalupe in 1934 to petition them to send a priest to help them in their spiritual needs. As a result of that meeting, a priest was sent to these areas and thus began the parish that is presently known as Our Lady of Sorrows Church on Kashmere.

During this time, the founding families sponsored several social events to raise funds for their new church. Two affiliated chapels were founded during 1939 and 1940, one at Colonia Villa (just west of the parish) and the other at Colonia Hidalgo.

Hard Times: The Depression, World War II, and the Aftermath

The depression brought increased resentment toward people of Mexican descent in the Southwest. Competition for scarce jobs and resources resulted in a search for scapegoats. The open border policy that had characterized the United States during the 1920s was later transformed by immigration restrictions, and the unskilled jobs that had formerly been open to Mexican and Mexican-American applicants disappeared. Many Mexican-American citizens were viewed and treated as unwanted outsiders. Schooling was difficult to obtain for both social and economic reasons, and few Mexican-Americans were able to finish high school. Some businessmen, however, especially restauranteurs, were able to survive by catering successfully to the Anglo population. By 1930 the people of Mexican descent in Houston had developed into three social classes: the long-time working class residents, the middle-class professionals and merchants, and the newly arrived, generally unskilled laborers. The long-time residents and their native-born children continued to work as unskilled and semiskilled laborers

Azteca Theater, 1920.

and craftsmen. The 1930 census indicates that of the 14,500 Mexican-Americans living in Houston, 568 worked in railroads, 382 in restaurant- and hotel-related businesses, 293 as laborers in road and street work, and 259 as construction laborers. In Magnolia barrio, women worked in textile plants making burlap sacks, as well as in other small industries.

Nevertheless, there was a small group of people who had come from Mexico as professionals. Others, or their children, managed to get an education after their arrival in Houston. A few graduated with civil en-

gineering degrees from the Rice Institute, now Rice University. Others became lawyers, but these were the exceptions. As one informed observer noted, "At that time, it was often the first Mexican-American doing this or the first Mexican-American being that." Others managed to parlay their entrepreneurship to achieve a comfortable and socially prominent status. The third group was composed of newly arrived people who came either from rural Texas or from Mexico. For them the work was hard, almost brutal. Even though they lived in a big city like Houston, trucks would

Ladies' English class, Rusk Settlement House, Second Ward, 1920.

come by to pick them up to work in the fields for a week or a month at a time.

As jobs became more scarce during the depression, more families faced insecurity and hardship. Job programs advertised that they were for "white" Americans only. Houston, Pasadena, and Galveston pooled their resources and formed the Tri-City Relief Association in order to create soup kitchens. When funds began to run short, Mexicans and blacks were refused assistance. A group of Second Ward residents met at Rusk Settlement House early in 1932 and formed the Club Pro-Repatriación. Their goal was to raise funds to help their more unfortunate countrymen return to Mexico. Eventually, city officials stepped in. Following federal policy, the local police rounded up and jailed Mexican aliens who did not have the proper documents, and the federal government deported hundreds of them.

The times brought a decrease in cultural events for Mexicans as well as for other groups. Members of the Sociedad Benito Juarez could not pay their dues, so in 1932 they lost the hall they had so proudly dedicated four years earlier. *La Gaceta Mexicana* had to cease

Reception of Houstonians for Miss Mexico, Brazos Hotel, 1920s. Photograph by Luis Suarez.

publication, and other newspapers came out only sporadically. The Fiestas Patrias were celebrated in a much less festive fashion. Increased ethnocentrism was reflected in the behavior of law enforcement officials. During early 1932, three incidents in which Mexicans were shot by police raised the suspicion and ire of the Mexican-American community. In one of these incidents, the individual was shot without evident provocation. Despite the participation of lawyers brought from San Antonio by the Mexican Consul in Houston and the testimony of nine eyewitnesses, the grand jury failed to indict the officers involved.

In order to counter some of the racism and to reassert themselves, a number of business and professional people founded the Latin American Club (LAC). Their choice of the term "Latin American" was inten-

tional and indicative of the need they felt for distancing themselves from the negative connotation that the name "Mexican" had in the Anglo mind. Their activities focused on incidents where the rights of people of Mexican descent were infringed upon both at work and by the police. In 1938 LAC became Council No. 60 of the League of United Latin American Citizens (LULAC). LULAC was founded in 1929 in Texas, and although it became the dominant Mexican-American organization in Houston, its members refused to use the term "Mexican" in their name. LULAC was especially influential in the 1940s and 1950s, speaking out against police brutality, pushing for better educational opportunities for Mexican-Americans, and urging them to take an active interest in the political process. In the 1950s Houston LULAC members were responsible for

Sarabia Bookstore, 1920s. Photograph by Luis Suarez.

expanding LULAC membership along the Texas Gulf Coast. A total of five Houstonians became national presidents of LULAC in the 1950s and 1960s.

Mexican-American women also became more active and visible. One particular female branch of LULAC from Council No. 22 became very important in the 1950s through its sponsorship of local grass-roots projects in Houston. Among their activities were fund raisers for clothing, meals, and scholarships for needy area children. LULAC continued to grow, especially in the 1960s, so that by the early 1980s there were seventeen LULAC councils in Houston alone.

One of the most obvious signs that the Houston Mexican-American community had come of age in the post–World War II period was the opening of radio station KLVL in 1950, the first Spanish-language radio

station in the Houston area. It was owned and operated by Mexican-Americans, a "first" for Houston. "La Voz Latina" became the broadcasting voice of the Houston Mexican-American community. The founders of KLVL, Felix and Angelina Morales, had come to Houston in the early 1930s from San Antonio. They first opened the Morales Funeral Home on Canal Street in the Second Ward, and by the late 1940s it had become a community landmark. After World War II, they decided that the Houston Mexican-American community needed some sort of daily mass media, since the only public media that existed at the time were weekly community newspapers.

The Moraleses applied for their radio station license in 1946, rallying community support for their effort. Members of Houston's Mexican-American populace

Mexican Inn baseball team, 1934.

sent letters of support to the Federal Communications Commission. Finally, in 1950, KLVL received its license, opening on a very tight budget and with little experience. The broadcasting tower and studio were established in Pasadena, but within a couple of years a Houston studio was built in the Second Ward. In the beginning the station's programming was bilingual; however, it gradually adopted more of a Spanish-speaking format. A large, receptive Spanish-speaking audience was discovered in the Houston and Pasadena areas, and Anglo businesses were eager to reach the growing Spanish-speaking population as advertisers.

KLVL likewise offered low-cost advertising for local Mexican-American businesses, and it addressed the needs of the Hispanic community with public service announcements as well as community programs and news. The station was often used to rally community financial support for Mexican-American families who had suffered some catastrophe, such as a death, illness, or destructive fire.

Of equal importance, KLVL allowed local Spanish-language artists to have a voice on the radio. For the first time the community was entertained by Mexican and Mexican-American music. Since 1950 this radio

Activity of KLVL Radio, Second Ward, 1950s. Photograph by G. T. Valerio.

station has been a fixture, symbolizing the growing sophistication of the post–World War II Houston Mexican-American population. Only in the late 1970s and early 1980s were other Spanish-language radio stations founded, and they were intended to be more cosmopolitan than KLVL by serving the growing Cuban, Puerto Rican, and other Latin American groups, as well as Mexican-Americans.

During World War II, a majority of Houston's young men of Mexican descent were away in the service. Yet the Fiestas Patrias grew in festivity and visibility during those years. Indeed, these celebrations curiously

served as occasions for the Mexican-American community to stress its contributions to the American war effort; they enabled members of the community to maintain a sense of personal identity amid the impersonality of urban American society—rather than to express loyalty to Mexico.

In the immediate postwar years, the celebrations of the Cinco de Mayo and especially the 16th of September celebrations developed a great deal of community support and enthusiasm. Returning decorated war heroes were publicly honored. By the mid-1960s, a parade down Main Street on the Saturday falling closest to September 16th was initiated. By 1969 an organization known as Fiestas Patrias was founded to organize this annual event. Fiestas Patrias and the Comite Patriótico are the two leading groups in Houston that now sponsor holiday celebrations. It should be noted, however, that various other groups such as LULAC hold their own celebrations in parks around the city.

In the period after World War II other new developments affected the inhabitants of the Mexican-American colonia. These were the dispersion of Mexican-Americans throughout the city of Houston and improved educational opportunities. Before 1950 Mexican-Americans belonged to a caste social system and were systematically shut out from housing and educational and work-related opportunities. They were "kept in their place," and when they walked into a store or restaurant away from their barrios, they were more than a little uneasy, never knowing whether they were going to be served or turned away. If a boy played on a school baseball team, he was afraid he would be barred from playing with his teammates in certain sections of the city. But fear began to dissipate in the early 1960s as people moved into new neighborhoods. Some Mexican-American veterans took advantage of the G.I. Bill and sought higher education. Their military experiences had awakened the desire for and expectation of equal treatment and equal opportunity, and they were no longer apologetic for being of Mexican descent.

By far the most widely acclaimed effort by Houston Mexican-Americans to increase their educational opportunities was the development of the "Little Schools of the 400" program. In the 1950s educators had estimated that in many areas of Texas fewer than 10 percent of all Mexican-American children who had started school ever graduated, owing primarily to the language barrier. A disproportionate and alarmingly high percentage of children speaking predominantly Spanish were failing in the first and second grades. By the time they reached the third grade, having already failed several times, they became discouraged and would drop out. It became evident to many that these children urgently needed to obtain a working vocabulary in English prior to entering the first grade.

To rectify this condition, LULAC stepped in under the direction of its national president, Felix Tijerina, a Houstonian. In 1957 the league established summer school pilot courses called the "Little Schools of the 400," which were designed to teach preschool children a basic English vocabulary of 400 words in a matter of six weeks. Educators had concluded that with such a vocabulary the Spanish-speaking child would have a fighting chance to complete first-grade work successfully. With the encouragement of the Texas Education Commission and the governing bodies of LULAC, the pilot program opened in Ganado, Texas, in the summer of 1957. The following summer, LULAC opened ten more Little Schools in other South Texas school districts. The program had excellent results. More than 80 percent of the children who completed the program passed the first grade on their first attempt. By the end of the summer of 1959, more than 1,500 children had completed the summer school course. The strength of the program rested largely on the fact that the teachers were bilingual and stressed full participation of the family in the educational process of the child.

The program, designed and initiated by Houstonians, became statewide when other members of LULAC from across the state registered as lobbyists and convinced the Texas Legislature to adopt this concept as the basis for the state's Preschool Instructional Classes for Non-English Speaking Children Program in 1959. Before that time, money for the program had come from whatever LULAC could raise from the business community. The Houston LULAC leaders involved in the program's development had for inspiration their own poor experiences in Texas public schools. By the summer of 1962 approximately 155 Texas school districts were participating and were instructing more than 18,000 preschoolers per year in the basic English vocabulary. Although the program is still a functioning entity and part of state law, its concept served as the model for even more effective programs: Project Head Start, initiated in the mid-1960s, and the Texas Child Migrant Program and Title I of the Elementary and Secondary School Act, begun in 1965. Thus, the "Little Schools" had an impact far beyond their modest beginnings in the late 1950s, and they have influenced the whole course of Mexican-American education since that time.

A representative of the "World War II generation" is Raúl Martínez, Harris County Constable for Precinct 6. Born and raised in Goliad County in South Texas, Martínez left home at age eighteen to join the Army during World War II and saw action in Italy. Upon his return to Goliad, he found little opportunity there, and he migrated to Houston in 1945. After working at several different jobs, he applied for and was accepted into the police academy in 1950. His application to the academy became a community-wide effort, because there were no uniformed Mexican-American policemen in the Houston Police Department at that time. Martínez also earned his college degree from the University of Houston, attending under the G.I. Bill. He served for twenty-three years in the police department and retired in 1973. At that time he was appointed Constable for Precinct 6. As constable he has helped his community and has been active in Mexican-American groups such as LULAC and the Political Association of Spanish-Speaking Organizations (PASO). Martínez has lived for more than thirty years in the Denver Harbor subdivision, where he is a very active, visible Mexican-American community leader.

Coming of Age: The 1960s and 1970s

World War II military experience, improved educational opportunities, and the growing sophistication of the city of Houston led the Mexican American community to increase its political activity. The Harris County PASO emerged between 1958 and 1961 as the Civic Action Committee and produced a significant chapter in Houston Mexican-American political history. It consisted of a group of concerned Houstonians who rallied around the 1958 gubernatorial candidacy of Henry B. González. State Senator González was not victorious in his gubernatorial campaign, but his activity sparked the political activism of Mexican-Americans that had started during World War II and had grown during the Korean conflict. Following the

González campaign, the Civic Action Committee grew as it sponsored poll-tax drives to make the Mexican-American vote a viable political force in the Houston region. It also began publishing a politically oriented newsletter that helped to keep the community informed.

PASO continued the tradition started by CAC of instructing members of the community in the electoral process, sometimes even showing people how to use a ballot box. PASO differed from other Mexican-American groups such as LULAC in that it actively helped political candidates whom it felt would best serve the interests of the Mexican-American community—especially liberal Democratic candidates. In the PASO organization of the early 1960s, membership was composed of entire families, thus drawing upon the strongest social unit in Mexican-American culture. PASO's voter registration headquarters on Navigation Boulevard became a community center during those years. PASO is still in existence and is perhaps the most viable Mexican-American political group in this region. Another such organization is the Harris County Hispanic Caucus, which began as a splinter group in the 1970s.

The civil-rights movements of the mid-1960s mobilized many people in the Mexican-American community of Houston. The most significant event was the Minimum Wage March that made headlines in Texas in 1966. It did not take place in Houston, but a large number of Houstonians were involved in its planning and execution. The affair sprang from the economic plight of Rio Grande Valley farmworkers who were making between forty and sixty cents an hour. In June 1966 a United Farm Workers Association called a strike—a *huelga*—against the growers of Starr County. They asked for a $1.25 hourly wage and union recognition. Houstonians in organizations such as LULAC, the G.I. Forum, and PASO responded to the call for help and encouraged their members to participate.

Many Mexican-American churches in Houston, both Catholic and non-Catholic, offered to serve as assembly points for gathering food and clothing from the Mexican-American community to help meet the needs of the Valley strikers. Houstonians transported the

PASO Voter Registration Drive headquarters, 1960s. Photograph by Alfonso Vazquez.

food to Rio Grande City, where the march was to start. More than forty Houstonians joined the seventy-five farm workers to begin the march to the state capitol in Austin to demand that a special session of the legislature be called. When the march began on July 4, 1966, two Houstonians—the Reverend James Novarro and Father Antonio Gonzáles—assisted labor leader Eugene Nelson in leading the march. All along the way from Starr County to Austin, some 491 miles in very hot weather, the marchers were joined by thousands of sympathizers. Finally, just outside of New Braunfels, the march was met by Governor John Connally, who told them that he would not call a special session of the legislature. Undaunted, the marchers went on to Austin, where they were met by such supporters as Senator Ralph Yarborough and Congressman Henry B. González. Houstonians were prominent in the crowd of some eight thousand people who descended on the capitol building to make one of the most significant appeals for social justice in Texas history. It was at this time that the term *Chicano* was increasingly heard. Originally used by and attributed to militants and activists, it eventually became almost interchangeable with the term *Mexican-American*. Even now, however, some people see it only as a label appropriate for young, politically active innovators.

Another event that generated Mexican-American political activism in Houston occurred just before the 1970–71 school year, when the United States Fifth Circuit Court ordered the Houston Independent School District to implement a desegregation plan involving the pairing (the exchange of students by means of busing to achieve a racial balance) of 25 elementary schools. The plan evoked strong opposition from the Mexican-American community, since of 260 schools in the district, the 25 schools involved in the pairing order were located mainly in the northeastern part of Houston in predominantly Mexican-American and black neighborhoods. The plan involved the pairing of 15,000 residentially segregated black students, 6,200 Mexican-Americans, and 2,300 Anglo students in neighborhood schools. Mexican-Americans claimed that they were being used in the pairing with predominantly black schools so that Anglos could avoid integration. Some members of the Mexican-American community felt that Chicanos had always been considered an ethnic group separate from Anglos for housing and jobs, but now were being considered white for integration purposes. The result was that Houston Chicanos boycotted the HISD schools in September 1970 and opened their own *huelga* (strike) schools.

Of the 6,200 Mexican-American elementary students affected by the pairing order, an estimated 3,500 to 4,500 were kept at home by their parents during the three-week boycott, and of these about 1,000 were enrolled in the *huelga* schools operated by the Mexican-American Education Council (MAEC). These *huelga* schools were to continue in operation until the end of the 1973 school year.

In order to understand the causes and effects of the strike, it is important to know some of the history of Mexican-American school segregation in Texas. The 1876 Texas State Constitution established separate schools for "white" and "colored" children but never sanctioned separate schools for Mexican-Americans. School segregation of Mexicans began around 1902, and eventually a tri-ethnic school system comprising black, Anglo, and Mexican-American schools became dominant across the state of Texas. Generally, the segregation of Mexican-Americans was enforced by housing patterns, as well as the customs and regulations of school districts throughout the Southwest, rather than by state law.

In 1948 the state ruled against segregation of Mexican-American students in *Delgado* v. *Bastrop Independent School District*. This ruling should have put an end to the tri-ethnic system, but it was not communicated to all the districts nor enforced. In 1954 the landmark decision of *Brown* v. *Board of Education of Topeka* determined that "separate educational facilities are inherently unequal." In early Mexican-American desegregation cases, attorneys argued that Mexican-Americans were white and therefore should not be segregated into a tri-ethnic school system. After the *Brown* decision Mexican-American school cases assumed a new dimension. Since Mexican-Americans were generally classified as whites, school districts began to integrate blacks and Mexican-Americans, while Anglos were assigned to all-Anglo schools. In order to apply the *Brown* decision, Mexican-Americans had to gain legal recognition as an identifiable ethnic minority group.

It was not until June 4, 1970, in *Cisneros* v. *Corpus Christi Independent School District,* that Judge Woodrow Seals ruled in Federal District Court in Houston that Mexican Americans are an identifiable ethnic minority for the purposes of public school desegregation. With this decision, Mexican-Americans became a recognizable legal population whose identity had to be considered when trying to put a unitary school system into operation. Judge Seals ruled that integration of blacks and Mexican-Americans failed to produce a unitary school system.

On May 24, 1971, the Mexican-American Educational Council (MAEC) tried to intervene in the Houston school case but was thrown out of court. The Mexican-American community was up in arms when Judge Connally accused Mexican-Americans of being racist: "Content to be 'White' for these many years, now, when the shoe begins to pinch, the would-be intervenors wish to be treated not as Whites but as an 'identifiable minority group.'"

The battle against pairing lasted until June 3, 1973, when the United States Supreme Court ruled that a unitary school system could not be achieved through the integration of blacks and Mexican-Americans. The decision in this case, known as the Denver School Case, finally ended the boycott and the *huelga* schools.

The Houston school walkout was a reflection of the times. In California, thousands of Mexican-Americans had also walked out of schools claiming poor facilities, poor education, and an alarming drop-out rate, which were present as well in Houston. It also appears that Mexican-American parents felt a certain racism and uneasiness at the prospect of being integrated only with blacks, claiming that they were also an educationally disadvantaged group. This reflected the mounting tension between blacks and Mexican-Americans.

Although the pairing plan by itself was unsuccessful, there were certain gains from the experience. It highlighted the inadequacy of the school system in meeting the needs of Mexican-Americans. The pairing order made Mexican-American parents realize that their children were not receiving good educations, and that these educational problems were not going to get any better by mixing with another minority with its own attendant educational problems. The school district responded to the demands of Mexican-American parents by hiring more Mexican-American teachers, even advertising in other cities in order to get them in sufficient numbers. From 1970 to 1972 the number of Mexican-American teachers in Houston public schools increased from 181 to 300.

The *huelga* schools fostered the development of Mexican-American leadership and unity. People donated books and supplies to the schools, teachers volunteered their time, and University of Houston psychology majors came and tested the children for placement. The boycotters were supported by the Mexican-American Clergymen's Association of Houston. In a letter the clergymen demanded recognition of Mexican-Americans as an identifiable ethnic group and gave their support to the school boycott: "In light of the apathetic slowness of 'due process' in achieving social change, the exercise of this right will expedite the final acceptance of our people as an ethnic minority." The clergymen called for integration of all, not just blacks and Mexican-Americans. As evidence of their support, they offered buildings and private schools to be used as boycott schools. The clergymen represented the Centro Social de Casa de Amigos of the Presbyterian Church, the El Mesias and Good Shepherd Methodist Churches, the Holy Name Catholic Church, and the Disciples of Christ. In a letter addressed to the Houston City Council, they said: "The Blacks and Browns are minorities that are often forced to vie against each other for the offerings of the majority." These clergy saw this as the reason for the growing number of violent incidents between blacks and Mexican-Americans in Houston schools and communities.

As with any kind of group effort, leaders emerge as part of the process. Leonel Castillo, then chairman of the Mexican-American Educational Council, and Joe Torres, principal of the *huelga* schools, were salient figures. Along with others, they provided inspiration in the face of many difficulties that had to be overcome. The success of the boycott and the *huelga* schools was not obtained easily, and the unified effort and unflagging cooperation that these leaders engendered were essential. In the aftermath, Leonel Castillo ran for city controller of Houston in 1972 and won.

Even as the *huelga* schools were unifying the Mexican-American community, a group of young people felt that the pace of change was too slow. Many of them were members of the Mexican American Youth Organization (MAYO); they formed the Raza Unida Party to challenge the traditional parties, especially the Democratic, which they felt had taken Mexican-Americans for granted for too long. It began in San Antonio and the Rio Grande Valley in 1970, but its activity soon spread to the whole state. In Houston the party became very active, particularly among younger Mexican-Americans who had received more education. They invited Ben Reyes to run for state representative on their ticket, but instead he ran successfully as the Democratic Party candidate.

Although the Raza Unida Party lost impetus after 1976, its considerable efforts at political education complemented those of PASO and contributed substantially to stimulating more Mexican-Americans to become politically aware. This increased participation,

The Eloy Perez Band in the 1960s. Photograph by G. T. Valerio.

in turn, helped make people more ready to react to perceived social and official injustices. An example occurred on May 5, 1977, the Cinco de Mayo. Joe Campos Torres, a United States Army veteran, was arrested by a group of Houston policemen for drunken disturbance in a Houston nightspot. He was subsequently beaten and thrown into Buffalo Bayou, where he drowned.

The reaction from the Mexican-American community was immediate and intense. An organization called People United to Fight Police Brutality was formed to protest the death and ask for justice. It had strong youth participation, but women also played a significant role. Mrs. Torres, Joe's mother, was very involved in People United during its first few months. The group organized marches within a few weeks after the homicide and handed out leaflets throughout the summer. In late summer 1977 the trial of the police-

men began in Huntsville, having been moved from Houston at the request of the defendants' lawyers. People United arranged transportation to bring members of the community to the trial. During this time, there were demonstrations being held on weekends. In October the verdict was in: the crime was ruled a "misdemeanor," and the police officers each received a one-dollar fine. The public outcry against the verdict could have been predicted. "A Chicano's life is only worth one dollar" became the new cry from the Mexican-American community, as they dramatized their outrage by pinning dollar bills to their clothing. The verdict itself led to still more demonstrations in which even more groups became involved. Finally, a federal court decided to try the policemen for civil-rights violations. The stage for demonstrations then became the Federal Building. Picket lines were orga-

Houston PASO members at Minimum Wage March, 1966. Photograph by Alfonso Vazquez.

nized and tension was high. In the end the federal verdict was as unacceptable to the community as the state verdict had been. In April the offending police officers were sentenced to serve a year and a day, a sentence that meant they could be paroled in nine months. The disappointment and anger throughout the community was evident.

A month after the federal sentence was imposed, about three thousand members of the Mexican-American community were celebrating the Cinco de Mayo in Moody Park. It was a year to the day after Joe Torres's arrest and death. A fight broke out among some of the celebrants. When some people tried to intervene, the smoldering anger erupted, rocks began

to fly, a police car was set on fire, and a riot was in full swing. Stores were looted and set on fire. The Houston police SWAT team arrived and pushed the crowds out of the park. During that night and the one following, about four hundred people were arrested. But the riot seemed to have had a somewhat cathartic effect, and the community's anger began to subside.

These groups, which had sprung from a united opposition to police brutality and a perceived lack of justice from the court systems, broke up. Some felt that the fight for justice should continue, while others were of the opinion that there was nothing more that could be done in the particular case of Joe Torres. They felt that some progress could be made through traditional channels, such as the appointment of more Mexican-American judges and community efforts to sensitize police officers to Mexican-American needs and culture.

Mexican-Americans in Houston in the 1980s

According to the official figures in 1980, the population of the Houston metropolitan area was 2.9 million and Hispanics numbered 400,000 (14.6 percent); however, Spanish-language radio stations, such as KXYZ, claim this figure is too conservative. They contend that they have one million Spanish-language listeners. Although Mexican-Americans live throughout the city (only 25 percent of the census tracts have fewer than 1 percent Spanish-speaking people), Magnolia, North Side, and Denver Harbor remain the Mexican-American barrios in the city, while Pasadena and Galena Park are suburbs with large Mexican-American communities.

Education continues to be the key to social mobility in the United States, and Mexican-Americans still lag behind. According to the 1980 census, in Texas only 34.3 percent of Hispanics over the age of twenty-five had finished high school;[1] in California, it was 43.2 percent, and in New Mexico, 49.1 percent. This means that for every one hundred Anglos who complete high school, sixty-six Hispanics finish in New Mexico, fifty-six in California, and fifty-three in Texas. In Houston there has been a considerable increase in the number of Mexican-American children enrolled in the Houston Independent School District, even as the number of Anglo and black children has decreased. In the school year 1977–78 there were 60,000 Anglo children, 91,000 blacks, and 47,000 Hispanics.[2] Five years later,

there are 50,000 Anglos, 86,000 blacks, and 58,000 Hispanics. Even though these figures are encouraging for Mexican-Americans, the dropout rates in grades 7 through 12 are 10 percent for Anglos, 8 percent for blacks, and 14 percent for Hispanics. In large part, the decreased number of Anglos can be attributed to white families moving to Houston suburbs where school districts are still predominantly white. The increased number of Hispanics is due in large part to the increase in the city's Hispanic population. Other school districts in the Houston area have 77 percent Anglo enrollment, 11 percent black, and 12 percent Hispanic. Catholic elementary and high school enrollment in 1982 was 62 percent Anglo, 13 percent black, and 25 percent Hispanic. A more telling indicator is enrollment at the University of Houston: in 1982, only 3 percent of its 28,000 students were Hispanic.

Houston Mexican-Americans are very active politically. They have elected Ben Reyes to the Houston City Council, and they have two Mexican-American state representatives: Al Luna and Roman Martinez. City controller Leonel Castillo was appointed commissioner for the Immigration and Naturalization Service by President Carter in 1977, and in 1979 his candidacy for mayor, though unsuccessful, generated much interest.

The Fiestas Patrias celebration in September is still the major social event for Mexican-Americans in the city in the 1980s. The parade, the ball, and family outings to the parks are all very well attended. Other social events are patronized by subgroups such as the Club Mexico Bello, which celebrates its sixtieth anniversary in 1984. They traditionally hold a Black and White Ball in January and a Debutante Ball in October. The Associacion de Charros de Houston, a Mexican horsemanship club, holds *charreadas* (a type of rodeo) regularly. The Institute of Hispanic Culture overarches Mexican-Americans and other Hispanics. Its most spectacular event is an elaborate ball called Noche de las Americas (Evening of the American Nations) celebrating Columbus Day. The diplomatic and international communities are invited, as are well-known political and media personalities in the city.

In spite of the efforts of groups such as these, the public image of Mexican-Americans in Houston is con-

1. The 1980 census figures lump all Hispanics under this label so that Cubans, with one of the highest educational ranks, are averaged in with Mexican-Americans and Puerto Ricans, who are very low.
2. Numbers rounded out to thousands.

Raza Unida Party campaign workers, 1972. Photograph by Alfonso Vazquez.

tinually blurred by the influx of immigrants from Mexico. The general public often does not distinguish between Mexican-Americans and the new arrivals. The latter often, but not always, come without documentation authorizing their residence and sometimes do not plan to stay in the United States. The problems faced by these people redound in many instances to Mexican-Americans.

The plight in the United States. The problems faced by these people redound in many instances to Mexican-Americans.

The plight of Mexican children who, without legal residence permits, were refused public education in Texas mobilized wide Mexican-American support and community concern. The Center for Immigrants was incorporated in 1978 to provide legal assistance to people who wish to rectify their immigration status. In addition to this advisory type of legal work, Isaias Torres and other staff attorneys of the center initiated a legal suit in Houston, joined with other suits within the state, to challenge the Texas law that allowed school districts to charge these children a prohibitive tuition. The case was decided locally in favor of the children, and after being challenged, the decision was upheld by the United States Supreme Court in 1982. Yet, the issue of undocumented immigrants from Mexico continues to draw unfavorable attention to the Mexican-American population of Houston and produce unpleasant reactions against them, regardless of the fact that they may be first-, second-, or third-generation Houstonians.

Mexican-American public identity is also blurred by the influx of people from other Latin American countries. Puerto Rican, Cuban, Salvadoran, and other Latin American communities have increased in numbers in recent years. These ethnic communities are often grouped in the public mind and media and simply labelled "Hispanic." The commonality of such groups is often confined to a greater or lesser use of the Spanish language and to carrying a Spanish surname, and their cultural heritages are clearly distinct. They do not share a historical tradition, and although they can collaborate as they do, for example, in the Institute of Hispanic Culture, they find it undesirable to lose their ethnic identity and immerse themselves in a single group labelled "Hispanic."

In their search for roots and identity, a group of Houstonians formed the Hispanic Genealogical Society in 1980. Rose Zamora Cope, a local businesswoman, is the 1983 president. The group meets at the Clayton Library. Other prominent Mexican-Americans include restauranteur Ninfa Laurenzo, who became the subject of a musical presented at Miller Outdoor Theater in 1982; executives Mary Medina, Manny Sanchez, José de la Cerda, and George Hernández; community center directors Felix Fraga of Ripley House, Rachel Lucas of the Chicano Training Center, Gloria Guardiola of the Association for the Advancement of Mexican-Americans (AAMA), and Rita Rodriguez of the Magnolia YWCA. Four well-known educators are Guadalupe Quintanilla, assistant provost at the University of Houston; Delia Pompa, director of bilingual education at the Houston Independent School District; Tina Reyes, member of the HISD Board of Education; and Dorothy Caram, who in 1983 was named vice-chairman of the Civil Service Commission.

Mexican-Americans were one of the earliest and are now one of the most numerous of the distinct cultural populations in the rich ethnic kaleidoscope of this international city.

Acknowledgments

The author wishes to thank Dr. Thomas H. Kreneck and the Reverend Roberto Flores, O.F.M., for their assistance in gathering and presenting this material. For greater detail concerning events from the 1900s to 1930s, see F. Arturo Rosales, "Mexicans in Houston: The Struggle to Survive," in *The Houston Review,* Vol. III, No. 2, 1981. For the 1960s, see Mary Ellen Goodman, *The Mexican American Population of Houston,* Rice University Studies, Vol. 37, No. 3, 1971.

CHAPTER 4

Chinese

Edward C. M. Chen and Fred R. von der Mehden

In the 1930s many complete families moved to Houston. Shown in this photograph, taken in 1925 in Los Angeles, is the Y. Y. Chan family. Edward, third person from left and standing, was the first of his race to graduate from the University of Houston in 1939; Charles, fourth from left standing, was the first Chinese graduate of the Rice Institute (now Rice University) in 1941. George, on his father's lap, was the first Chinese graduate of a Houston high school, San Jacinto High, in 1937. He later graduated from Rice with a degree in chemical engineering and was the first Chinese naval officer from Houston in 1943.

*I*n 1980 Houston celebrated the centennial of the first Chinese people to live in the city. However, the City by the Bayou has only recently become the home of large numbers of Chinese residents. The Chinese community in the United States initially grew slowly; before the Gold Rush in California there were fewer than fifty Chinese reported in the entire United States, although centuries before, explorers from Imperial China had reached these shores. The first immigrants to America from the Celestial Kingdom did not come to the South but found their way to Hawaii and then the West. They were primarily young men without families who came to the continental United States to work in the gold mines and on the railroads. Life was hard for these newcomers, most of whom planned to make their fortunes and then return to China. At first they worked mostly in unskilled jobs, and they were discriminated against in housing and employment. In the gold mining towns violent battles often erupted between Chinese and other miners over water and land rights. In the cities, too, their clothing, skin color, and strange ways made them targets of ridicule and curiosity. Although some Chinese students, diplomats, and other visitors also came to America, most people associated the Chinese with mine and railroad work.

As the gold and silver mines became exhausted and major railroads were completed, most of the Chinese on the mainland returned to their homeland. In addition, exclusion acts (laws limiting Chinese residence and citizenship) made it difficult for them to immigrate or stay. Later the Chinese immigrants who were allowed to come could not even bring in their wives. As a result their total population fell by more than a third between 1882 and 1900, and the official number of immigrants in 1900 was only ninety-one. Those who remained settled in Hawaii, the western United States, and the areas near New York. Prior to World War II half the Chinese in America were in three cities: Honolulu, San Francisco, and New York City. They tended to be shopkeepers, restauranteurs, household servants, agricultural workers, and laundrymen, with the younger generation beginning to obtain the education that would take them out of these traditional occupations. Yet even at this time many thought of themselves as transients who would one day return to China.

As late as 1940, foreign-born members of the community in the United States outnumbered the locally born. Continued discrimination, symbolized by the fact that they were the only group unable to obtain citizenship unless born in the United States, did not make them feel welcome. In California they, along with the Japanese, were part of the "Yellow Peril" described in the newspapers as dangerous to United States security and the American way of life.

World War II brought major changes to the Chinese communities. Citizenship laws were relaxed, and more Chinese began to come to America. Their numbers increased by almost 50 percent in twenty years, rising to 120,000 by 1950. In the next thirty years their population rose to at least 800,000, more than a 1,000-percent increase in half a century. In 1940 the Chinese population of Houston was less than 1 percent of what it is today. Beyond this growth in numbers, the Chinese began to move out of their traditional geographic areas and occupations. They began to leave the old Chinatowns and become more integrated into the general community. Their long-standing interest in education led increasing numbers of young people to enter colleges and universities. Higher percentages of Chinese completed high school and college than almost any other group; and the sons and daughters of shopkeepers and laundrymen increasingly became teachers, professionals, and technicians. Other changes were taking place as Chinese political strength showed itself in the election of Hiram Fong of Hawaii, the first United States senator of their race. These developments paralleled the history of Chinese families in Texas and in Houston.

The Chinese in Texas

The first large numbers of Chinese also came to Texas to participate in the expansion of the railroads. Four years after the end of the Civil War, some 250 laborers came south from St. Louis by steamboat to work on the Houston and Texas Central Railroad. The January 22, 1870, *Harper's Weekly* noted: "On the 26th of December [1869], the first detachment of Chinese laborers engaged to work on a railroad now building in Texas, numbering 250 men, arrived opposite Council Bluffs, Iowa. The river was covered with a pack of broken ice sufficiently strong to prevent the passage of boats. A plank walk was laid across the uneven surface on which the Celestials passed over to the eastern side of the river, carrying their baggage on poles balanced over their shoulders in true Oriental fashion." In the next fifteen years, others followed to help build the Southern Pacific Railroad, Texas Central, and various spur lines. Since the Chinese were considered better, more industrious workers than other groups, the planners of these railroads were anxious to hire them. At one time there were as many as three thousand men employed by the railroads, but local discrimination and legislation had reduced that number sharply by 1890.

Even before the railroads were completed, the more adventurous Chinese became interested in a permanent life in their newfound state. Some began to look to farming, and when railroad construction slowed, the first large Chinese agricultural community developed in the Brazos River Valley. These workers were primarily sharecroppers or contract laborers and did not own their own land. Others came to the towns of West Texas; the first urban areas with sizable Chinese populations were railroad centers such as El Paso, San Antonio, and some small towns such as Toyah and Bremond. The first Chinese voters, totaling 150 men, took part in elections in Calvert in 1874, although they were not United States citizens.

Most of these early immigrants were young men, usually brought in as unskilled contract workers. They came, as did other Chinese of that period, from four counties in Kwantung near Hong Kong. With the exception of truck farmers and railroad workers, those who settled in Texas chose mainly urban areas, involving themselves primarily in the laundry and restaurant businesses. They were targets of white attacks because of their domination of these occupations and the presence of gambling and other alleged questionable practices, such as smuggling and opium smoking. In 1910 there were only thirteen Chinese women noted in the census figures for Texas.

From the period of railroad construction to World War II, the number of Chinese in Texas was small. Although census figures for minorities are often low, there were only 595 Chinese counted in 1910, and 1,031 in 1940.

The population only remained as high as it did because of Pershing's Chinese, a group of 527 men who joined with the American army when it invaded Mexico in search of Pancho Villa. The Chinese who resided in northern Mexico had been severely mistreated; reportedly, 303 were massacred in Torreon in 1911. Of the 527 who came out after the war, many settled in Texas. Thirty-six of these came to Ellington Field near Houston.

Between the world wars the Chinese in Texas went through changes similar to those their countrymen faced elsewhere in the United States. More women immigrated, diluting the previously almost all-male population. Occupational patterns were diversifying, and fewer Chinese went into the traditional laundry business. American-born Chinese began to make their presence felt. Whereas early in the century only one-sixth were locally born, by 1940 the percentage had increased to almost one-half. One thing that did not change was continued discrimination. Although they were classified as whites, many Chinese found it difficult to own land because of their alien status; they were also kept from public swimming pools and other facilities. However, discrimination was not as bad as it had been earlier when Judge Roy Bean reportedly freed a white man for murdering a Chinese on the basis that there was "no law against killing a Chinaman." Yet during this time the Chinese community in Texas matured, as they formed commercial, family, and political associations and made formal efforts to maintain ties with China.

Texas has been a major beneficiary of the growth in the Chinese population in the United States since World War II. During the war years the prewar number doubled, and in the 1950s and 1960s the population tripled from the wartime years. Further change in the composition of the community came with this growth. The previous domination of immigrants from South China has been challenged by newcomers from other regions, and divisions have appeared based on language, politics, and background. The percentages of the sexes have almost evened out. For Houstonians, the most important development has been the rise of the city as the new center of Chinese activity in Texas; more than half the Chinese in Texas now reside in Harris County.

This cartoon from Puck *magazine shows American workers of various nationalities building a wall against the Chinese in the early 1880s.*

The Chinese in Houston

In 1870 crowds of curious Houstonians gathered to see the arrival of 250 Chinese laborers who were traveling through the city on their way to work on the railroads. Not until a decade later, however, did the census report seven actual residents in the young city. All of these first citizens were in the laundry business, an activity monopolized here by the Chinese in the late nineteenth century. Most of these early residents were male. The 1880 census lists a family consisting of Mr. and Mrs. (Anna, Caucasian) Wah Yuan and son, Lincoln (four months), Chinese. Lincoln Yuan was the first Chinese-American born in Houston.

The Houston Chinese community grew very slowly in the prewar years. Until the late 1930s there were fewer than 50 men, women, and children; by World War II they numbered only 121. During the war many people of all races come to the city, and the number of Chinese more than doubled in that period. They came from the surrounding states of Arkansas, Mississippi, and Louisiana, as well as from other parts of Texas. Many had owned small stores in black neighborhoods in the South, and when they came to Houston they opened similar businesses in the predominantly black neighborhoods. These were family enterprises with

everyone involved in long hours of work. Still, the community was small in total population, in spite of new laws that allowed more Asians into the United States. It was not until 1955 that the population reached 1,000.

During the past quarter of a century Houston has grown explosively, and the Chinese have more than kept up with these increases. By 1965 there were more than 2,500; by 1975, more than 10,000; and by 1980 at least 20,000 and perhaps 25,000. The composition of the Chinese population of Houston showed changes similar to those in the rest of the country. More immigrants from places other than southern China began to appear. Many came from mainland China, through Taiwan and Hong Kong; more recently new arrivals have often been from Southeast Asia. Most of the "boat people" who escaped from Vietnam have been of Chinese origin, and today Houston has the second-largest Indochinese community in the United States (after Los Angeles).

Houston has never had a traditional Chinatown similar to those in San Francisco and Los Angeles, where there are centers of both commercial and residential activities. Here, the Chinese have tended to live and work throughout the city. The first residents established themselves in the downtown area. In the 1930s and 1940s, many Chinese opened groceries in the

The 1889 Houston city directory had a section devoted to local business advertising. The bottom ad on the page tells of the first Chinese export-import company in Houston, which had been opened that year by Him Lee. His company, Hop Lee Wah, received some publicity in Harper's Monthly *during 1889, as follows: "Nearby on a sidewalk, a Chinese Peddler displayed his wares. John had his pigtail neatly pinned up and his blouse and shoes are a model of cleanliness. 'Anytling a day?' he asks, exhibiting wonderful fans and cushions, brushes, teapots, Chinese lilies and what not. He tries to be very persuasive in his pidgin-English." Many immigrants, even as some do today, took an easily understood Anglicized first name, just as this peddler had done.*

black areas on Houston's east side. These shops were both living and working places; the family's living quarters would be located above the store. The lack of any Chinese ghetto in those years can be seen by the fact that the children of that early period graduated from three different high schools: San Jacinto, Austin, and Sam Houston.

The great expansion of Houston in the post–World War II era has also meant that the Chinese have moved to all parts of the city. Chinese restaurants exist from Memorial to Pasadena, and from Westbury to the area near Intercontinental Airport. Professionals now work at NASA and the University of Houston/Clear Lake City, in downtown offices, and for corporations throughout the area. Chinese families today live in every part of metropolitan Houston. Houston does have a small commercial Chinatown along Chartres Street on the eastern edge of the downtown area. The first Chinatown—an area of shops, restaurants, and cultural activities, not residences—was near the present Alley Theatre location on Smith Street. The growth of Houston made expansion difficult there, however, and the Chinese Merchants' Association decided to move to its present location in the early 1950s. A few of these businesses have been there since the beginning, while others are signs of efforts to rejuvenate the area. A new theater has been built for showing films and presenting cultural events, and it has been particularly attractive to the new Indochinese population who use it as a community center.

Chinatown has not become the magnet for Houston's Chinese that many of its merchants have wanted. In part, this is due to the somewhat unattractive surroundings of warehouses, vacant lots, and an elevated portion of U.S. Highway 59 that borders the area. Perhaps more important, the Chinese are spread too widely throughout the city to make effective use of this one area. For now, Chinatown is a place of good food, Chinese groceries, films, souvenirs, and the offices of the Chinese Merchants' Association. However, as Houston's corporate buildings move in its direction and the Chinese community continues to grow, there will probably be greater activity there.

Diversity Among the Chinese in Houston

Throughout the world there has been a tendency to look upon the Chinese as a closed group who have few serious internal divisions. Historically, other communities in Texas have pictured them as a close-knit society, and there is no doubt that the local Chinese have helped one another in times of need. However, this view also does a disservice to the great variety that exists among the Chinese of Houston. The mosaic includes differences in language, place of origin, politics, generation, economic activities, and religion.

Language and Place of Origin

The Chinese written language is based upon characters, each with its own meaning. Those who can read Chinese, from whatever part of China they come, understand these characters. However, Chinese speak a variety of dialects that may be unintelligible from one group to another. The major dialects that have come to the United States are variations of Cantonese— the language of most of the immigrants prior to World War II—and Mandarin, the official language of China. Mandarin is spoken in the populous region of northeast China and on the island of Taiwan, from which many new arrivals have come. Other Chinese have come from Southeast Asia, where their native languages were Thai, Vietnamese, Indonesian, or others. As a result, even those from Asia may not be able to speak to one another, although they may have a common written language.

These linguistic variations are also found in Houston. Many adults from the older community speak Cantonese, while most of those who have arrived during the past twenty-five years speak Mandarin. In addition, there is a growing Vietnamese population of Chinese origin. Many younger people, however, are unable to read or write any Chinese. Like their counterparts in other ethnic groups, these second-, third-, and fourth-generation youth are comfortable only with English. The fact that Chinese are not concentrated in any one area of Houston also inhibits daily use of the language. Only Bellaire High School offers Chinese, although there have been private efforts to introduce both Cantonese and Mandarin to young people.

The diversity of the local Chinese population has also been reflected in the variety of Chinese restaurants. Twenty years ago, all of Houston's Chinese restaurants were Cantonese. Now Szechuan, Hunanese, Mandarin, and Sino-Vietnamese menus are available.

Politics

During the twentieth century, China has gone through major political changes. In 1911 the ancient Chinese Empire came to an end and a republic was declared. Rather than bringing peace and progress, though, the

In 1900 the Chinese population in Houston had reached fifty. Two years later, the effects of the extension of the Chinese Exclusion Acts were felt, and on April 28, 1902, the Houston Chronicle *stated that the number of Chinese in Houston had decreased to twenty-seven. Both political parties pushed such legislation through Congress with slogans like "The Chinese Must Go." Some advertisers, such as are shown in the cartoon, picked up the slogan for their own purposes.*

years that followed were ones of chaos with no government recognized throughout China. Local military leaders (warlords) controlled their own areas. Finally in 1927 Chiang Kai-Shek, as leader of the Kuomintang Party (KMT), united most of the country under his rule. This turned out to be only a short period of peace and unity. In 1931 the Japanese took control of Manchuria in northeast China; and in 1937 they began their invasion of China, which resulted in the occupation of the most populous and developed regions of the country. During this period there was also civil war as the Communists, under their leader, Mao Zedong, fought to bring down the government of Chiang Kai-Shek. When the war with Japan ended in 1945, the civil war spread, ending with a Communist victory in 1949. Following their defeat the KMT, or Nationalist Chinese, fled to Taiwan, a Chinese province that had been under Japanese control for almost half a century. There they set up a government that they declared to be the government of all of China. The United States con-

tinued to recognize the Nationalists as the rulers of all China until 1978, when President Carter moved to recognize the Communist government in Peking (Beijing). The complex politics of the Chinese in Asia have naturally had an effect on Houston's Chinese community. There are two consulates: one from the Communist People's Republic of China, and an unofficial one representing Taiwan, called the Coordination Council for North American Affairs. In fact, there are three different groups in Houston in the mid-1980s. Among those who express support for one side or another, the largest number favor the government on Taiwan. Many of these people can be seen at the Nationalist celebration called Double Ten, for October 10, 1911, when the Chinese Empire collapsed. A much smaller group is attempting to develop contacts between the local Chinese community and the People's Republic of China. The third division consists of those who are apolitical or uninterested in these issues. The attitudes of various Chinese groups toward events in China do not detract from their loyalty to the United States, and many Chinese are deeply involved in local politics in Houston.

Economic Activities

As noted before, the first Chinese in Texas worked on the railroads and in the mines, and those who followed held the traditional occupations of launderers, restauranteurs, truck farmers, and household servants—the same kinds of occupations held by their countrymen in other parts of the United States. These were not necessarily the jobs they wanted. Local discrimination, however, kept them from many opportunities, and their inability to gain citizenship limited their possible employment in positions that restricted aliens. For example, state legislation in New York prohibited noncitizens from participating in twenty-seven occupations. Many states would not allow aliens to become doctors, lawyers, architects, or even barbers—activities that required a certificate or license. As recently as World War II, many labor unions would not accept Chinese as members, keeping them from skilled trades.

In Houston similar restrictions existed, and the restaurant and grocery businesses became the main economic activities of the Chinese. At the turn of the century there were ten Chinese restaurants in the downtown area. While this dropped to only one later, by 1940 there were twelve, and now there are perhaps three hundred Chinese-owned establishments in the city. They now serve a wide variety of Chinese cuisine, from the more subtle Cantonese to the spicy Hunanese, and also varieties of American, other Asian, and European food. They vary from small family-run restaurants to large places with banquet facilities.

The second major business, the grocery store, has also continued to grow, although somewhat limited by the development of supermarket chains. In 1949 there were 42 Chinese-owned groceries, and by 1980 they numbered more than 100, after reaching a peak of 300 in 1967. In addition, Vietnamese of Chinese origin have been active in the operation of convenience stores, such as 7-11 and Stop-N-Go markets. In Houston many of the groceries have been small stores in minority areas. The family has often lived above the place of business; all members of the family, no matter what their age, have helped in running it. Long hours are usual in these operations, and many well-known doctors, lawyers, and professors grew up working with the rest of the family while they were going to school. Interestingly, the traditional laundry business, often associated with the Chinese, is no longer an important occupation. Early Chinese laundries frequently had hotels as their major customers; when the steam laundry came into being, they went into other businesses. The 1980 telephone Yellow Pages listed only one laundry with an Asian name, and it was not owned by a Chinese. Nor are many Chinese still involved in household labor or farming.

In 1940 only 2.8 percent of the Chinese employed in America were in technical or professional fields, and in Houston there were no technical or professional Chinese in the general work force. There was one Chinese student at Rice University studying architecture and one studying chemical engineering. By the 1970 United States census, almost a third were in these technical and professional occupations. The average income of Chinese was above the national average, and a higher percentage were college graduates. In 1980 more than 500 students at the University of Houston were studying science, engineering, or computer sciences; more than 250 were studying business, economics, or accounting; and pharmacy and architecture each had 50 students. There were about 50 students in the humanities and human science areas. The professional areas of law and optometry each had 10 students.

It is possible to observe in the economic activities of the Chinese many of the basic divisions mentioned previously. People involved in the traditional grocery and restaurant businesses tend to come from the older Cantonese community. On the other hand, a high percentage of the foreign-born professionals are from Mandarin backgrounds. Younger Americans born to Chinese professionals often speak only English. These divisions affect the languages spoken in commercial

In 1916 General John Pershing went to Mexico to capture Pancho Villa. Chinese merchants in Mexico helped his troops to survive, so he brought the Chinese back into the United States as refugees. Because of the Exclusion Acts, they could not become citizens; in fact, it took them more than five years to gain permission to become legal residents. They earned their keep by helping to build the army and air force bases used during World War I. This picture shows General Pershing meeting with the Chinese at Ellington Field near Houston in 1920.

and professional organizations and other relationships. A more subtle distinction has developed along class lines. Whether they were the older generation of American-born or were immigrants, Chinese Houstonians tended to come from poorer families and entered the commercial trades upon their arrival. While their children went on to college and the professions, they worked long hours in restaurants, groceries, and shops. Today, many of the newcomers to Houston are from higher-status families in Taiwan and mainland China and work predominantly in the professions. They tend to consider the older commercial generation as lower in status. There is, consequently, a recognizable relationship among language, place of origin, economic activity, and class.

Religion[1]

In traditional China, Confucianism, Taoism, and Buddhism were known as the "Three Teachings." Although each school of thought differed from the others, the Chinese believed that all three beliefs were united into one. Together they satisfied the intellectual, emotional, and religious needs of the Chinese people.

Confucianism was a social philosophy. It was concerned with good government and harmony in society. The family served as an ideal social model, for just as children owed obedience to their parents, so the people as a whole owed obedience to their ruler. At the same time, of course, rulers had to care for their subjects, just as parents had to care for their children. No two people were equal in Confucian society, but all were bound by ties of mutual obligation. Confucian

1. Professor Richard Smith of Rice University was of great help in supplying background on traditional practices.

The first grocery store owned by a Chinese person in Houston was the Quong Yick, opened in 1930 on Dowling Street by C . Y. Chu. Mr. Chu was the first Chinese naturalized in Houston after the repeal of the Chinese Exclusion Acts. This store grew into a chain of five stores.

love (*jen*) extended to everyone, but not in the same measure. Family loyalties were more important than loyalty to neighbors or the state, and devotion to parents (filial piety) was the highest Confucian virtue. Confucians believed that proper behavior could be encouraged by music, ritual, and the arts; but above all, self-improvement required humane wisdom gained from reading the Confucian classics. "In education," said Confucius, "there are no class distinctions."

The second belief was Taoism (pronounced *dowism*), and it was very unlike Confucianism. It was a playful philosophy of freedom, individualism, and communion with nature. While Confucians sought moral knowledge, Taoists sought innocent ignorance. While Confucians valued ritual and self-control, Taoists treasured freedom from restraint. And while Confucians stressed hierarchy, Taoists emphasized equality.

Like both Confucianism and Taoism, Buddhism was concerned with the elimination of selfish desires. But as the third belief held by the Chinese, it was a religious philosophy in ways that the other two schools of thought were not. Chinese Buddhism appealed to the masses. Its moral values were, in many ways, similar to those of Confucianism; but where Confucianism expected people to act properly simply because it was the right thing to do, Buddhism promised rewards and punishments after death. According to Buddhist doctrine, life was a continuous cycle of rebirths. If persons had done good deeds in their previous existence, they would be born into a better life in the next. On the other hand, if they had been evil or unkind, they would be punished by rebirth as a lesser being, perhaps even as an animal or insect.

By the time Buddhism reached China from India, it had developed a vast system of deities, all reflections of the Buddha spirit. This fit perfectly well with the long-standing belief in various gods and demons. In China Buddhism not only supported Confucian moral values and provided valuable social services, but it also became a part of the universal system of ancestor worship.

Much of this traditional religious pattern has not been maintained among the Chinese of late twentieth-century America. Most second- and third-generation citizens have dropped many of the old ways, and the Chinese youth have generally become integrated into American culture, as is true of nearly all young people who grow up in this country. There are Chinese who continue to support Buddhism, and many of the values so important in traditional China remain powerful in the Chinese community today, including the strong role of the family and education. At the same time, Christianity has increasingly become a part of the local Chinese way of life. As late as 1953, W. Kung reported in *Chinese in American Life* that there were probably fewer than 17,000 Chinese Christians in the United States and Hawaii, or 7.5 percent of the total Chinese population. While this number may be too small, it does reflect a traditional lack of strong interest in organized religion in China. However, this same report noted that young people were beginning to become involved in local church activities.

The small community of Chinese who lived in Houston before World War II also displayed an interest in Christian activities. The first organized church group came into being in 1940 when the First Baptist Church started a Chinese mission. From that time, the major Christian element among Houston's Chinese has been Baptist. In time, three primarily Chinese Baptist congregations were established with more than 1,500 regular members. The Chinese in the United States became involved in Christianity for a variety of reasons. Some saw in church gatherings the opportunity to learn both the English language and American ways. As Chinese churches grew, they provided fellowship and community to newcomers to our city. Many Chinese turned to the Baptists because of the attraction of its evangelical content and the missionary activities of the church both in China and Houston. Throughout the United States, efforts of missionary groups have tended to be the initial influence on the development of these Chinese congregations.

Today Houston's Chinese community reflects the variety of religious interests of the population as a whole. While the Baptist churches have the largest membership, there are also Presbyterian, Church of Christ, Lutheran, and Catholic assemblies. Services at these churches are in Cantonese, Mandarin, English, or Vietnamese, depending on the composition of the congregation. There is also a Buddhist Association with its own temple and members. These religious groups offer more than religious services. They have active parishioners who see in their church a center for a wide variety of social activities similar to other churches in the city. While the first Chinese congregations in the United States were very weak financially, Houston's Chinese parishioners have generally been very generous in their support.

We do not know how many persons maintain the older religious ways of China. Certainly there are few outward signs of traditional beliefs. Instead, the Chinese population here has tended to become part of the local culture. The younger people reflect American patterns, and many of Houston's older generation were those responsible for establishing Christian congregations in the city.

The Chinese Family

In many ways the Chinese family is like others in this country and city. It contains fewer children now than previously, and family ties are looser than in the past. Relationships, however, show subtle differences, and the Chinese identify more fully with others who have the same family name. Traditionally the Chinese have shown strong support for the family group, and parents have encouraged their children toward education and personal achievement. Young men and women have been discouraged from "wasting their time" with activities that do not aid personal achievement. For their part, Chinese children feel a need to please their parents, particularly in attaining an education. Many older Chinese in Houston were expected to work long hours in the stores owned by their parents or relatives. The children of today are not expected to work as much in family businesses, and discipline is

The 1940 census showed 121 Chinese in Houston. As depicted in the 1942 photograph, taken at the Wah Kew Association headquarters, 1911 Louisiana, there were several families with children and grandchildren. E. K. T. Chen, fifth adult from the left, was the first Chinese professional in Houston—a professor at the University of Houston. Mr. Chu, sixth adult from the left, was the owner of the Quong Yick; Mrs. Chu is the first adult on the left. Under the center flag is Albert Gee, a prominent restauranteur for many years in Houston. Next to him are Vice-Consul and Mrs. T. L. Quang, who came to represent the Republic of China in 1932. At the far right is George Leo, wearing his military uniform. He served under General Claire Chennault in the "Flying Tigers."

less strict than it once was. Because of this change, many older Chinese think the children of today have too much freedom and independence.

The Chinese, like other Asian people, give considerable importance to the large or extended family that exists beyond the parents and children. Of special importance to the Chinese are the family associations—people with the same name such as the Chens, Wongs, Engs, Lees, Joes, and Gees. Some confusion arises because the same name may be spelled in many ways, such as *Chen, Chien,* and *Chan.* Historically these associations provided a sense of security, identity, and a general feeling of community among the newcomers to America. They helped people to get started in their new homes, settled disputes within the group, and generally brought newcomers into the system, even aiding them in times of need. For example, associations were very important in keeping Chinese off welfare rolls during the depression. Family associations in Houston go back some thirty years, but the great growth of the Chinese people here has expanded their number and changed their character. At present there are approximately a dozen such groups, the most active including the Joes, Gees, Chens, Engs, and Lees. These groups are not highly organized but remain loose associations of families with the same heritage who gather together primarily for social occasions. The most important gathering is the family banquet at the lunar New Year, when perhaps hundreds of cousins, uncles, and others who are related by a common surname gather for a great feast.

The family associations of Houston continue to perform other functions. When members get into trouble, the association may step in to help. It also provides rewards, such as prizes and scholarships to family members who achieve good grades. Other activities of particular groups include credit unions and informal mediation services and, especially, helping to preserve the heritage and sense of identity for the family in this new society.

This last goal has not been easy in contemporary Houston; the Chinese population has exploded, and as was mentioned earlier, the Chinese live in many neighborhoods of Houston. People of the same name do not necessarily know one another as they did some years ago when Houston was smaller. Also, the older associations were mainly Cantonese and were led by the commercial elements of the community. The new-comers are from Taiwan and other Mandarin-speaking areas and have different social and educational backgrounds. The associations are facing difficulties, there-fore, at the same time that the Chinese have grown from a small, close-knit group to a large, varied so-ciety. Yet the family has been one of the main reasons for stability among the Chinese in Houston, and nothing illustrates this better than ethnic crime rates in Houston.

Crime

In spite of dramatic early stories of Tong Wars and fic-tional characters such as Fu Manchu, the Chinese have developed a well-deserved reputation as law-abiding citizens. Statistics for the twentieth century show that arrest rates for serious crimes committed by the Chi-nese have been well below the average for the rest of the population. The Chinese have more often been the *victims* of murder, burglary, rape, and other violent crimes. Chinese women have been even less involved in criminal incidents than Chinese men and also all women in general, and a study of serious federal crimes in America from 1934 to 1960 found very few Chinese women involved in wrongdoing. During one nine-year period not a single Chinese woman was sen-tenced to prison. Equally impressive has been the gen-erally small number of youths accused of juvenile de-

linquency; study after study has noted the remarkably low level of juvenile crime among all Orientals in the United States.

This pattern has also tended to hold true for Hous-ton, where violent crime perpetrated by Asians has consistently been below that of other elements of the population. For example, there were 359 homicides in Houston during the first half of 1979, and not one Ori-ental was accused. There were 3 cases in which Asians were, however, the victims.

The explanation for low crime rates among the Chi-nese in general and their youth in particular has been based upon their close family life. The pattern reflects the encouragement, sense of responsibility, affection with firmness, and pride in heritage that characterizes the Chinese upbringing. Respect for family, education, and the social order have all been ingredients for de-veloping healthy attitudes. Many sociologists who are aware of these familial traits of the Oriental groups believe that the lack of a strong family life can offer a partial explanation for the increase of crime among other ethnic communities and especially among those people who do not have a group of which to feel a part.

The Chinese history of good citizenship has come under considerable pressure in cities such as San Francisco, Los Angeles, and New York. The Immigra-tion Act of 1965 brought a great influx of newcomers into ghetto-like Chinatowns. Some young people who were unable to obtain jobs turned to street gangs, and the very size of the new population made it difficult to turn to traditional ways of controlling them. Family associations had grown so large that many people did not know one another, and the "small-town" atmo-sphere of the old Chinatowns no longer existed.

Fortunately, this has not been the experience in Houston, in spite of great increases in the number of Chinese in the city. It is true that the traditional family associations are not as tightly knit as they once were, and not all the Chinese know one another as they did a generation ago. However, the absence of an over-crowded Chinatown, along with the many opportuni-ties for jobs, education, and advancement that Houston provides, have meant that newcomers have not been

A Chinese basketball team was formed in Houston. They were called the Whiz Kids and were affiliated with the Dragoneers, a youth group.

strained to the extent that they have in other places. In this environment traditional family values and ties continue to play a role in making the Chinese community a model of good citizenship.

Education

The Chinese have a strong commitment to the education of their children. Originally illiterate and unskilled workers who were discriminated against by other Americans, they have sought to provide their youth with tools to compete in the modern world. Even when looking at the small prewar Houston Chinese community of fifty-two boys and girls, we see this drive for education. In the decade after 1933, when the first Chinese children attended public schools in Houston, the city had its first Chinese high school graduates and the first Chinese students to graduate from Rice Institute and the University of Houston. Not only did these individuals obtain their degrees, but

they began a tradition of graduating with honors in Houston high schools, colleges, and universities.

In the years since, Chinese have become faculty members of all the major colleges and universities in Houston, and the number attending as students has risen dramatically. Almost every Chinese boy or girl graduates from high school. By 1980 there were approximately one thousand Chinese students at the University of Houston and ninety at Rice University, with others at neighboring institutions. Chinese students earned more than fifty doctorate and seventy-five master's degrees in the 1970s. Few other ethnic groups can compete with the Chinese in their drive to give their children the gift of an education, and few take more pride in their accomplishments.

However, the community seeks more than a modern Western education; the Chinese have long sought to give their children a sense of their own heritage. As early as 1938 and again in 1946, there were short-lived attempts to hold a Chinese language school to give

In 1954 the Chinese American Citizens Alliance (CACA) established a lodge in Houston; approximately 20 percent of the members were professionals. Shown in this illustration are the first president, Edward K. T. Chen; the vice-president, Albert Gee, who later became the first grand president of the national organization to come from outside California; and Hobert Joe, who later established a chain of supermarkets in Houston and served as president of the Texas Retail Grocers' Association.

children some training in speaking, reading, and writing their native tongue. In 1970 the Institute of Chinese Culture was formed, and since then it has held classes in Chinese language and culture for people of all ages. On Saturdays students ranging in age from the young to the old attend classes in the Cantonese and Mandarin dialects at Rice University. Those whose heritage is Chinese are not alone in trying to learn about this nation of almost a billion people. Bellaire High School offers Chinese language classes; Memorial High School has classes on Asia; and local universities give courses in Chinese history, political science, philosophy, and art.

How Chinese Are the Chinese?

Observers of ethnic groups in the United States usually focus on the factors that make them different and the extent to which their members retain traditional ways from the "old country." A corollary is the question of how much they have become assimilated into American society—that is, the degree to which once-distinct people, such as the Germans, Russians, and French, have come to resemble the general populace called "American." Of course, the Chinese have had greater difficulty in assimilating fully, because their features and color always distinguish them from other groups, no matter how they may act and feel.

In portraying the Chinese in Houston, one can ask who is changing, what is changing, and what is still Chinese in character. *Who is changing?* is perhaps the easiest question to answer. The most Americanized tend to be those who have been here the longest and who are the children and grandchildren of immigrants. Parents and grandparents often complain that the youth of today are losing sight of their Chinese heritage and that they eat, play, think, and work more like other Americans.

To answer the question *What is changing?* one needs to look at language, way of life, and customs. In spite of efforts to maintain the Chinese language through private schools, it is normally only spoken fluently by those born in China. The youth born and raised in the United States have generally not been as interested as their parents in their Chinese cultural heritage, and have experienced difficulty in speaking their parents' or grandparents' native language. Similarly, traditional customs and lifestyles brought from China become less important to immigrants the longer they live here and as the next generation seeks to become Americanized. This attitude of not wanting to be different is to be found in the children of other ethnic groups as well.

What, then, is left that makes these people Chinese, other than features and color? Many of the older generation and immigrants speak and read the language, although they may differ in dialect and ability. Newcomers often read newspapers, magazines, and books from the People's Republic of China or Taiwan. There are distinct Chinese cultural likes and dislikes; for example, many older local and foreign-born Chinese are interested in Chinese culture as it is manifested in music, Chinese opera, painting, ceramics, films, and so on, although the youth are less excited by these pursuits than are their parents.

Traditional customs brought from China are declining in importance. Only a minority celebrates the moon festivals, such as the August Moon Festival, when special cakes are made; the Red Egg Ceremony, related to birth; weddings in the old style; or the burning of incense in their homes. In general, women, older people, and new immigrants are more likely to participate in these activities. Most Chinese in Houston continue to celebrate the lunar New Year, when large banquets and parties are held. Often, however, they use this time to entertain their non-Oriental friends. At the same time, this celebration is less elaborate in Houston, or even in San Francisco and New York, than it is in parts of modern Asia, where it lasts several days and involves such customs as exchanging greeting cards and gifts, setting off firecrackers, and even paying one's debts before the start of the new year.

Another area in which one may see the maintenance of some Chinese ways is in their tendency (like so many other Americans) to join a wide variety of ethnic associations. These have become important for social events, protection for the group, fellowship, and a sense of identity. There are many Chinese churches, as previously mentioned, plus the family associations and such organizations as the Chinese American Citizens Alliance, Chinese Professional Club, Taiwan Cultural Association, Chinese Merchants' Association, and on and on. Each has a special function for its Chinese members, but that function may relate more to particulars of life in Houston than to its members' all being Chinese.

While some traditional customs and lifestyles are weakening, three interlocking elements of Chinese culture remain as the foundation of community life and are vital to maintain. The first is the role of the family, both the parent-child relationship and the extended family. This is the basis for the discipline, goals, and values of the child and is valued above all else by most of Houston's Chinese. Second is a desire for education; the family encourages and pressures the child to obtain the best schooling possible in order to gain a better life. This leads to the third element, a very strong achievement motivation. Many older Chinese remark that they have not found the time for hobbies and sports, and that they are not "leisure-oriented." They spend their time developing their businesses, families, and societies. While these goals are not unique to the Chinese, the community does emphasize their importance to a greater extent than do many other groups in Houston. And most important, they define these goals of family, education, and achievement as the core of what it means to be Chinese in America.

Indochinese

Fred R. von der Mehden

Dancers in native Cambodian costume waiting to perform at the 1981 Asian American Festival.

The Indochinese arriving on our shores are among America's most recent immigrants, the majority coming here only in the past decade.[1] Like the Germans of the 1840s, the Jews of the 1940s, and the Hungarians of the 1950s, most left their homeland to escape political repression. To most Americans they are mysterious and exotic, a people whose heritage is largely unknown and whose recent past is clouded by a long and controversial war. In this chapter we seek to dispel many delusions regarding the Indochinese and to explain the heritage, customs, and present lifestyle of Houston's new neighbors.

The Historic Heritage

The Indochinese are composed of three major elements, each with their own history, language, and customs: the Cambodians (now often called the Kampucheans and earlier the Khmers), the Laos (including the Hmong and other tribal groups), and the Vietnamese. Each group also varies internally in its cultural and social heritage. The Indochinese were joined together only by a relatively brief period of French colonial rule, and all have suffered through the postwar conflict that wracked Indochina and the recent imposition of communism. We are therefore not discussing a single society, but several communities with quite separate heritages.

This is not the place to provide a detailed history of Indochina. (See Suggested Readings at the end for a list of books.) However, the very recentness of their immigration emphasizes the importance of understanding the region in which most Indochinese have spent the majority of their lives. The following brief histories are meant to present a limited view of the environments that helped to shape these new Houstonians.

Laos

Laos is a landlocked state approximately the size of Kansas. Its history has been one of dissension and external pressure. Divided into two kingdoms at the beginning of

1. The author wishes to thank Bui Tien Khoi for his help in preparing this chapter.

the seventeenth century, it saw parts of its land dominated or annexed by Thailand, Vietnam, and China. Finally, at the end of the nineteenth century, it came under the control of the French, who made it part of their Indochina possessions. It remained largely a neglected colony with little attention being paid to education, economic development, or the establishment of a sense of national unity. The development that did take place was among the Mekong Lao people, lowlanders who composed approximately two-thirds of the population. Various tribal groups were usually left to themselves, but even lowland Laos often found communication with the people of northern Thailand easier than with neighboring Vietnam or Cambodia.

French control was first broken by the Japanese during World War II and was not firmly reestablished after the war. A growing sense of Lao nationalism finally led to an initial grant of autonomy and finally independence. However, this was not the signal for unity. Even in the 1950s, many Laos did not know that they lived in a country called Laos, and many who did were divided along political, ethnic, and cultural lines. Divisions between the Mekong Lao and tribal elements persisted. Anticommunist nationalists experienced internal conflicts and were opposed to the communist-dominated Pathet Lao. The Pathet Lao in their turn were heavily supported by the North Vietnamese communists, who stationed large numbers of troops in the provinces bordering their country. These tensions periodically broke out into warfare between communist and noncommunist forces, and Laos remained a battleground until the victory of the Pathet Lao and their Vietnamese allies in 1975. Even today there are minor antigovernment insurgency activities in the hills.

Aside from this internal dissension, what was it like in the Laos that these refugees left? Laos was and is a quite poor country, even by Asian standards. Its average per capita income is less than $100, and more than 85 percent of the population are farmers. There are no railroads, only poor roads outside the heavily populated areas, very little industry, and not much in the way of natural resources. The population is small—approximately three million—and there are no large cities. The two major capitals of Vietiane and Luang Prabang are only overgrown towns (in 1958 the populations were

Scene from Vietnam of more peaceful prewar days.

only 60,000 and 10,000, respectively), whose citizenry was increased by war in the countryside until Vietiane had some 200,000 in 1970.

The Laos gained little in the way of education or health from colonialism, and the situation did not improve with independence. Following World War II the government made efforts to expand education, and literacy had risen to almost 30 percent by the late 1950s. It did not increase dramatically after that, however, partly because of civil conflict. Secondary education, largely neglected by the French, was developed, although only 2,000 students were receiving training at that level in the late 1950s. Even now, under the communists, only 14 percent of high-school-age students are in secondary schools.

The Laos that the refugees left was a land divided by warring factions; it was poor, primarily agricultural, strongly committed to tradition, and less influenced by the West than were most other parts of Southeast Asia. At the same time, it is important to note that, given the diversity to be found in Laos, any individual Lao refugee may be quite different from another.

Cambodia (Kampuchea)

Cambodia has experienced a long and often glorious history, exemplified by the magnificent ruins of Angkor Wat. Today it is a relatively small ravaged state bordered by two historic enemies on the east and west—Vietnam and Thailand. Once a formidable empire (from the tenth to the fourteenth centuries), it later came under attack from the Thais and Vietnamese, losing territory to them and at times control of its own government. Finally, feeling endangered by those neighbors, Cambodia sought protection from the French in 1863. During the French

Angkor Wat in Cambodia symbolizes the great civilization that is the heritage of the Khmer people.

era Cambodia, like Laos, received little attention from the colonial administration. While it was able to maintain its monarchy (in name at least), economic and social development lagged. The administration remained mostly in French and Vietnamese hands; the Chinese and French dominated the economy, and education was severely limited, particularly past the primary grades.

Relatively untouched by the Japanese occupation and the disturbances in Vietnam, Cambodia gained its independence in 1953 under the leadership of King Sihanouk, later titled Head of State. During the next two decades, there were major efforts to modernize the country; but there was also the constant threat of being drawn into the Vietnamese war as both sides violated Cambodian territory. After the fall of Sihanouk in 1970, increasing communist pressure forced the new government back into the cities. Ultimately, the capital of Phnom Penh came under siege and fell in 1975. What followed was one of the great tragedies of modern times. The victorious communists under their leader, Pol Pot, forced men, women, and children out of the cities into the war-stricken countryside and systematically set out to eliminate supporters of the former regimes, including civil servants, military officers, professionals, and the educated. These atrocities account for the generally low level of education of many Cambodian refugees. We will never know the total number that died from starvation and execution, but estimates are between one and two million, with some figures as high as three million. Finally, after numerous border incidents, a small group of communist dissidents backed by the Vietnamese military marched into Cambodia, ending Pol Pot's rule in January 1979. Vietnam continues to maintain approximately 180,000 troops in Cambodia, and most Western states refuse to recognize the government of Phnom Penh as a completely independent state. Meanwhile, remnants of the Pol Pot regime, along with other antigovernment forces, continue to carry out attacks on the Vietnamese and their loyal Cambodian troops, particularly in the border regions. Any refugee leaving his or her homeland during the past dozen years has fled violence and disorder, and many of them are very fortunate to be alive at all.

Even before the disorders of the 1970s, Cambodia was one of the poorest states of Asia. With a population at that time of six to seven million (there was no accurate postwar census), it had an economy based on agriculture. The principal crops were rice and rubber, and fishing was another major activity. Approximately 90 percent of the population was rural before the war drove people into the cities. Unlike Laos, it did have one major city: Phnom Penh, which had a population of about 700,000 before hostilities and more than one million prior to the forced exodus in 1975. Also differing from the poeple of Laos, the population of Cambodia is largely homogeneous, approximately 85 percent being Khmer before many Chinese and Vietnamese were forced out during the seventies. If the people remained poor during this period, there were major strides in education; by 1970, approximately 60 percent of the adults were literate, and nine new universities and colleges had been established (with tertiary teaching in French). All of the economic and social advancements initiated in the postindependence era were brought to a standstill and then reversed during the seventies, and today a ravaged Cambodia seeks to rebuild something of what existed before, this time under the "tutelage" of the Vietnamese.

Vietnam

Vietnam's history has been heavily influenced by foreign occupation and domestic division. While united in language and ethnicity, the country was constantly faced with internal and external pressures. For eight centuries it was occupied by the Chinese, and even after the end of Chinese rule in 939 A.D., Vietnam had periods when it was a vassal of its powerful neighbor. The northern and southern sections of the nation were divided for lengthy periods during the sixteenth and nineteenth centuries. Though the country was united briefly under the Nguyen Dynasty after 1802, the divisive nature of its society gave the French opportunities to penetrate into the region. Cochin China (the far south) was annexed during the period from 1862 to 1867, while Annam (the central region) and Tonkin (the north) became "protectorates" in 1884. With the exception of a brief time in 1945, Vietnam was under French rule for the next seventy years.

French administration was far more intense in Vietnam than it was in the rest of Indochina. It established a sizable European civil service, maintained a tight hold on the economy (and allowed the Chinese to control much of the lower and middle levels of economic life), and severely limited political expression. Paris considered Vietnam a vital economic and political prize and was very reluctant to allow any degree of autonomy. It was in this environment that Vietnamese nationalism was born in the second decade of this century. What followed were periods of both nationalist and French violence, as moderates were unable to develop freely under colonial repression. It was a fertile ground for the growth of communist and other radical movements. In the post–World War II years the French continued to be reluctant to allow full independence, and conflict dominated the region until the defeat of colonial forces at Dien Bien Phu in 1954.

The Geneva Accords, which temporarily ended warfare, provided for a "provisional" division at the seventeenth parallel between the north—the Democratic Republic of Vietnam under the communists—and the Republic of Vietnam in the south, first under Ngo Dinh Diem, and under a series of military leaders after 1963. Relations between the two regions deteriorated during the 1950s as it became obvious that a peaceful unification of the country was not possible, and late in the decade the communists launched an all-out effort to unite the two Vietnams forcibly. More than fifteen years of fratricidal warfare followed, during which the United States became more deeply involved. Under Presidents Kennedy and Johnson, American activity increased until late 1969, when this country had 540,000 men in Vietnam, plus supporting units in Thailand and the Philippines. Responding in part to domestic pressure in the United States, President Nixon began withdrawing troops after his inauguration, and the last units left Vietnam in 1973. In 1975 the communists launched a major campaign, and their troops swiftly overcame South Vietnamese opposition, taking Saigon (renamed Ho Chi Minh City) in April of that year.

Most Vietnamese who came to the United States were from the south, although many had fled the north in 1954 when the country was divided. They are people who have faced colonial repression and lengthy civil war almost all their adult lives. We can, however, make some of the same observations about them that we did about the Laos and Cambodians. As was Cambodia, Vietnam was ethnically homogeneous, with approximately 90 percent of its population of almost 20 million being Vietnamese. Important minorities were the Chinese (800,000 to 1 million), the Cambodians (400,000), and hill tribes (70,000 to 100,000). At the beginning of the renewed fighting in the late 1950s, the country was predominantly rural, but violence in the countryside brought a major influx of people into the cities. Ultimately the urban population reached about 50 percent, and Saigon swelled to more than 3.5 million.

The fighting also badly hurt the agricultural economy as South Vietnam went from a net exporter to a major importer of its main crop—rice. The second export earner, rubber, was also reduced markedly. The country was never a major industrial center, the north having that role under the French, although military-oriented services became increasingly important. The south, however, was more affluent than the north, and per capita income reached approximately $175, compared with $90 for its communist neighbor.

Education received far more attention under colonial rule in Vietnam than it did in the rest of Indochina, although literacy never reached 20 percent under the French. Still, there were a few good secondary schools and professional and technical institutions. After independence, considerable activity took place in the educational field, and literacy rose to more than 80 percent. Secondary schools were given particular priority, and by the 1970s there were approximately 35,000 students in tertiary education.

In sum, the Vietnamese refugees who came to the United States tended to come from a more urban, educated, and economically developed society than did their Lao and Cambodian counterparts, but all had similar backgrounds of an environment of violence and instability.

The Exodus

The experiences of the Indochinese people in the past several decades have been filled with tragedy and promise, none more so than the mass exodus since 1975. During this period, more than one million Indochinese have fled their countries, taking refuge throughout the world. There have been three distinct periods of immigration to the United States, each reflecting differing circumstances in the homeland and each leading to variations in the type of immigrant. The first and smallest wave consisted of people who were already here at the time of the fall of Saigon in April 1975. They were mostly students, professionals, "war brides" of men formerly stationed in the region, and officials on temporary assignments in the United States. In early 1975 fewer than 30,000 lived in this country, with fewer than 100 in Houston. In our region they included 20 to 40 wives of former servicemen, 30 to 50 students, and a small number of instructors. At the time they were but a small proportion of a sizable Asian immigration that had taken place in the postwar period. From 1965 to 1974 the Vietnamese (who were and are by far the largest group of the Indochinese) constituted only 17,225 out of a total of 713,397 Asian immigrants. In the year before the fall of the South Vietnamese government, Vietnamese numbered only 3,194 of about 400,000 newcomers to the United States.

The collapse of anticommunist forces in Indochina during the spring of 1975 signaled the first major surge of refugees from Laos, Cambodia, and Vietnam. During those weeks, about 131,000 fled Vietnam (including a small number of Cambodians), thousands having been airlifted by the United States in those last difficult days. Almost immediately 32,000 came to this country, and in the next two years, a total of 144,758 arrived, almost half of whom took up residence in

Thousands of Vietnamese escaped, often in unsafe vessels. Large numbers of the "boat people" died or were robbed by pirates during their attempts to leave Vietnam.

California. Many Indochinese went to other countries, with France accepting the largest number.

At the time of this exodus, there were mixed views in the United States about welcoming these new-comers. President Ford and major newspapers such as the *New York Times* and *Christian Science Monitor* argued that we had a moral obligation to aid those who had put their faith in us during the long Indochinese war, and that the United States had always welcomed victims of oppression. Other local groups and politicians, particularly in California, worried openly about the impact of these new immigrants on jobs, welfare, and government services. Some argued that they would be right-wing activists, while others cautioned about the dangers of tropical diseases accom-panying the refugees. Some of these comments had obvious racial overtones.

What was this second wave like? They were young—nearly 50 percent under eighteen, and 38 percent un-der fifteen—with somewhat more males than females. About 50 percent were Catholics, and 27 percent were Buddhist. Around two-thirds were from an urban environment. Approximately 35,000 were heads of households, and a large proportion (62 percent) came with their families. They were better educated than most immigrants to the United States; 23 percent of the heads of household held university degrees, and al-most half had secondary educations. More than 50 per-cent had average fluency in English. Many were from the professions, government, and the military, al-

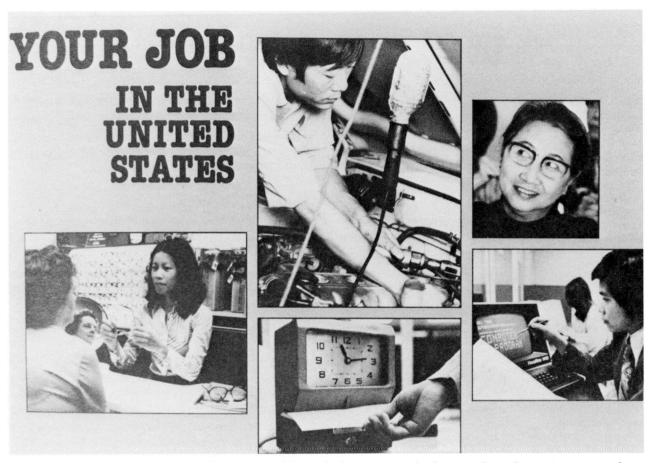

YOUR JOB
IN THE UNITED STATES

Pictures from posters and booklets prepared for Indochinese arrivals, showing them the environment of their new homeland.

though there were also fishermen and farmers. At the time there was considerable debate as to whether these people would be long-term wards of the state and might put a major strain on welfare programs. However, they tended to be very work-oriented; a study in 1977 showed that although one-third still received some government aid, this amounted to only 10 percent of their total income. The more urban and educated composition of this group made them somewhat easier to assimilate than the next exodus.

The biggest wave of refugees leaving Indochina began in late 1977 and was in many ways unlike the first two. Events in Southeast Asia had made life untenable for many in these communist states. The rising conflict between Vietnam and Cambodia had eliminated the

domination of the infamous Pol Pot regime that was responsible for mass deaths in Cambodia, but it also had opened up possibilities for leaving that war-torn country. Tension and violence between China and Vietnam put strains on the latter's Chinese population, which was suspect for both its loyalty and its capitalist tendencies. The Vietnamese in Laos began aiding the communist government there in efforts to control tribal elements. These and other factors led to a massive outpouring of refugees from Indochina. More than 250,000 Sino-Vietnamese fled across the border into the People's Republic of China; initially 80,000 Cambodians sought safety in Thailand, and another approximately 80,000 Laos made their way across the Mekong River into Northeast Thailand. Even today, tens of thousands remain in camps on the Thai border.

The most dramatic pictures of this flight, however, came from the "boat people," Vietnamese refugees who took to often unseaworthy craft to seek haven abroad. We are not sure how many died in the attempt, but the low estimate is 30,000 men, women, and children. In July 1979 the flow started; over 6,000 people left by boat, more than during the entire previous year. In spite of the high loss of life from sinkings, illness, and pirates, and an average cost of around $2,500, the number rose dramatically during the next months. By the end of the year almost 14,000 a month reached rescue ships and land areas in Southeast Asia, and the following June the number was 56,000. Their greeting in Southeast Asia was not always hospitable, as local governments saw them as an added burden to fragile economies and a danger to delicate domestic racial balances. Nor, obviously, did the communists in Vietnam want them, for as more than one observer noted, 56,000 people could not leave a totalitarian state in one month without, at least, the tacit approval of the state.

Unwelcome in Southeast Asia, these refugees sought homes in the West, and many countries other than the United States stepped forward to accept them. In addition to the 265,000 who went to China, 40,000 went to Australia, 63,000 to Canada, more than 100,000 to Western Europe, and a smattering to other regions throughout the world. Of the half-million Indochinese who came to the United States, most arrived in this third wave. Once here, the largest number settled in California (approximately one-third), although there have been efforts to discourage this movement. The next largest number settled in Texas (40,000 in 1981 by official statistics), followed by Washington (20,000), Pennsylvania (18,000), Illinois (17,000), and Minnesota (15,000), with forty states having fewer than 10,000. As we shall see, the Texas figures were understated.

In less than one decade, Houston had received a sizable proportion of this exodus. From fewer than 100 prior to 1975, approximately 5,000 Indochinese had settled in the area by 1977. By 1980 the number had risen from 16,000 to 20,000 as a result of the third wave of immigrants. Continued immigration directly from Southeast Asia, combined with an increasingly large secondary movement from elsewhere in the United States, raised that number from around 40,000 to 50,000 by 1983. While the first two waves were primarily Vietnamese (with a large proportion from Saigon), the final wave changed the pattern so that by 1980, only about two-thirds were from Vietnam. Of the rest, about 21 percent were Laotian, and 7 percent were Cambodian. The religious background has also changed over the years; early Vietnamese residents tended to be more heavily Christian than later settlers. The present pattern is approximately 30 percent Christian, 30 percent Buddhist, and 40 percent Confucian (heavily Vietnamese). Other demographics tend to reflect the national situation; about two-thirds of the people are under twenty-five years of age, and a majority of them are male. Finally, the third wave has been more rural, less well-educated, and has experienced several years of communist rule.

Arrival

The Indochinese who came to Houston arrived under a number of different circumstances. The Vietnamese who were here prior to 1975 came voluntarily—either accompanying husbands who had been servicemen in Southeast Asia, or seeking job opportunities. Their assimilation was relatively easy, given their family relationships, education, and professional ties. The second group, the ones who came after the communists' victory in 1975, also came by a number of different means. Some were fortunate enough to have families or immediate sponsors and were able to fly directly to the United States. (By mid-May approximately 14,000 Vietnamese had found homes in the United States through family and friends.) The largest contingent of refugees came first to centers such as those at Camp Pendleton, Camp Elgin, and Fort Chaffee prior to their arrival in Houston. Those who escaped Indochina in 1977 and in the years following were involved in a more difficult and ultimately more systematic process. Most had to spend some time in camps in Indonesia, Thailand, Malaysia, and the Philippines, where health, food, and housing were initially poor. There were many cases where the local population refused to allow refugee boats to land, while along the Thai border with Cambodia, fighting often overflowed into the camps. After a time international efforts led to a more structured process: while waiting in Southeast Asia the refugee received an initial orientation, English lessons, health screening, and other processing. Once the refugees gained medical approval and sponsorship in the United States, they were transferred to the United States. Each had to pay back the cost of his or her transportation.

Refugees are still leaving Indochina. But there has been some effort to discourage Laos from going abroad, and conditions have become somewhat better in Cambodia. In addition, the government of Vietnam has not been as active in encouraging flight as it once was. There is now an "Orderly Departure Program" by which 200 to 300 people are allowed to leave Vietnam each month if they have family ties abroad. A number of them now reside in Houston.

An integral part of the overall Indochinese refugee program has been cooperation between the United States government and private voluntary organizations. Government programs involved include the Bureau of Refugee Programs of the Department of State, the United States Department of Health and Human Services, the Texas Department of Human Resources, and public educational institutions, as well as a variety of other programs that deal with America's needy. A range of voluntary organizations have aided refugees in finding jobs and housing and in adjusting to American life. In Houston the most active voluntary organizations have been the Catholic Charities, the YMCA, the International Rescue Committee, and various Protestant and Jewish groups and congregations. The Harris County Refugee Council, composed of representatives of local voluntary agencies, businesses, federal, state, and local government, refugee associations, and educational institutions, coordinates most of the program, and the agencies make decisions about the number of refugees the area can accept (although many now come from other areas of the United States through secondary migration). The council also attempts to aid communication, understanding, and the study and service programs that deal with refugee problems.

Over the years, the process of settling the refugees has been refined. Voluntary agencies, with the help of small per-capita grants from the Department of State, act as sponsors for incoming refugees and seek out others to act as sponsors. The federal government provides the state's share of public assistance costs; initially the grant was for thirty-six months but is now for a diminished period. Most refugees in Harris County receive such support for much less than the authorized time, although more individuals who arrived after 1977 are on welfare. Other federal, state, and local programs provide aid in health, education, and housing. For example, the Houston Community College system provides training in English as a second language and vocational education and guidance, while the Houston Housing Authority (supported by the Department of Housing and Urban Development) provides public housing for refugees.

Private sponsors, however, have been the main reason that the refugees have been so successful in assimilating into Houston. Individuals, religious organizations, and charitable groups have all become involved in the process. While not required to give financial aid or to maintain any legal responsibility, sponsors are expected to help the refugees in finding housing and jobs, in settling into their new homes, and generally in becoming acquainted with the mysteries of Americans and that strange subculture, the Texan. Many of these contacts have developed into long-term relationships, with both learning something of the customs, history, and attitudes of the other. As the refugees become settled they gain greater independence, and the growing Indochinese population now provides continuing internal support that the earlier migrants lacked.

Why Houston? This city has become the center of the second-largest urban concentration of Indochinese in the United States—behind only Los Angeles. The many reasons for the choice have often been interdependent. The refugees who arrived before 1975 had come through Fort Chaffee, Arkansas, and Houston was one of the nearest metropolitan centers in the region. The semitropical nature of the city was also attractive to a people accustomed to a warm climate, and in subsequent years the climate has drawn many secondary migrants from the Midwest. Later, like other Americans, they were drawn by job opportunities. Some observers have asserted that there is a certain self-selection process going on as the more work-oriented come to Texas, where fewer welfare programs are available than elsewhere. Some newcomers came to Houston because they wanted to live near or with relatives; and this factor, combined with climate and jobs, has led to a large secondary migration that is not reflected in official statistics of the Indochinese population here. In addition to these voluntary movements, there have been government-sponsored programs such as the Cambodian Cluster plan, which has made Houston one of five cluster cities chosen for settlement. Finally, it should be noted that the Houston Indochinese community is gaining a reputation as a strongly integrated society. For example, the Vietnamese here can take pride in publishing five magazines and three newspapers—one with 10,000 readers—and maintaining a regular radio program.

Problems and Achievements

Most newcomers to our city have some difficulty in getting acculturated, but the combination of distinctively different cultural backgrounds and abrupt and traumatic departures from their homelands has made the process particularly hard for the Indochinese. Problems may vary among the refugees, depending upon their rural or urban backgrounds, education, time of arrival, and so on; but language, jobs, housing, and nostalgia for what they left behind have been especially pertinent. Before we assess these difficulties in detail, we might peruse a survey of several hundred Vietnamese here in Houston to provide some useful background. This poll was not a scientific sample and must be viewed only as illustrative of the situation.[2] Among the questions asked was "What do you think have been your two greatest difficulties here in Houston?" The choices to be checked were hous-

2. The author and Bui Tien Khoi conducted the poll using a short written questionnaire in English, Vietnamese, and Cambodian. We received several hundred replies.

ing, crime, language, jobs, schooling, "homesickness," and "other." Overall, the two problems checked most often were jobs and language, in that order, with homesickness third. What was most interesting were the differences between those who had arrived in this country by 1978 and those who came later. For the former, language and jobs remained important, but homesickness was checked the most frequently (more than 50 percent). Housing was specified by only two respondents and schooling by none, showing adjustment to the community. However, like other Houstonians, a sizable minority of the Indochinese mentioned crime, although it received few votes from the newcomers. For those arriving since 1979, jobs and language were important, being checked by almost 80 percent of the respondents. What these admittedly unscientific results seem to show is that during the first years the immediate problems of jobs and language are uppermost in the refugees' minds, whereas after a time they become less important and other problems take their place. It may also be possible to explain the homesickness variation (less than 20 percent among the newcomers) by hypothesizing that those leaving in 1975 remembered a precommunist Vietnam, while the newcomers had fled a country ruled by the communists.

Language and Education

Language and education are excellent examples of the problems and achievements of the Indochinese community. Even after seven years in the United States, many still express real frustration with English. For those who came from Vietnam in the early years, the transition to English was made easier because the Vietnamese language had been romanized under the French (although phonologically it provides greater problems than Lao or Cambodian). Many people had been educated in European-style schools, and a significant percentage had dealt with Americans during the war. Those from Laos and Cambodia were less fortunate, because of their generally rural backgrounds, the larger percentage without much formal schooling, and the necessity to learn an entirely different script.

Whatever their condition upon arrival, the refugees have generally displayed an intense desire to learn English in order to obtain jobs and enter into the life of the community around them.

The learning process is taking place on three levels. Children have joined the regular curriculum, augmented when necessary by English-language instruction. Once students conquer the language, they have often made considerable progress, as evidenced by scholastic awards, good grades, and a high proportion of college entrance. Traditional respect for learning and teachers and a pattern of hard work have aided their transition into the American system. Factors contributing to their difficulties have included educational methods different from those in Indochina, including communist schooling for recent arrivals, and problems in acculturating to our social system. However, the very progress noted by many of their teachers and administrators may lead to problems at home. Tensions arise between the youth, who can speak English and relate to American culture, and older members of the family, who are accustomed to respect and who now find themselves dependent on their children and grandchildren for translating both the American language and lifestyle. Many parents express increasing dismay at the "Americanization" of their offspring.

A second group is composed of adults who seek both language and skill training. English classes are available through the school system and various voluntary agencies, and they vary in length and intensity. Vocational training comes largely through Houston Community College, which also teaches English as a second language. After achieving sufficient language capability, a Houston Community College student can receive schooling in a variety of skills to become a machinist, welder, computer operator, air conditioning repair worker, auto mechanic, body repairman, or other skilled worker. The jobs they have secured have initially paid from $5.00 to $8.50 per hour. Several thousand refugees have gone through classes at the Houston Community College, San Jacinto College, and other area schools.

A third element is the regular college student. All of Harris County's colleges and universities have experienced a major growth in Indochinese students. The largest student body is at the University of Houston, with approximately six hundred Vietnamese students alone. (The Vietnamese have, by far, the largest percentage of college students among the Indochinese.) Following the pattern of other Asians in the United States, they tend to major in engineering, computer sciences, and accounting, with very few concentrating on the humanities or social sciences. Some Asian-Americans who have studied this situation fear that the Indochinese will be trained only for technical jobs and will therefore not be prepared to compete for positions in higher management. Whatever the case, Houston's institutions of higher education must be prepared to welcome a major influx of Indochinese students during the coming decade.

Housing

A significant problem for many within the Indochinese community and a major achievement for others has been in the area of housing. There is almost universal agreement as to the problems in obtaining adequate housing:

1. The large size of many families reduces opportunities for rental. This problem was compounded until 1983 when more housing became available, reversing a steadily declining vacancy rate in Houston (down from 8.4 percent in 1975 to 6.6 percent in 1979, and ranging between 1 and 4 percent throughout early 1982) and a traditional inadequacy of public housing in the area. This not only affects large families but also many young men who attempt to reduce costs by crowding into apartments.

2. The low income of the refugees limits their possibilities for housing, although there are subsidies available. Those housed in hotel rooms find themselves without cooking facilities, adding to costs unless the manager is tolerant regarding groceries and hot plates. In public housing, the Indochinese face problems if they cannot find employment, or their rents increase as their salaries rise. Like other Houstonians, the Indochinese find high interest rates a hindrance to home ownership.

3. Language difficulties impair the refugees' ability to articulate grievances, and ignorance of our laws hinders their being able to recognize their rights as tenants.

4. Violence and vandalism have been rampant in housing projects, and the Indochinese have expressed considerable fear for their personal safety and that of their possessions. Many will not leave their apartments in the evening, and past problems with authorities in Asia make them reluctant to turn to the police. However, violence has not all been one-sided, as evidenced by recent problems with young people who are no longer contained by traditional controls.

5. Cultural differences are often a problem; other residents in densely populated hotels, housing projects, and low-cost housing areas complain about the refugees' living habits. The most frequent complaints arise over issues of sanitation, the growing of vegetable gardens (and attendant flooding), strange smells from exotic cooking, drying fish, and noise standards. Issues of violence and cultural variations are often expressed in racial terms between the Indochinese and other minorities who feel that the former are "foreigners" participating in programs that should rightfully be limited to Americans.

Along with these problems, there have also been some remarkable accomplishments. By carefully saving and combining the incomes of the extended family, many Indochinese have been able to purchase homes. This is particularly true of those who arrived between 1975 and 1977, many of whom had the advantages of education and urban work experience. A high percentage of these families (some say up to 80 percent) now own their own homes, primarily in the west and southwest parts of Houston in areas such as Alief and Almeda-Genoa. Some subsidies have been available, such as those provided by the Church World Service. Some of the more affluent have purchased property for investment, renting it out to other refugees.

A striking innovation in housing is the Khmer Village, a collection of brick cottages off the Eastex Freeway just outside Loop 610. (There is also a second group of houses nearby.) Under the leadership of Mrs. Yani Rose Keo of the Catholic Charities resettlement office, these rather dilapidated cottages were refurbished and rented to approximately forty-five Cambodian families for a relatively small amount paid through the Catholic Charities. The Khmer Village provides more than just housing; its residents also find themselves with fellow countrymen and receive help with English, careers, and orientation into American society.

Two aspects of this housing situation are most encouraging. First, a strong desire for independence and a family environment has led the Indochinese to make major efforts toward home ownership. Second, the Indochinese are not congregating into an ethnic ghetto; once they are financially able, they are spreading out into the city and its suburbs. Like other Houstonians, they seek good schools, a secure environment, and an opportunity to lead independent lives.

Employment

Indochinese refugees have faced the problem of obtaining a job—almost any job—in order to feed themselves and their families, and getting the right kind of employment. The latter goal varies according to the background of the individual. Desirable employment has been most difficult among those who held white-collar, high-status positions in Southeast Asia and who had expectations of finding similar work in the United States. This has been a very important factor, for the Indochinese came from a society where white-collar employment was held in considerable respect, and blue-collar work had little status. The refugees who came to the United States in 1975 and 1976 included a considerably higher percentage of professionals and managers and a much smaller percentage of blue-collar workers than the general population. A majority of heads of families of this group also had at least a secondary school education, which in Southeast Asia was a key to a white-collar job. This pattern changed with the refugees who came after 1977, but a random survey of the Vietnamese in Houston in 1982 still showed that a high percentage held white-collar positions in Vietnam.

What the refugees found when they arrived in the

United States was that employers often discounted past experience and education. For example, the doctors who initially fled (approximately 1,500 in number) discovered that it was difficult to enter practice in this country. Overall the refugees found that their first jobs were well below their previous positions, although those with blue-collar skills were generally more fortunate. This has been a very traumatic experience for husbands who feel underemployed and for wives who, in a white-collar family in Indochina, did not have to enter the work force, particularly in menial jobs. In the United States, a significantly higher percentage of refugee women work than is true of the general population.

For most Indochinese arriving on our shores, the problem has been not the right kind of job, but any job at all. Initial unemployment among the refugees was very high—almost one-third—with about three-quarters of the group underemployed. This pattern decreased rapidly over time, and a survey of those who came between 1975 and 1977 showed that fewer than 5 percent of heads of households were unemployed after twenty-seven months. The situation was somewhat different for the last group of immigrants, who tended to be less well educated and more rural in background. However, the Indochinese have shown themselves to be very hard workers. In fact, their strong work orientation has often caused tension with other Americans who find them "over-industrious." Reports by employers in Houston are generally very positive; once Indochinese workers know the rules and our attitudes toward time, they prove to be very conscientious employees.

The refugees still face many obstacles in finding employment, including a lack of language skills, difficulty in getting formal certification and in having their experience accepted, problems with transportation and learning about a modern urban society (particularly for many rural Laos and Cambodians), trade union and licensing restrictions, the need for citizenship or permanent-alien status for some activities, and a lack of knowledge about the job market.

Economic recession is a particular problem for the Indochinese. Those who came in 1975 and 1976 arrived during a business downturn, and the newcomers face the even more serious economic problems of the post-1980 recession. Last-hired/first-fired policies hit the newly trained skilled workers, and some families that sponsored other refugees have found themselves with serious economic burdens. When added to the traumas of flight and acculturation, this becomes a difficult psychological problem for the refugees as well.

The Indochinese in Houston today hold occupations of endless variety—ranging from skilled physicians to those who pick up trash along the freeways. The majority, though, hold blue-collar and service jobs. With the aid of training at Houston Community College, sizable numbers are employed as machinists, welders, and draftsmen at various machine, tool, and electronics firms. (In 1982 approximately 90 percent of the refugees who graduated from HCC were hired.) Those who came in the early years are more likely to be in professional, business, or technical occupations, but the survey of Vietnamese in Houston mentioned earlier also found many newcomers employed in white-collar jobs such as clerk, accountant, photographer, and medical professional, along with a large proportion of students. A particularly interesting result of the study was that while parents tended to look forward to skilled worker jobs for themselves, they have very high aspirations for their children. When asked what occupation they would like for their offspring, the overwhelming answer was engineering, with medical professions second. This corresponds to an earlier study of Indochinese who arrived in the United States between 1975 and 1977, wherein the author expressed the belief that many refugees were transferring their own future aspirations to their children.

The Indochinese, particularly the Vietnamese, have also gone into private business. While many are involved in managing convenience stores, others own restaurants, grocery stores, machine shops, architectural firms, laundries, apartments, tailor shops, theaters, liquor stores, and beauty shops. Major shopping centers for the Vietnamese include the Crystal Palace on Main Street, the Vietnam Plaza on Austin Street, the Vietnam Center on Milam, and the Indochinese Center on Milam; but Vietnamese-owned operations tend

Many Vietnamese restaurants and shops have opened throughout Houston. They are usually small, family-oriented businesses. Photograph by Cary Wintz.

to be found throughout the city today. These are usually family-operated establishments in which the whole family works. Many are found in areas that normally cater to Houston's growing Asian population, which now numbers more than 130,000 people. Because there are not currently any Indochinese banks, the finances for these firms normally come from savings and the aid of the extended family. In the first half dozen years since their arrival, approximately a hundred Vietnamese firms were established, and the number is burgeoning. Few have expanded beyond the "Mom and Pop" type of store, but there are a few successful larger firms. Given the work ethic of this population and the sizable Chinese ethnic element among the Vietnamese here (in Southeast Asia, the Chinese tend to be the entrepreneurs), the city can expect an expanding number of Indochinese enterprises.

Acculturation

A major problem for most Indochinese in Houston is adapting to American customs and lifestyles, although some have discovered greater obstacles than others. Acculturation is, for example, normally more difficult for those who come from basically rural and agrarian environments, those with little previous contact with Americans or Europeans, and older men and women more steeped in traditional ways. The young, particularly those who arrived young and entered directly into our school system, have adapted the most easily. For most adults, however, tensions have arisen on several levels: acculturation into American lifestyles, interaction with Americans, homesickness, and changing loyalty patterns from the "old country" to their new homes.

Acculturation is made difficult for the Indochinese by the isolation fostered by differences in language and customs, and by their uncertainty about the new culture in which they find themselves. Texans and other Americans vary markedly in manner and lifestyle from the ways traditionally followed in Indochinese homelands. This is not the place to provide a detailed account of those differences (see the appendices for analyses of variations among the three ethnic groups and possible problems with students), but a hint of the difficulties faced by these newcomers may be obtained from some of the following "Do's" and "Don'ts" formulated in a federal government document for the Vietnamese:

DO . . expect Americans to be surprised if you visit them without being invited.

DO . . expect more informality in the classroom. (DON'T interpret this as a lack of politeness or respect.)

DO . . expect Americans to be upset if they are standing in line . . . and you move in front of them.

DO . . expect Americans to smile and say "thank you" when you say that you enjoyed the food or you think someone's dress is pretty. It is not the nature of Americans to be self-effacing.

DO . . expect that Americans will disapprove if you let your young children urinate outside.

DO . . expect Americans to be on time for business appointments.

DON'T . . be surprised to find that the manner of working is different here.

DON'T . . be surprised to find that while Americans believe in equal opportunities for all, they do accept the fact that inequalities exist.

DON'T . . be surprised to see American husbands washing the dishes or caring for the baby and American wives doing carpentry or repair work.

DON'T . . be surprised if Americans stare or giggle at two young men who are holding hands or walking arm in arm.

DON'T . . be surprised to find that Americans may express displeasure in public.

DON'T . . be surprised to see that many elderly people prefer to live apart from their children.

DON'T . . be surprised if you find that many of these do's and don'ts are not true in all cases.

Many Indochinese are deeply concerned that they, and more particularly their children, will lose their attachment to important values in their culture. The preservation of that heritage is a much discussed problem in refugee circles. This effort is made difficult by the lack of contact with home governments, the often fractured leadership of the communities, the pervasiveness of the American lifestyle, and the absence of wage-earner parents—leaving the children to listen to rock music, watch television, and eat Big Macs. Central to the fears of the older people is the weakening of their native language over time as future generations become less fluent. Many see language as the foundation for maintaining their heritage. At this time these efforts to preserve the various cultures is somewhat haphazard in Houston. The most important ways in which refugees have kept their attachment to traditional values and customs have been the various associations that they have formed, the family, and the observance of special ceremonies and days.

The people of Cambodia, Laos, and Vietnam have for centuries celebrated a number of important occasions, some religous holidays, some family observances, others national in character. While many of these, such as marriages and birth and death rituals, may not be observed by the general public, others have long been times of widespread celebration. The most well-known and important in Southeast Asia and now in the United States have centered on New Year's Day. For each community the date and means of commemoration vary. The Lao New Year is celebrated in April or May and is called Pi Mai; the Vietnamese have Tet in February; and the Cambodians have their festivities, Chaul Chhnam Tmey, in April. During this time, the Laos clean their houses, altars, and statues of Buddha, pour water on one another with great glee, and give special respect to their elders. In Laos this activity lasts for two weeks. Tet is traditionally the birthday for all, as everyone becomes a year older on that day. Over a period of several days houses are specially decorated, people attempt to make a new start in their lives, special respect is given elders, and visiting and festivity take place. The Cambodians have three days during which they celebrate religious ceremonies, visiting their family and friends and generally enjoying themselves. There are other special dates as well. The Christians follow practices known in other Catholic societies; the Buddhists commemorate Buddha's birth, enlightenment, and death; the Cambodians pray for the souls of the dead on All Souls' Day; and there are various politically important dates such as Vietnam's National Ancestors' and Founders' Day. Each of these and other days gives the community the opportunity to reestablish its ties to the past and remember its heritage.

Difficulties with the American population have arisen over a series of economic and social issues. A large proportion of our society has not welcomed the refugees, particularly after the influx of large numbers after 1978. At that time, a national Harris Poll found that 62 to 72 percent of the respondents believed that "We had too many problems resettling Vietnam refugees right after the war, so it would be a mistake to let more of them come settle here." The majority of every region and political orientation—liberal, middle-of-the-road, and conservative—were in agreement, with the exception of those who were college educated. It also became apparent that many of those American citizens who were on welfare feared that the refugees already here were obtaining support "rightfully theirs," or at least aid beyond what American citizens would receive under similar circumstances. There were other economic elements, such as the presence of fishermen along the Texas Coast, that created worries about the impact of the newcomers on local people's livelihoods. Differences in customs and physical makeup, when combined with the Indochinese emphasis on industriousness and lack of observance of local mores and procedures, have also caused tensions in housing and jobs. However, the history of

America is replete with conflicts over newcomers, from the anti-Irish sentiments of the nineteenth century and prejudice against Southern and Eastern Europeans early in this century to the antipathy shown to Haitians in the 1980s. History also tells us that these tensions tend to diminish over time.

To combat these problems of isolation and separation from the mainstream, the Indochinese in Houston have engaged themselves in a wide variety of associations composed largely of their own people. The first of these grew out of religious organizations joined when the refugees first arrived. Since that time religious activities have developed in a major way. The various groups have established their own congregations—the Vietnamese Catholic Conference, Vietnamese Buddhist Association, Vietnamese Christians Association, and Huyen Quang Buddhists Family. The Catholics are the best organized, and the Catholic Conference has membership from nine churches, each with a Vietnamese priest (Holy Rosary, Notre Dame, Sacred Heart, St. Christopher, St. Jerome, St. Luke, St. Vincent de Paul, St. Mary, and St. Peter House of Prayer).

In recent years, secular organizations of all kinds have proliferated; they deal with cultural affairs, veterans' activities, specific professions, education, the martial arts, and so forth. These include such associations as the Lac Viet Cultural and Civic Organization, Vietnamese Society for Culture, Vietnamese Doctors Association, Vietnamese Dentists Association, International Martial Arts Association, Cambodian Mutual Assistance Program, Cambodian Association in Houston, Laotian Association in Houston, Vietnamese Ex-Officers Association, Vietnamese Students Association of both Houston and the Houston Community College, Overseas Supporting Force for Reconquest of Vietnam, Human Love Association, Voice of Vietnam, Texas American Vietnamese Education Association, Truong Son Scout Association, and Vietnamese Fishermen Association. Obviously, the Vietnamese are far better organized than the Laos and Cambodians because of their earlier arrival, better education, larger numbers, and more urban backgrounds. The ethnic orientation of these associations reflects both a degree of isolation from mainline Houston groups and a desire for mutual support.

Finally, the refugees have faced the persistent problems of "homesickness" and ambiguity about establishing permanent residence in the United States. Many older Indochinese feel quite nostalgic about the old country and have romanticized conditions there as they were in the past. The forced and abrupt means of their departure and immediate need for jobs and housing led to an initial concentration on gaining a livelihood; but as their situation has improved, homesickness has tended to increase. Despondency and other psychological problems have often resulted. The impact may be greatest on the older population, on those most isolated from the American community, and those who have not acquired positions with the status and income that they held back home. This situation is not unique among the Indochinese, but it needs to be recognized by members of the general community who relate to them.

Many Indochinese also feel a certain ambiguity about their ultimate loyalties. Like so many other political refugees that came before them, they dream that conditions in the old homeland will change and that they will be allowed to return. They continue their ties with relatives by infrequent correspondence and by sending financial aid to their kin in Indochina. Indigenous language magazines and media help to remind them of what they have lost. Other groups have experienced a similar pattern: a period of transition from the expectation of return, to the decision that their permanent home is here in the United States, or, simplistically put, a change from refugee to immigrant. We already see many of the early arrivals applying for American citizenship and participating in political action. In Houston the sizable Asian population has tentatively discussed possible political coalitions; in the future we can expect them to be a potent force. However, the sorrow over the loss of friends, relatives, and a familiar way of life will remain.

Goals

A major clue to the goals of such a heterogeneous population as the Indochinese can be found in the tragic personal experience of so many refugees. In light of these histories, we should not be surprised that their paramount concerns should be security for the individual and the family. Providing the foundation for a sense of security is an amalgam of new and old values. Both the nuclear family and the extended family have traditionally been important to these communities, and the fact that many families were broken up by the exodus has reinforced the centrality of the unit. Even more than before, parents' aspirations for the future have been transferred to their children, and they place strong emphasis on educational attainment. We can expect a steady influx of Indochinese students into our colleges and universities and more award-winning children in our lower schools.

As we have already seen, securing an appropriate job is another important goal of the Indochinese. In addition, safety from crime and owning one's own home will become more important as other concerns are resolved.

Finally, the refugee communities regularly discuss the preservation of their traditional cultures and languages. While they have not given up the hope of returning "home," many are looking toward citizenship and greater involvement in their new homeland. In the coming decade Houston must be ready to assimilate an Indochinese population that is likely to reach at least 100,000; the better we understand their histories and values, the easier the process will be.

Japanese

Fred R. von der Mehden

Japanese residents of Houston gathered in front of the Sawamura residence during the visit of Mr. Tsurumi in the mid-1930s. Photograph from the Institute of Texan Cultures (gift of Hope Kobayashi).

*T*he Japanese who first came to the United States were considered quite strange and exotic. For almost three centuries, their homeland had cut itself off from the rest of the world, and when it was opened to the West by Admiral Perry in 1853, it was a mutually fascinating experience. Since that time, Americans of Japanese ancestry have moved into the mainstream of American life, and a modernized Japan has become the major trading partner of the United States. This chapter attempts to present the history of Japanese settlement in the United States, Texas, and Houston; the role of the Japanese in this city; and some perspectives on what the Japanese who live in Houston are like.

Japanese Immigration Into the United States

Like other immigrants from Asia, the Japanese who came to American shores first settled in Hawaii and along the West Coast. As agricultural laborers under contract to the government of Hawaii, they arrived in the islands prior to Hawaii's annexation by the United States in 1898. Over the past century, they have become the largest ethnic group in the islands, rising to positions of prominence in economic, professional, and political life. In Hawaii, Americans of Japanese ancestry have been elected to the United States House of Representatives, the Senate, and the governorship of the state. At this time, approximately a quarter of a million Japanese live in Hawaii, which also hosts an increasingly large number of Japanese tourists. (Today hotels and shops often have signs in both Japanese and English.)

The Japanese who came to the mainland were of two types. Initially, most of these early travelers were students from upper-class families who had been sent abroad to learn about the West and then return home. However, this element was soon outnumbered by the laborers who began arriving around 1869. Ultimately, most of the latter turned to agricultural pursuits, particularly truck gardening and nursery activities. Discriminated against in education and jobs and prohibited from obtaining citizenship, the urban Japanese tended to become house servants, gardeners, and restaurant and small shop owners.

Before World War II, the Japanese remained a very small part of the national population, reaching only approximately 280,000 in 1941, of whom slightly more than 125,000 lived on the mainland. Their small numbers, however, did not alleviate strong anti-Japanese attitudes, particularly on the West Coast. They, along with other Asians, became characterized as the "Yellow Peril" and were objects of distrust and dislike. The reasons for this suspicion varied from antagonism toward Japanese military activities in Asia, to reactions from farmers and labor organizations to Japanese competition. As a result, cities made numerous efforts to limit their activities; Los Angeles, for example, refused to allow the Japanese on public tennis courts, and San Francisco attempted to segregate them in the schools. Pressure from local interests led to the "Gentlemen's Agreement" of 1907–08 between the Japanese and American governments to limit Japanese immigration to the United States. Later the state of California passed the Alien Land Act of 1913, which prohibited those ineligible to become citizens from owning land; and a federally established quota system all but stopped immigration.

While these tensions subsided somewhat after World War I, the Japanese attack on Pearl Harbor on December 7, 1941, led to the most tragic period in the history of the Japanese in America. The United States government, reacting to the wartime hysteria and the pressure of economic and nativist interests, evacuated approximately 100,000 Japanese from the West Coast region, including 70,000 American citizens. Viewed as necessary to the economy of the islands, the 157,000 Japanese in Hawaii were not moved. The unfortunate people living in California, Washington, Oregon, and parts of Arizona were forced into concentration camps with such speed that they lost some $400 to $500 million dollars in the sale and theft of homes, businesses, farms, and personal property. Very little of this was returned after the war, and even today the United States Congress is arguing the issue of compensation. In spite of this treatment, some 18,000 Japanese Americans served in the armed forces; the war's most decorated American unit was the Japanese 442nd Infantry Battalion (3,600 Purple Hearts, 810 Bronze Stars, 550 Oak Leaf Clusters, 342 Silver Stars, 123 Divisional Citations, 47 Distinguished Service Crosses, 17

Legions of Merit, 7 Presidential Unit Citations, 1 Congressional Medal of Honor, and almost 10,000 casualties). Meanwhile, many of their families had to remain in the camps until 1945, when they were closed after the United States Supreme Court finally held that Japanese-American internment was unconstitutional.

Most of the Japanese returned to the West Coast after the war, but they came into a changing environment where far less antagonism prevailed. In part this was due to the arrival of about 20,000 war brides in the United States, and to the experiences of thousands of Americans who had become entranced with Japan during the occupation of that country. Many Americans were also embarrassed about the internment of Japanese and Japanese-Americans during the war. After the end of the quota system Japanese immigration into the United States increased, and by the end of the 1970s about three-quarters of a million Japanese were residing in this country. This growth did not lead to a reassertion of discrimination against the Japanese as people (although some Americans have been unhappy with Japan's trade policies); a combination of court rulings and a generally more open society helped wither away the laws and practices of former years. Asians of all backgrounds suffer from some discriminatory attitudes and practices even today, but the level is significantly below that of the prewar period.

Go East, Young Man

The postwar years showed a movement of more and more Japanese away from their previous centers of Hawaii and the West Coast. In 1940 only 15,000 Japanese lived in other parts of the country; but only thirty years later, the number had increased by more than 100,000. In part this was due to the evacuation itself; some escaped internment by moving east prior to the official orders; later, others refused to return after their incarceration. Eastern states such as Illinois, New York, Connecticut, New Jersey, and Virginia experienced large influxes of new Japanese residents. Texas and the Southwest also began to attract a sizable Japanese population interested in the opportunities provided by the Sunbelt. The number

of Japanese in Texas, New Mexico, Oklahoma, Louisiana, and Arkansas, which had been only 38 in 1900 and 1,250 in 1940, reached almost 12,000 in 1970, according to census figures. Texas was by far the largest recipient of new Japanese residents, growing from 13 in 1900 and 458 in 1940 to more than 6,000 in 1970. (It should be noted that census figures on minorities are often low.) By 1980 the total Japanese population, including foreign residents, was approximately 10,000, mostly concentrated in Houston, Dallas, San Antonio, and El Paso.

Texas had never been the home of a large Japanese population prior to the war. Even the temporary work provided to many Chinese on the railroads had not attracted the Japanese. The immigrants from Japan who settled in the state were involved in rice farming, an occupation in which they had considerable skill. At the beginning of this century, a number of Japanese-sponsored rice colonization schemes were initiated in Del Rio, Garwood, Port Lavaca, League City, and Webster. While most of these efforts failed, those in Garwood and Webster led to permanent settlements, the latter becoming the original seedbed of Japanese expansion into Houston. The Webster colony was founded by a man of considerable prominence in his mother country: Seito Saibara was a member of the samurai class, a lawyer, a Christian in a Buddhist land, former member of the Japanese House of Representatives, and onetime student at the Hartford Theological Seminary. Starting in 1903, he established his settlement in southwest Harris County. He hoped to attract about 1,500 new settlers, but hardships and immigration laws kept the number between 60 and 70; even in 1980, Webster had slightly more than 2,100 people, only 5 percent of whom were Asian. These original settlers kept largely to agricultural pursuits, broadening their interest from rice to citrus fruits, truck gardening, and nursery work. Other latecomers eventually turned to owning restaurants, food distributorships, and shops in the city of Houston.

These early immigrants were generally not landless workers or peasants. Of the first nineteen families that settled in Harris County, only one head of household came from a family that rented more land than it owned. Most of the men who came to the area, though, were not first sons and therefore could not inherit the family land

Kiyoaki Saibara, left, and an unidentified rice-field worker are shown tending their crops near Houston about 1906. Photograph from the Nancy Saibara Collection, Institute of Texan Cultures.

in Japan. Nor were they uneducated; all had at least an elementary-school education, half had attended high schools or professional institutions, and one had graduated from college.

The Japanese who came to Harris County did not have an easy time. The flat lands of the region were unlike the hills and mountains of their homeland. Their efforts to grow citrus fruits were frequently defeated by the weather; and as in the agricultural colonies established by other ethnic groups in Texas, internal dissension often caused splits in these small communities. The Japanese also suffered from racial discrimination, although it was not as virulent as on the West Coast. The most serious problems were in the Valley and West Texas, and it was an El Paso state senator who initiated a Texas version of the Alien Land Act in 1921. Even that act was less damaging to Japanese immigrants than was its California counterpart, since it did not apply to land already held by Texas residents at the time of its passage. Also, the Japanese were not segregated officially and were allowed in theaters, restaurants, and hotels. These conditions were due in part to the small size of the Asian population in the state and city, the relative isolation of farming enterprises, and major efforts by Japanese leaders to Americanize themselves and their children. As Seito Saibara told his grandson, Robert (who was later to become the first Japanese-American to be promoted to lieutenant colonel in World War II): "I hope the day will never come when there shall be armed conflict between Japan and the United States. If there should be, your duty lies with your native America."

Even during the war that did come, the treatment of Japanese persons in Harris County was not as bad as it was in California and other areas on the West Coast. It was certainly not a comfortable period, and most first-generation men were interned for periods of a few weeks to more than a year; but local Japanese were generally allowed to go about their business uninterrupted. After the war, the rescue of the Texas "Lost Battalion" by the 442nd was viewed as a debt of honor by many Texans, and when a Japanese veteran of that unit was refused the purchase of land in Tomball, various veterans' organizations came to his aid. The war

was a turning point for the Japanese in Houston. A number of other Japanese began to move in during and after the conflict, and the community in Texas doubled in the 1940s and more than quadrupled in the next decade. A new generation of Japanese-Americans began to lead different lives.

The Japanese in Houston Today

The Japanese in Houston today consist of three groups. Perhaps the largest, numbering approximately one or two thousand, is temporary residents—businessmen, doctors, government officials, students, and their families (see Appendix). They are usually here for only a few years before returning to Japan or being assigned to other overseas posts. In addition, the city hosts large numbers of tourists and other visitors from Japan. Houston has become a major center of Japanese economic interests. This is not entirely a postwar phenomenon; even the early settlers maintained close contacts with Japanese representatives in the United States. Before the war, the consulate in Chicago and later New Orleans looked after national interests in the Gulf Coast region, and holidays such as the Emperor's birthday were often honored by local Japanese.

The opening of the Port of Houston brought shipping from all over the world to the city, and one of its major customers was Japan. A listing of departures and arrivals for any two months of the 1930s usually shows ten or twelve ships bound to or from Japan or Houston. The war halted this trade, and it was not until 1951 that the first postwar Japanese ship docked at the port. Before the war, exports to Japan were mostly cotton, and there were Japanese branch offices and the semiofficial Japan Foreign Trade Bureau in the city. Perhaps a sign of change could be seen in the arrival of the Japanese ship in 1951, which showed the Port of Houston receiving its first foreign load of steel ingots—not tea, as might have been expected historically. Since that time, trade has increased enormously. As the figures below show, exports to Japan out of the Port of Houston between 1960 and 1980 increased more than six times, while imports grew from less than $25 million to

The Japanese Art Store, 715 Main Street, in 1911. The photograph originally appeared in the Business Album of Houston *(1911); that album is now in the Houston Public Library collection.*

more than $1.6 billion. This last amount is even more impressive when one considers that approximately two-thirds of Japanese goods reaching Houston come by rail, truck, and plane from the West Coast. Today Japan is Houston's second-largest direct trading partner, surpassed only by Saudi Arabia with its large oil interests. There is considerably more variety in our Japanese trade: imports consist primarily of autos, iron and steel products, and machine tools; exports are corn, cereals, petrochemicals, and machinery. In the past twenty years the pattern of trade has displayed some interesting changes. For example, imports of autos from Japan totalled less than $400,000 in 1960 but were more than $477 million in 1980, while exports in 1960 were almost 50 percent cotton, an item that accounted for approximately 1 percent of exports in 1980.

To handle all of this activity, more than a hundred Japanese firms have opened branch offices in Houston. These companies handle an amazing variety of products, including oil-field needs, tires, houses, autos and trucks, machinery, food, ceramic tiles, iron, steel, elec-

Table 1
Port of Houston Trade with Japan,
1960–1980

	1960	1970	1980
Imports	$24,613,293	$159,137,868	$1,670,128,568
Exports	64,560,086	125,587,610	393,623,937

tronics, and nuts and bolts—literally everything from soup to nuts. Houstonians know these products and firms by trade names such as Sony, Toyota, National, Daiwa, Mitsui, Fuji, Toshiba, Honda, Japan Air Lines, Hitachi, Mitsubishi, Kawasaki, Datsun, and so on. Other businesses that cater to both Japanese and American needs are several shipping companies, eleven banks (the largest foreign representation in Houston), eight restaurants, and numerous grocery stores and translation services catering to the Japanese community.

The average Houstonian may now wake up in his or her Japanese-built home, turn on the Japanese radio, eat breakfast prepared with Japanese home appliances, drive to work in a Datsun, Honda, Toyota, or Subaru, deal with several Japanese firms during the day, then return home to look at the Japanese television, perhaps stopping along the way to dine in a Japanese restaurant.

By the late 1970s, the Japanese foreign community was making itself known in the city. The number of Japanese companies with branches in Houston rose from thirty-eight in 1979 to eighty three years later, and a sizable consulate staff and the Japanese External Trade Relations Office (JETRO) were in place. Though the Japanese live in many parts of Houston, the Memorial area has become a center of considerable activity of this foreign community. Many Japanese families reside there; the office of a Japanese trade association and cultural center (complete with a small library and film collection) has been established on Memorial Drive; and a Saturday school in Japanese language and mathematics has been opened there. Local fish shops even provide signs in both English and Japanese for shoppers looking for *sushi* (raw fish).

This predominantly business community has not been well integrated with the general Houston populace or the local Japanese-American community. This is due in part to the temporary nature of that group; other contributing factors include the tendency for Japanese overseas to interact primarily among themselves (much like Americans do when they live abroad) and language difficulties on all sides. For instance, many local Americans of Japanese ancestry do not know the language of their forefathers. The Japanese consulate and Japanese-American societies work vigorously to develop a better understanding, however, and as more Houstonians travel to the Orient there is less mutual ignorance.

The second largest group living in Houston comprise the progeny of those who came to the Houston area in the first half of this century—the old-timers. Before we discuss this group, it would be useful to define certain important terms employed to designate the different generations of Japanese in the United States. First-generation immigrants are called *issei,* and their children are referred to as *nisei.* The third generation are the *sansei,* and the fourth are the *yonsei.* Most of Houston's first *issei* are now gone, although a new postwar generation of *issei* have now settled in the city. The present progeny of these pioneers are of the *nisei, sansei,* and *yonsei* generations. This is a relatively small group, which in the mid-1950s consisted of only twenty-seven families and slightly more than a hundred individuals. However, it provides an excellent example of growth and assimilation.

Through the decades, these Houston-area Japanese became more and more Americanized; even the older generation became assimilated into the local culture. At the same time, children began to differ from their parents as the old country had less influence in their homes, customs, and lifestyles. American and Texas food, speech, and sports became far more attractive to the youth. Some older-generation leaders such as Seito Saibara had encouraged the community to accept the standards of their adopted country, and the local environment accomplished much of the rest. The small size of the Japanese population here meant greater interaction with other elements of the commu-

A small group of Japanese were photographed in the mid-1920s in a formal pose. Photograph from the Institute of Texan Cultures (gift of William Kagawa).

nity, unlike their counterparts on the West Coast. In addition, the Japanese-Americans moving into the city did not congregate in one isolated residential area, but made their homes in various parts of metropolitan Houston. This meant that the youths were able to learn English more quickly, and it accelerated the process of assimilation.

Further aiding this assimilation was a reverence for education, found in most Asian immigrants. While the efforts to foster interest in Japanese language and customs among second- and third-generation youth were less than totally successful, *nisei* and *sansei* children readily took to American education. They attended local high schools, and by the mid-1950s this small

group had more than thirty college graduates and two doctorates, in spite of some problems of discrimination. Upon the advent of World War II, many of these well-educated youth became officers in the United States armed forces, including three brothers who were graduates of Texas A&M University. Today these descendants of Harris County rice farmers are American in language and interests and have largely left the land to become businessmen, educators, and professionals.

The third group of Japanese living in Houston consists of those who have taken up permanent residence since World War II. This population is composed of Japanese-Americans who have moved to the Southwest

Table 2
Japanese in Harris County and Texas, 1979

Harris County

Government	56
Businessmen and families	83
Students and visiting scholars	193
Green card holders [1]	261
Others	17
Total	610

Texas

Temporary visitors	3,200
Green card holders	1,000
Japanese-Americans	5,000 [2]

1. Includes international marriage
2. Mostly concentrated in Houston, San Antonio, College Station, Dallas/Fort Worth, and El Paso

from the West Coast and Hawaii, a few from other parts of the country, and new immigrants to the United States. It is a very heterogeneous community, consisting of Japanese "war brides" (there are also a few European war brides of Japanese veterans), individuals who decided to take advantage of the Sunbelt economy after the war, businessmen and their families transferred to Houston by their companies, and others. It is difficult to assess the total number of these newcomers, but they probably do not exceed 1,000. There is no strictly Japanese residential neighborhood; most of these families live on the west side of town in middle-class and relatively affluent areas, reflecting their often technical business and professional occupations.

Being Japanese in Houston in the 1980s

When the question is asked, what is it like to be of Japanese ancestry in Houston in the 1980s, no single answer is possible. For the majority of Japanese residing in Houston, this is a temporary stopping place on the way to another assignment overseas or back in Japan. Japan is home, and there is a close attachment to that country, its language, customs, and heritage. Most of the men have their primary contacts with local and Japanese business associates, and socially they tend to gather with other countrymen except for official functions. Some of these individuals are alumni of American colleges and universities, and they interact with Houstonians more easily. Their wives (few foreign Japanese women work outside of the home) try to cope with a strange environment and language, while their children tend to do exceedingly well in American public schools. Their educational capabilities, small numbers, and middle- to upper-class backgrounds minimize overt discrimination, a pattern generally mirrored in attitudes toward Japanese-Americans. However, their values and goals remain those of the professional and business sector of modernized Japan.

The growing Japanese-American population can be characterized in terms of education, occupation, residency, internal organization, and social behavior. While it is a varied community, the people tend to be well educated, with a relatively high percentage of them in technical and professional occupations. (Houston has a smaller percentage of Japanese-American teachers than in the western United States.) The group is, overall, more prosperous than their counterparts in Hawaii and on the West Coast, who include a discernible element at the poverty level. Most live on the west side of Houston, with a scattering in suburbs to the north and around Clear Lake City.

Internally the community is not well organized; there are few churches, clubs, or societies. The Japan Society is composed primarily of non-Japanese who are interested in Japanese culture, art, politics, and society. At one time there was a club composed of war brides, but it has not met for a number of years. A Japanese Citizens' League exists and is quite active, but it by no means includes all Japanese-Americans in the area. No organization of those who fought in past wars has been formed, although there is a list of local veterans of the 442nd. In other words, this is a group of individuals and families that is only in the process of

Some Japanese at a picnic in Harris County Park around 1930. Photograph from the Institute of Texan Cultures (gift of William Kagawa).

forming itself into a community. It has no real focus, and its high level of adaptability into the American culture has weakened old ties.

Looking at the values of the Japanese-American population, we should probably differentiate among generations. While the *issei* and *nisei* may still maintain many old-country values, the *sansei* and *yonsei* have become highly acculturated. This is probably particularly true of those in the Houston area, with its highly mobile general population and small and somewhat fragmented Japanese community. The same ethnic ghettos of Asians are not found here as they are in the western part of the United States; but even there, the younger Japanese-Americans display a high degree of acculturation. As Harry Kitano notes in his book on the Japanese Americans:

Sansei *are, on most measurements of acculturation, almost identical to the Caucasian group. Their test results, achievement and interest preference, and social values are typically American. They are members of Little League, fraternities, sororities, and other organizations designed on American models, although these are still primarily ethnic in their membership. But even these structural barriers are breaking down.* Sansei *college students now sometimes join non-Japanese fraternities and sororities, and intermarriage is increasing, although the preference of most remains to marry within the group. In general, however,* Sansei *thinking and behavior are American.*

At the same time, many young people have taken the opportunity to visit Japan and are more forceful than

their parents in criticizing discrimination when it occurs. In spite of this, older-generation Japanese are dis-
turbed by this loss of cultural heritage and seek ways
of reminding the youth of their background. Still, it
would be a mistake to argue that traditional values
have been submerged completely by the American experience. The Japanese emphasis on family has remained strong, and racial separation has reinforced
particular community values. While American urban
attitudes toward marriage and the nuclear family have
had their impact, the more traditional family structure
is stronger than in the general population and has been
the basis of explanations for the relatively low levels of
crime and juvenile delinquency among Japanese in the
United States—a pattern that is well known in Japan
itself. Education, upward mobility, and achievement
have also been highly prized by all generations, making the Japanese model citizens. As a result, in spite of
racial barriers, Japanese-Americans have experienced
considerable material success; as Kitano ends his
study: "When we look back on the past prejudice and
discrimination faced by the Japanese, we find that even
their most optimistic dreams have been surpassed.
Such a story may give us some optimism for the future
of race relations in the American society."

The Japanese in Houston reflect this sense of
achievement.

Greeks

Donna Collins

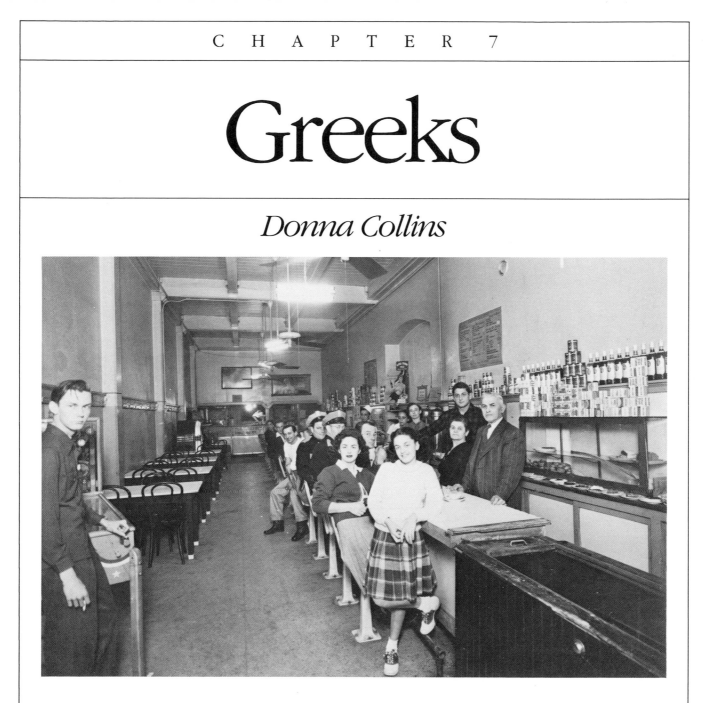

Preston Cafe, 605 Preston, in 1947. The restaurant was owned by Stelios Demetre, pictured here with his family, employees, and customers.

The Greek Festival has become a Houston tradition, when the city looks forward to sharing in the heritage of its Greek community for three days each October. Those who attend the festivities get a glimpse of the Greek-American spirit, reflected in the traditional music and dancing, food, and gaiety, as well as in the Greek Orthodox faith that undergirds the community. In this brief introduction to the Houston Greek community, I will attempt to familiarize the reader with Greek immigration to Houston, the early days of the Greek community here, and the growth of the community from its small beginnings to its present size and prominence in Houston.

Greek Immigration to the United States

There are several complications involved in determining how many Greek-Americans live in the United States, or even how many Greek people immigrated to this country. For example, American authorities consider an individual's nationality to be determined by the country of his birth, while Greeks look to his heritage. To the Greeks, a person born of Greek parents in Turkey is a Greek, not the Turk he is classified as being by American immigration authorities. Many of the people who have immigrated to the United States from Turkey, Bulgaria, Egypt, and other non-Greek territories have actually been Greeks, and this discrepancy is not reflected in immigration statistics. A second complication is that many Greeks who came to America returned to Greece; some of them later reentered the United States one or more times. As a result, some of the statistics on immigration represent a recounting of the same person. The United States census of 1970 found about 450,000 Greek-Americans. This figure appears to underestimate the actual number, since it includes only those people who immigrated from Greece proper, and even then, only the first two generations. Other sources estimate that there are from 1.3 to 1.5 million Greek-Americans.

At any rate, immigration from Greece has never been of the magnitude of immigration from other European countries such as Germany, Ireland, and Italy. Greek immigration was no more than a trickle until the years 1881 to 1890, when about 2,300 Greeks entered the United States. Each decade that followed saw an increase in Greek immigration until the quota laws of 1921 and 1924 effectively limited immigration from southern and eastern Europe. Immigration has again increased since the relaxation of the restrictions in 1965 (see Table 1), and these more recent immigrants will be considered in a later section of this chapter.

Overpopulation, agricultural problems, economic depression, wars, and political instability contributed to the exodus of Greeks to America. Those Greeks from areas within the Ottoman Empire emigrated to avoid military service or to escape persecution. For example, one woman who emigrated from Turkey in 1913 said that when she came to America she could sleep at night without fear because she felt safe for the first time. The majority of those who left Greece, however, were uneducated peasants from rural areas who came to take advantage of the economic opportunities in the United States that were lacking in their homeland. Immigration reached such proportions that by 1910 an estimated one-fifth to one-fourth of the total labor force of Greece had left, and about three-quarters of the men between the ages of eighteen and thirty-five had departed from Sparta.

Another factor in immigration was the dowry system. Parents traditionally had to provide sizable dowries for their daughters, and until the young women were provided with dowries that would enable them to wed, their brothers were not supposed to marry. Many Greek men thus came to America, where it was much easier to raise dowries for their daughters or sisters. A few Greek women also came to find husbands outside the context of the dowry system; but Greece's emigrants were overwhelmingly male, about 95 percent according to some estimates.[1]

Even though the Greeks came mostly from rural areas, they preferred to settle in the cities when they arrived in America rather than seek agricultural employment. They had known only hard times working on the soil and

---

1. This gender imbalance is reflected in Houston's census figures as well. By 1930 there were 248 men and 78 women who were born in Greece; the Greek-born population was 75 percent male.

Table 1
Immigrants to the United States from Greece and Turkey

Period	Turkey	Greece
1871–1880	404	210
1881–1890	3,782	2,308
1891–1900	30,425	15,979
1901–1910	157,369	167,519
1911–1920	134,066	184,201
1921–1930	33,824	51,201
1931–1940	1,065	9,119
1941–1950	798	8,973
1951–1960	3,519	47,608
1961–1970	10,142	85,969
1971–1975	6,629	56,191

Source: United States Immigration and Naturalization Service Annual Report, 1975 (Washington, D.C.: 1976), pp. 86–88.

wanted to make new lives. In urban areas they could also find the companionship of other Greeks, which they understandably sought. This was the case in Houston as well.

The Early Days

The first Greeks known to have come to Houston arrived in about 1888. These were the Polemanakos brothers, who established first a series of fruit stands, then later a confectionary on Main Street. A few years later, according to the 1900 census, Houston had 18 people born in Greece and 20 born in Turkey (a large percentage of these were probably Greeks); these figures jumped to 132 and 155 by the census of 1910. Following a pattern typical throughout the United States, the few Greeks who settled in Houston attracted others from their home-towns, who came to join their *patrioti* (people who come from the same village or island). In Houston many early settlers came from Coroni in the Peloponnesus; somewhat later, a large group came from the island of Patmos, although many other regions and islands are also represented here.

These first settlers were all males, either bachelors or married men who had left their families behind in Greece. Typically they sold fruits, nuts, and candies from pushcarts or stands in the central market; others ran tai-lor shops and cleaning shops, shoeshine parlors, pool halls, and saloons; a bit later, several entered the motion-picture theater business. The most common Greek busi-nesses, however, were confectionaries and small cafes in the downtown area. Regardless of the specific type of business involved, the Greeks sought economic indepen-dence by becoming small businessmen. Usually a new-comer found his first job working for a Greek who was already established in business. He might shine shoes, wash dishes, tend bar, or serve as a clerk in a confection-ary or bakery shop. As soon as the newcomer learned enough English and earned enough capital, he set up his own business in which he, in turn, hired more recent arrivals. Frequently the employee, and even the proprie-tor, lived on the premises. A son describes his father's experiences, which were typical:

When he arrived from Greece, he worked at this shoe-shine parlor, and his pay was a dollar and a half a week. It had a second-story storage room and that's where my dad lived. His blankets consisted of news-paper during the winter months, and that's how he kept warm.[2]

Although the men occasionally gathered at the local version of the Greek *kaffeneion* (coffeehouse) to play cards, gamble, and pass the time in conversation with compatriots, the rule was hard work with very little time off for relaxation. The men worked to support them-selves and to send money back to their families; but pri-marily they struggled to make their fortunes so that they could set themselves up in business back home when they returned to Greece. Most never intended to remain in the United States. Since there was little or no commit-

2. This interview and the others quoted in this chapter were conducted orally by the author in 1981. Respondents in-cluded first- and second-generation men and women from the Houston Greek community.

A saloon on Milam Street was one early Greek business. The proprietor is leaning on the bar in the foreground.

ment to America as a permanent home, ties to Greece remained strong.

The first Greek woman arrived in Houston in 1903 under rather unusual circumstances, as reported by her daughter:

My mother came here looking for her father, because he had left the family at home in Greece and come, and he was working here. At first he would send money, and then he didn't for a long time. She decided she was going to take it on herself to come here and find her father.

She found her father operating a candy and fruit stall in the city market, and two years later she married the young Greek man who was his assistant.

At her wedding, she was the only woman there. And my mother had to set the table and everything. The kumbaro (wedding sponsor) was cooking in the kitchen, and he'd come out there and do the stefana, you know, his part in the ceremony; then he'd run to the kitchen and stir the food they were going to serve.

Gradually more Greek women came to Houston, usually the relatives of the men and women already here. In some cases they had been chosen as brides from photos sent to their brothers in Houston, who arranged the marriages for them. Other men sent word back to Greece that they sought brides, or returned to Greece to marry and then brought their wives back with them to Houston. The arrival of women marked the beginning of the Greek community, in the true sense of the word. As long as men were living here without families, there were no ties to keep them in America. Once they married and their children were born here, returning to Greece became less and less pressing. A commitment to Houston as home then became possible.

In spite of this attachment, the dream of returning to

Greece possibly died hard. In fact, many men did go home after they made enough money to enter into business in Greece. Others tried to do so, but returned to Houston—sometimes repeating the process several times.

My father's dream was to go back to Greece. His dream was not to stay here. This was, from an economic sense, his downfall, because he put all his eggs on the other side of the ocean rather than over here. And so his years of hard work and toil and sacrifice were not as rewarded as they might have been had he invested in the United States. Dad always harbored a thought of returning to Greece. He felt that he was Greek, and that he belonged in Thessaloniki, so he always harbored the idea that at retirement he would get his boys and return to the old country. And of course the longer he stayed and the more he saw us assimilated, the more he realized that the dream was impossible.

Perhaps because of the supposedly temporary nature of their settlement, the Houston Greeks at first had only a rudimentary community with virtually no institutions; there was not even a Greek Orthodox church in Houston for many years. Religion has always provided a center for ethnic communities in the United States; for the Greeks of Houston the closest Orthodox church, Sts. Constantine and Helen, was in Galveston. Services were occasionally held in other churches and in halls around town, but for weddings and baptisms, as well as for special holidays like Easter, they rode the interurban train to Galveston. Although it often had the spirit of an outing, an adventure, this long trip was also inconvenient. As more women arrived, there was more demand for weddings and baptisms, and church attendance was stressed more than it had been when the settlement was made up strictly of men who were working long hours to establish themselves. Eventually it became clear that Houston Greeks would have to build a church.

Establishing the Church

In 1916 the Pan-Hellenic Benevolent Brotherhood Elpis (Hope) was formed for the purpose of establishing a Greek Orthodox church in Houston. Its membership was about twenty-five men, but its inspiration came from a woman, as reported by a second-generation man:

My grandmother forced my father to get all the Greeks together to form a Greek church. Everybody approved that there would be a church—they'd raise the money. Daddy went around and asked everybody to donate to the church. He was taxing everybody what they were worth, so one was worth $10, the other $25.

They were far from wealthy, and it was a struggle to raise enough money to erect the church. Contributions were solicited and received from individuals and businesses, both Greek and non-Greek. In addition, a letter was placed in the two national Greek-language newspapers, the *Atlantis* and the *National Herald*, that stated, in part:

We are hereby making a request to all the devout compatriots in the United States who wish that our race be immortalized in this immense democracy and who wish to preserve our beautiful and holy religion and language which were saved through the long and bitter years of slavery [under the Turks], to come forward and contribute their mite so that we can realize this holy and noble objective.

Contributions from out-of-town Greeks—from Brenham, Austin, Beaumont, and Port Arthur—ranged from one to ten dollars.

Membership dues in the Elpis were one dollar a month, and to quote the secretary of the organization, "Sometimes they paid it, sometimes they didn't. Then we start from the beginning, nothing for the arrears—no penalty!" The officers of Elpis wrote and asked the Greeks of Dallas–Fort Worth to lend the plans of their church "to save the architectural costs, since our treasury isn't in a very good state." Perhaps the best description of the situation was given in a letter to a Greek who pledged money to the building fund and moved to another state without paying it. Reminding him of his obligation, the letter stated that the church was in debt and that "the local compatriots have given and are continuing to give every day—not from what

The interior of the present Annunciation Greek Orthodox Church, 3511 Yoakum.

is left over, not from their excess amounts, but by actually sacrificing in order to accomplish this holy objective."

Inaugural services were held at Annunciation Greek Orthodox Church in February 1918. The frame building at 509 Walker, across from City Hall, served as the focus for community activities until the present structure on Yoakum was built in 1952.

A Note on Orthodoxy

The Eastern Orthodox church represents a very ancient faith that goes back to the early days of Christianity. Christendom was originally divided into five sees—Rome, Constantinople, Jerusalem, Antioch, and Alexandria—each headed by a bishop or patriarch. These bishops governed the church together and were equal in power, with the Pope as the Bishop of Rome honored as "first among equals." Eventually differences in doctrine and practice between eastern and western Christianity, represented respectively by the four eastern patriarchs and the Pope, resulted in the schism of 1054 that divided Eastern Orthodoxy and Roman Catholicism.[3] The spiritual head of the Eastern Orthodoxy is the patriarch of Constantinople, and he is called the Ecumenical Patriarch; he is accorded the honor of first rank among the patriarchs but in no way rules or controls them.

3. Among the issues that precipitated the schism were the primacy of the Pope, which was not recognized in the East, and the Western church's addition of the "filioque" to the Nicene Creed. The statement in the creed was originally, "The Holy Spirit proceeds from the Father," to which the Western church added, "and the Son" (in Latin, *filioque*). Eastern Christianity felt this addition was unwarranted.

For several reasons, Orthodox people gradually established national churches with separate hierarchies and jurisdictions. For example, many of the Orthodox countries fell under the domination of the Ottoman Empire, and those that in time freed themselves established national churches so that they would be removed from the jurisdiction of the Ecumenical Patriarchate, which remained under the control of the Turks. Eastern Orthodoxy is thus now composed of a number of national churches—Greek, Romanian, Armenian, Russian, and so on—that are identical theologically, in dogma and in liturgy, but that differ primarily in the language of their church services and in their separate administrative jurisdictions. Immigrants who belong to these different Orthodox churches have come to America bringing with them their separate jurisdictions; as a result, one sees not a single American Orthodox church, but many ethnic Orthodox churches. There is no theological reason for their remaining separate in the United States, but ethnic tradition remains strong, and many of the people involved see little advantage to the administrative unification of the various churches.

Perhaps one of the main factors inhibiting unification is that in America the churches serve a social as well as a religious function; they provide a center for ethnic communities such as the Greeks, Russians, and Syrians. Much of the social life of Orthodox people revolves around their local church and its activities, and the church is truly a central feature and a unifying force for these communities. Historically, it has been the one institution that has consistently helped them maintain their ethnic community and identity; ethnic schools, fraternal and philanthropic organizations, and newspapers may come and go, but the church is constant. This was the case in Houston's early Greek community as well.

Social Life of the Early Community
Family Life

During the early days of the community, marriages were usually arranged; in fact, this was often the case even up to the time of World War II. A friend or relative of a man looking for a wife would approach a family that had a daughter of marriageable age, and they would discuss the matter. Of course, the family was not always receptive to the particular *proxenia,* or arranged marriage. If the suitor was acceptable, the parents would speak to their daughter.

A bunch of us went on a picnic, and this older man picked up his godchild—he was taking the boy out to dinner. We didn't have a car, so he gave us a ride home. I didn't notice that he paid any particular attention to me, but the next morning my mother got this phone call—that's how fast it was. This lady said, "Mrs. J., please pardon me for calling but Mr. So-and-so met your daughter and he is sending her a proxenia, *an offer of marriage." My father had already passed away then, and my mother said, "Well, he's my age! He would be good for me, but not my daughter!" This lady said, "I know that, but I had to tell you." She had to deliver the message.*

The rules were more flexible for boys, but for girls there was no such thing as dating—except perhaps after a couple became engaged, and even then they would be accompanied by one of the brothers of the girl. Even as recently as World War II, many girls were not allowed to date. For example, one woman could not take a date to her senior prom when she graduated from Rice; she could attend the party only because her brother agreed to be her escort.

In general, it was preferred that community members marry other Greeks, and many of the men returned to Greece to find brides. However, since there were few Greek women in Houston, and because of personal preferences, some of the early settlers—and some of their children as well—married non-Greeks. In some cases, these families eventually drifted away from the community; but frequently the non-Greek wife took an active part in the community and its affairs. For example, the largest single contributor to the building fund for the first church was the American wife of a Greek, and the first president of the American Hellenic Women's Society was a non-Greek as well.

Family roles were very traditional. The men worked

hard to support their families. In fact, they worked such long hours that the people we interviewed, when asked about their fathers, often had few memories of them except that they were "always at work." The husband was the undisputed head of the household. ("If Dad said 'no,' even if Mama wanted to say 'yes' it had to be 'no,' and that's the way it was with us.") The women remained at home, quite literally, and raised their children. According to one report, until about 1925 the men even did the grocery shopping because the women were expected to "stay in."

Most of them were at home, just mothers and wives. They sure didn't leave the house at all, just to visit each other is about all. All she did was raise her family the best way she could and made real good citizens and Christians.

In addition to this restriction, many of the women were hampered by knowing very little English. Men had to learn English to run their businesses. Women, since they were never forced to learn the language, relied on their husbands and children in situations where English was necessary.

Gradually the Greek women began to move out of the confines of the home and to interact more with the outside society. They also tried to take a more active role in the Greek community, even though the men officially ran its affairs as parish council members. Women frequently faced strong resistance when they attempted to increase their role in the community, but the men's disapproval did not prevent them from accomplishing their goals. As one young wife noted:

Some of the women were getting together a little organization to collect money for the church—nickels and dimes. The men heard about it, and they called us all together and told us we should stay out of it; it was none of our business. They said we didn't have a permit to organize and that they'd call in the police to arrest us if we continued. Then they took us before the icon of the Virgin Mary and made us swear we'd never do it again. On the way home I was so scared I could hardly stand up, my knees were shaking so.

But we didn't necessarily stay in! I'd go out about my business during the day and get home a little before my husband was due. I'd come in the front door and my mama would take my coat and hat and say, "Dinner's almost ready, hurry and get into your housedress—he'll be home in a few minutes!"

The women raised money for the church in various ways, but their primary role was the care of the sick and the needy, a community extension of the women's traditional family role of caring for others. By the time of World War II, they also took a more active role outside the community as well—selling war bonds and rolling bandages to help in the war effort.

Organizations

Eventually a number of fraternal and charitable organizations were established by the community; each of these had a different emphasis. The first was the American Hellenic Educational Progressive Association (AHEPA), a national organization that originated in Atlanta in 1922. It was established to help combat discrimination against Greeks, which was felt particularly in the South. The Ku Klux Klan, mirroring the nativist sentiment throughout the nation at the time, was antiforeign as well as antiblack, and Greeks were often victims of its attacks. AHEPA originally had two main purposes: to Americanize Greek immigrants, thereby making them good citizens, and to present a better image of the Greek community to the surrounding society. In accordance with these objectives, English was designated as its official language, and all AHEPA meetings were conducted in English. The Houston chapter of AHEPA (Number 29, Alexander the Great) was founded in 1923. Auxiliaries were formed for women (Daughters of Penelope), young men (Sons of Pericles), and young women (Maids of Athena).

A few years later, the Greek American Progressive Association (GAPA) was formed. As is apparent from its name, GAPA and its auxiliaries placed Greek heritage first in importance. Refusing to buckle under to the tide of antiforeignism that was sweeping the United States, the GAPAns were determined that their Greek heritage and identity would not be lost in America. Ac-

Ninth annual Christmas-tree party given by the Houston chapter of Order of AHERA, December 23, 1932.

cordingly, they insisted that their meetings be conducted only in Greek. Because of this, immigrants were able to take part in community affairs and assimilate themselves gradually into the larger society; so GAPA in Houston served as a vehicle for adjusting to American society.

Both AHEPA and GAPA accepted the fact that their members were in fact Americans and that their first allegiance lay with this country, but they differed in the emphasis they placed on their Hellenic tradition. Needless to say, there was tension throughout the na-

tion between these two organizations. GAPA, whose goals—although worthy—were perhaps too idealistic, has disbanded on the local level in Houston. AHEPA eventually lost its Americanizing emphasis. It has become a fellowship organization that emphasizes Hellenic heritage, thereby coming full circle by incorporating some of the goals of GAPA.

Another organization is the Philoptochos ("friend of the poor") Society, a church organization that grew out of the informal charitable work of the women of the Greek community. Until recently there were also

The Juniors of GAPA band performed at a number of functions in the 1930s and early 1940s.

two local societies in Houston whose membership was made up of *patrioti* and their descendants. These were the Patmian Society of St. John the Divine, made up of people from the island of Patmos, and the Agia Markella Society, informally called the Chios Society since its members were from the island of Chios. The Patmians have traditionally been a large and very recognizable group in Houston whose members—bound by ties of blood, marriage, and godparenthood—maintained close relationships with one another. The Patmian Society, established in 1927, has had hundreds of members in the past and has sent assistance for schools, hospitals, and public improvements to Patmos. The Chios Society was established in 1946 to help people on Chios recover from the ravages of World War II and the Greek civil war, and it has sent money, medicine, and other aid. Relations with *patrioti,* less important for the younger generations than for their parents and grandparents, tend to decline as the years pass. For this reason, both these societies have virtually disbanded.

Social Life

The social life of Houston's Greeks in the early days revolved around visiting other community members, as well as around celebrations associated with engagements, weddings, baptisms, church holidays, and namedays. For Greeks, religious holidays are marked by many traditions. Easter is the most important holiday for Orthodox Christians. Preparation for Easter begins with Lent, a period of strict fasting accompanied by prayer. Holy Week has several special services: on Tuesday the beautiful hymn of Kassiani is sung; on Wednesday church members are annointed; on Good Friday evening the flower-covered *epitaphion,* representing the tomb of Christ, is carried in procession around the church; at Easter midnight service the priest, in darkness, brings forth from the altar the Christ candle and the congregation lights individual candles from it to celebrate the Resurrection. Following the service, greetings are exchanged: "Christ is risen!" "He is risen indeed!" and red Easter eggs are cracked. Feasts, including traditional foods such as lamb, mark the end of the Lenten fast.

Other holidays are also marked by distinctive traditions; for example, St. Basil's Day (New Year's) is celebrated by cutting the *vasilopita,* a special bread with a coin inside. The person who receives the piece with the coin is thought to have good luck for the rest of the year. On the celebration called Elevation of the Cross, community members bring *vasiliko* (basil) from their gardens to the church to celebrate the finding of the cross by St. Helen.

One of the big events of the early community was the nameday celebration. Greeks traditionally did not celebrate birthdays; instead, they had an open house on a person's nameday, which is the feastday of the saint whose name he bears. For example, St. Nicholas's day is December 6, so everyone named Nicholas in the community was honored on that day. Nameday celebrations were held only for men. Usually the women of a family spent weeks cooking and cleaning the house inside and out, top to bottom, in preparation for the nameday of the head of the house. On that special day, all the community dropped in to wish him well, and then stayed for refreshments. Sometimes there was also music and dancing. Similar festivities accompanied engagements, weddings, and baptisms, and the whole community was often invited informally to these parties.

Community picnics, sponsored by various organizations such as the AHEPA and the Patmian Society, were also popular. A bit later, the community dance, attended by the whole family, was especially well attended. It was the one event that young girls, who were not allowed to date, could attend where they could have some fun—under watchful eyes, of course.

It was chaperoned, you know; the old folks were there, and the lights were always bright. One of my good friends said, "The Greek dance is the only place in town you can dance and get a suntan!"

Big festivities were also held on March 25, Greek Independence Day. For the Houston community, this day was especially significant because it coincided with the feastday of the church, Annunciation of the Virgin Mary. The community often had a parade through the downtown area, the Greek school children marching along with the members of the AHEPA and GAPA (AHEPAns on one side and GAPAns on the other, as one might expect), all wearing the Greek colors of blue and white. The parade ended at the church, where special services were held. Often, March 25 festivities included lengthy recitations and plays put on by the students of the Greek language school, all performed in Greek. The plays typically depicted famous incidents from the Greek war of independence, such as "O Horos tou Zalongou," which told of the brave Greeks who, faced with defeat, threw themselves over the cliffs rather than surrender to the Turks. The student taking part in these plays might take the role of a brave Greek soldier or maiden, a famous Greek hero, or even an infamous Turk. Both Greek and American flags were displayed prominently throughout the proceedings.

Neighborhoods

In the early days, most of the Greeks in Houston lived in two neighborhoods—one in the east end around

Harrisburg and the other downtown near the church; a bit later, a third area of settlement developed in the Heights. None of these areas, however, was ever predominantly Greek. In each neighborhood, there might be a Greek family in every other block or so, just near enough so that families could visit and children play together. The Greek mothers were very protective of their children and did not let them stray too far. As a rule, the children played with other Greeks, mostly relatives, who tended to live nearby.

Prejudice

Perhaps this geographic dispersion, along with the fact that the community was small, partly explains the lack of prejudice against Greeks in Houston. The children had some problems being accepted in school because they were considered "foreigners" (many, if not most, spoke only Greek when they entered the first grade), and a few recalled being hurt by the teasing of other children; in general, though, the Greeks here had surprisingly few of the problems with prejudice and discrimination faced by their compatriots in many other areas of the country. In fact, a number of Greeks moved to Houston to escape harassment by the Ku Klux Klan elsewhere. Because of their small numbers, the Greeks may not have seemed so threatening to others. Had the community been larger or centered in a "Greek" area of town, Houston Greeks would not have had to integrate themselves into their neighborhoods and to socialize to the extent that they did with non-Greeks.

We *lived in a Ku Klux Klan neighborhood . . . and it's a rarity for anybody in a Ku Klux Klan neighborhood to be a foreigner. They'd have the KKK rallies over at the park and we'd go as children and listen to them. The old man that was talking, he'd walk us home! He had to pass my aunt's house, she lived right across the street from the park, and·they'd cross us over.*

Language

Learning English was not necessarily easy for the immigrants, since it differs quite a bit from Greek. Many people laugh when they remember the language problems of the early years; a typical example is that immigrants were told by fellow Greeks that they could always get something to eat if they ordered "ham and eggs," but they grew very tired of eating ham and eggs before they learned how to ask for anything else. The frustration and embarrassment that their parents felt over not speaking and reading English still remain vividly in the minds of many Greek people; yet Greek was the only language spoken in most of the homes, and this was a matter of great importance to the parents. Many of the women spoke only Greek, and so their children spoke Greek, too. And since many of the community's members planned to return to Greece to live, it was thought to be more important for children to speak Greek than it was for them to learn English. Above all, it was a matter of pride in their heritage.

Public School and Greek School

As a consequence of this emphasis on speaking Greek, many children began school in Houston unable to speak English, and many of them had trouble with school the first year or two. Most picked up English quickly and made good progress in school, but the experience of this second-generation man was not unique:

When I went to the first grade, I couldn't speak a word of English—I flunked the first grade. By the time I finished that first grade, even though I flunked it, I could speak English, and I'd gotten away from my Greek. Then we moved to Greece, and I flunked the first grade in Greece because I'd forgotten enough of my Greek. Then we moved back to the U.S., and because I'd forgotten my English, I flunked it again! I'm a three-time flunkout in the first grade! But when I finally finished the first grade, I went to the fourth.

All the Greek children were also expected to attend Greek school after American school: 3:30 to 6:00 five days a week, and all day long during the summer. Since they already spoke Greek, the purpose of the school was to teach them to read and write it properly—if not elegantly, at least grammatically. Their lessons included not only the Greek language, but also instruction in woodworking for the boys, embroidery for the girls, and religion and the Bible for everyone. They were not necessarily excited about going to Greek school after they had been in school all day already; but looking back, most view it as an important and formative experience, and one of their most vivid memories of childhood in the Greek community.

Community Characteristics

Until after World War II, the Houston Greeks were a very small, close-knit, and cohesive community. The community began to grow slowly in its early years as the few original settlers sent for their relatives to come from Greece. A man might bring a brother to Houston, then another, then his mother and sisters, then perhaps his mother's brother and family. Later he would return to Greece to marry and bring back his wife, who would then send for her sisters to join her, or her brothers, or parents, and so on. Because of this pattern, many people in the early community were related to one another; virtually everyone had aunts, uncles, and cousins in the community, not to mention their in-laws and *kumbari* (people related through godparenthood). These overlapping relationships reinforced one another and were joined by ties of friendship as well. And the children who were born into the community quite literally grew up together, since their social life was restricted largely to Greek community activities, not to mention their going to Greek school together daily for years. As a result, the first Greeks in Houston report that "everybody knew everybody," "we were like brothers and sisters," and the community was "like one big family." People shared the good times and the bad times; if a Greek needed help, the community responded. All community members knew that they were invited to a baptism or a wedding, and on one's nameday, he did not have to ask people to "drop by." No doubt, there were also

some problems with this togetherness, such as one sees in a small town; but overall, community members look back and see the earlier days as a very happy time and the Greek community as "a good place to be."

Growth of the Community

As was true throughout the United States, World War II and its aftermath brought many changes to the Greek community. During this period, many traditional patterns had been altered. Some of these mirror the changes in American society, such as shifts in women's roles. Other changes, however, are unique to the Greek community. One significant development has been the increasing importance of education. Although first-generation Greeks generally were uneducated, their children and grandchildren are characterized by high scholastic accomplishment. Most are college educated, and many have also received advanced degrees. Consequently, Greek-Americans now tend to be professionals—doctors, lawyers, engineers, and teachers; some have remained in their families' businesses, but these younger Greeks now run the family restaurants with MBAs as well as with the plain hard work that sustained their fathers and grandfathers.

Women's roles have changed as well. In earlier years, many Greek people felt it was not necessary for women to have as much schooling as men; but today Greek women are as well educated as their male counterparts. Greek women also work outside the home, although perhaps not yet to the degree one sees in the wider society. Women are taking a more active part in Greek community affairs as well. After World War II they were permitted to become members of the church in their own right, rather than through the membership of their fathers or husbands. Now women may also serve as members of the parish council, a role that would have been unheard of a generation ago.

Reflecting changes in women's roles, family patterns have also been altered. Although the ideals of family closeness and respect for elders remain in force, traditional family structures are not as predominant as they once were. Wives now frequently work, even after childbearing; but this pattern probably reflects the realities of today's economy—which requires two incomes to support a family—as much as it does the desires of women to take on roles other than those of wife and mother. Husbands now take more of a part in housework and in child care, again reflecting changes in the larger society.

The Greek language is gradually dying out among Houston's Greek-Americans, and this situation is a matter of great concern to community members. Students now attend the Greek school only one afternoon a week for a couple of hours, and this does not compensate for the fact that the language is used by few families at home. Second-generation people still speak Greek, but in many cases their children can understand it better than they can speak it. As the generations proceed and the *giagias* and *pappous* (grandmothers and grandfathers) become a smaller proportion of the community, the ability to speak Greek becomes less and less important. Nevertheless, many people are disappointed that maintaining their language in America is so difficult. The problem comes from relying on a formal institution like the Greek school, rather than the home, for teaching the language. As one person commented:

I think the Greek school is important, but unfortunately we did not appreciate it when we were growing up and I think our kids didn't appreciate it at the time. When you're in school all day and then you have to go to Greek school, it's not fun. They do have opportunities here in the community to learn it, but—as with everything—they're so involved in their everyday living that they don't take time to do that. I think that Greek people appreciate Greek school after it's too late.

Another institution that has changed in the Houston Greek community is the Greek Orthodox church, which has become less ethnic in several respects. First, services are no longer conducted totally in Greek, but typically half in Greek and half in English. This division is necessary because now one finds in the community both people who speak little English—older people, especially women who never learned it, and recent immigrants—and people who speak little Greek, such as young third-generation people and converts into the church. The church is also more open to non-Greeks than it was in the old days; overall, community members have a very positive attitude toward converts, whom they feel are "some of the best, most sincere, and devout members we have." Greeks are proud of their Orthodox heritage and increasingly happy to share it with others. The Orthodox church has traditionally not favored proselytizing, but many younger people are beginning to reconsider this perspective. (When asked what the goal of the Orthodox church should be, older people said, "Keeping the young people in," and young people said, "Spreading the good word about our faith. We have something precious that we should share with others.") This approach has been accompanied by other Americanized activities such as Bible study groups and covered-dish dinners, as the church has responded to the changing needs and interests of its parishioners. More and more, people are able to separate the Greekness and Orthodoxy of their heritage, and they are choosing to stress the latter. In the past, community members would have been much less likely to comment, as some do today, "I'm Orthodox first and Greek second."

Links with *patrioti* are of decreasing significance, and community members no longer have the preponderance of Greek friends that they did in the past. Parents encourage friendships and dating among Greek young people but do not force the issue to the extent that they once did. There are also more marriages outside the group than in the past; about half the marriage ceremonies conducted in the Greek Orthodox church in America are for "mixed" couples. These marriages bring many non-Greeks into the church as converts. Most community members now seem to have the attitude that marriages to non-Greeks are inevitable, and it is best to accept the inevitable graciously.

The customs that remain strong in the community are primarily those related to church holidays such as Easter, Christmas, or St. Basil's Day. The traditional cuisine, of course, continues in special Greek ways of preparing food, and hospitality toward guests is essential. Greek music and dancing also continue to be popular, perhaps more so in urban America than in urban Greece. A recent immigrant commented:

When I was growing up and turned on the radio, mostly what I listened [to] was American music— Presley, Sinatra, Brenda Lee, Connie Stevens. The radio station played this kind of music. So growing up in the city I had the American influence in music, and also the dancing. Believe me, that I didn't know Greek dances! We were dancing the cha-cha, tango, waltz. And when I come here, most of the time I'm dancing the Greek dances! I love to dance the dances that I'm *used to dancing, but they [Greek-Americans] don't dance them!*

Those customs that have continued can be adopted rather easily by non-Greeks who marry into the community, and so it is relatively simple for them to take part in "Greek" activities. Since the alternative would probably be losing the Greek who marries a non-Greek, the community is stronger because it can (and does) incorporate outsiders as members.

Of all the areas of change since World War II, however, the most significant has been the tremendous growth of both the Greek community and the city of Houston. During the postwar period, the Greek community has kept pace with the rapid expansion of Houston both in population size and geographic dispersion. For example, the 1950 census reported that Houston was home to 540 people of foreign stock (that is, the foreign-born and their children) whose country of origin was Greece; in 1960 this number had increased to 1,440, and in 1970 to 1,743; and the 1980 census should show another increase. Again the reader should bear in mind that these figures greatly underestimate the number of Greek-Americans in Houston, since they include only those from Greece itself and only the first and second generations. Members of the Greek community estimate that there are currently about 10,000 Greeks in the Houston area. In addition to the vast increase in the size of the Greek community in recent decades, the community's members have become more dispersed geographically, and they live in all parts of Houston.

Each of these two factors has created problems for the Greeks of Houston. When newcomers came into the community in the past, they were usually relatives or at least *patrioti* of people already living here, so they were not really strangers and were easily integrated into the community. Now they are Greeks from other cities in the United States who have been transferred here or who have come for further education; they do not have the automatic ties with the community that newcomers had in the past, and their numbers are so large that the old-timers are overwhelmed. Formerly the community was like one big family, but now the old-time Houstonians, who grew up in a situation where everybody knew everybody, do not know eight out of every ten people they see at church. Needless to say, this situation is very disconcerting for a community that was small for so many years; and under these conditions of rapid growth, it is very difficult to maintain a sense of community.

Compounding this problem is the geographical dispersion of the Greek population. When many parishioners live fifteen or twenty miles or even further from the church, which is the community's social center, and when those miles are plagued by traffic jams, it becomes more and more difficult for them to participate in community activities and institutions such as the parochial school, afternoon Greek school, and meetings of organizations such as Greek Orthodox Youth of America (GOYA) or AHEPA. Consequently, a number of community activities are being decentralized; for example, the Greek school has a satellite campus in Alief, and Bible study groups meet in many areas of town rather than only at the church. This decentralization helps develop and maintain the sense of a special community within the larger city of Houston.

These changes in the Greek community that have grown out of its being located in Houston, with the consequent population boom, dispersion, and transportation problems, are probably more significant for Houston's Greeks than are the cultural changes the community has seen over the three or four generations that Greeks have lived in the city. Cultural patterns can be replaced by alternative ways of doing things, which can become traditions in themselves; but people have to be able to get together with each other to have a community, and the people involved have to be a relatively stable group that is not overwhelmed by large numbers of newcomers.

In spite of these changes, the Greek community appears to be irrepressible, and new organizations and programs are constantly being established to meet the needs of community members. For example, within the past few years several important new groups have been established—the Young Adults League, a church organization for people eighteen to thirty-five years old; the Over-35 Singles' Group; and the Hellenic Professional Society. In addition to these organizations, a program has recently been instituted in which newcomers get together periodically to meet each other and become familiarized with the Houston Greek community. In the past, a formal program such as this would have been unnecessary, but members realize that the community has become so large and complex that such a program is now needed.

New Immigrants

The postwar Greek immigrants differ from those who came to the United States in the first period of immigration, up to the 1920s. A larger number are women; the immigrants tend to come from urban rather than rural areas, especially from Athens; and in general they are much better educated than the earlier immigrants. Many come to the United States to further their education, because it is very difficult to attend college in Greece.

In order to get into [college], you have to prepare yourself for a very long time. The entrance examinations are very hard. And they do so in order to have fewer people go to the schools. They decide that "This year, we will accept so many—100 candidates for civil engineering or 120 for electrical engineering." You realize how few can go! So they make the exam so hard that it's no way. Many people from the age of fourteen or fifteen prepare for the entrance into college. For the last three years in high school, during the evenings you have to go for tutoring. The students

pay the teacher by the hour. If your parents' income is not so high, they have to make sacrifices. Many families, they do sacrifice to give their kids something that they didn't have.

My prime objective when I came here was to get a job; I could not go to school [because] I didn't have the money. So what I've done is get a job to maintain my living. And after I fulfilled this, I tried to fulfill my desire to go to college. At night, it took me about nine years to do this. Sometimes the desires and the determination overpass the hardships. You see, this is what happened with me.

Others who have graduated from college in Greece come to this country seeking advanced degrees. Of course, not all the recent immigrants come with such high levels of education, and there is still some immigration from rural areas as well. A final difference is that earlier immigrants came here with the intention of eventually returning to Greece; about half actually did so, whereas the recent immigrants left Greece with no clear intention of returning. This difference perhaps explains why they have not developed the same sort of community structure the early immigrants had, with close social ties and strong institutions.

The more recent arrivals are similar in many other ways to those who came before them, and they are repeating many of the traditional patterns already discussed. They are usually independent businessmen, primarily owners of restaurants and service stations; those with higher levels of education are professionals—engineers, doctors, professors. In any case, they work hard and put in long hours to make a better life for themselves and their families, just as the earlier immigrants did. The new immigrants also tend to have traditional family patterns, with the husband the breadwinner and definite head of the household, and the wife staying at home to raise the children.

Nevertheless, the two groups do not have a lot of contact, because of a number of misunderstandings between them. For example, although the Greek Orthodox church has traditionally been a unifying feature for the Greek community in Houston, this institution has not necessarily served to unite the two groups; most of the difficulties seem to lie in their

The engagement party of Anastasia Markou and George Caridas, 1930. The blessing and party were held at a local hall. The table has koufeta *(favors of candy-coated almonds) and sweets.*

different attitudes toward the church. The Greek-Americans see the church as the center of their community, and they cling to it with a passion their forefathers may not have felt in Greece. The church reminded these early immigrants of home and served as a central institution for their communities, preserving their heritage, customs, and language as well as their traditional faith. Over the years the church has come to serve more of a social function for some, a place to get together with other Greeks. Others, however, see the church as a major influence in their lives, not because of its Greekness, but because of its Orthodoxy; their identification has been transformed from

Greek Orthodox to *Orthodox* who just happen to be Greek. Both groups feel that the church has a primary role to play in the Greek-American community.

Recent immigrants, on the other hand, have a different perspective. They are usually less church-oriented than the Greek-Americans, for several reasons. First, they do not need the church as a source of identity, because their identity as Greek is secure. "Of course I'm Greek—I speak Greek! I'm *from* Greece!" Because of this attitude, they fail to see the significance of the church for second-, third-, or fourth-generation Greek-Americans as a source of unique identity in American society. Second, many consider themselves rather sophisticated and take a dim view of religion in general, which they see as superstition. Even those who do not subscribe to this view, however, bring with them from Greece memories of a different type of church: one that is state supported and thus can be taken for granted in a way not possible in the United States. As is the case with other American churches, the Orthodox church here is supported by the donations of its parishioners, so the new immigrant is met by drives to raise money for church operating expenses; he frequently interprets this to mean that he must *pay* to become a church member. Some immigrants also resent what they see to be the aloofness of Greek-Americans, and particularly the use of so much English in the church. To them this is not Greek Orthodoxy, and it represents a debasement of their Hellenic heritage. In spite of these areas of contention, the new immigrants are definitely Greek Orthodox; for example, they would never consider not having their children baptized Greek Orthodox, and a number even return to Greece for baptismal services.

From the point of view of Greek-Americans, their grandparents and parents and they themselves have worked very hard and made many sacrifices to build the church and the community. They feel that the newcomers do not want to support the church with their time or money but want it to be there when they need it for weddings and baptisms and at Easter. The recent immigrants, in turn, think that the Greek-Americans are not willing to share the church, that they want to run it and are not interested in the needs of newcomers. Another point of contention lies in their different approaches to being Greek. The recent immigrants say of the Greek-Americans, "They think they're Greek? They don't act like Greeks, they can't speak Greek, many of them have never even been to Greece!" On the other hand, Greek Americans say, "How can they be Greek? They hardly ever even come to church!" Greek-Americans do not want to admit how truly American they are in many ways, and recent immigrants fail to realize how important the Greek Orthodox church has been for maintaining Greek identity and community in America.

Given the nature of relations between these two groups, there are several possible ways the community may develop. One alternative is that two separate Greek communities may emerge, one "Greek-American" and the other "Greek Greek." For example, there has been a movement recently to form a second Greek Orthodox parish in Houston, one better suited to the needs of recent immigrants with church services in Greek and more of an "old-country" ambience. If this church is not built, there is some question about whether the immigrants can maintain their Greek identity outside the context of the Orthodox church. The relative ease of travel to Greece now can possibly overcome this problem. Many of the recent immigrants keep their ties by returning to Greece each summer for extended visits; and their children learn the Greek language and learn about their Greek heritage directly in a way that is not possible in a couple of hours of Greek school each week.

Another alternative is that the recent immigrants, as they have children, may draw closer to the Greek-American community. They may find that their children will need to be baptized, to be brought to church for communion, to participate in youth groups, and to learn the Greek language in the afternoon Greek school. In some cases, this is already happening. A second development that points to an integration of the two groups is the establishment of the Hellenic Professional Society, an organization composed of professionals of Greek heritage who are interested in furthering Hellenic culture in the United States. This organization was originally made up of recent immigrants, primarily engineers, who were motivated by the Cyprus crisis in 1974 to organize as a forum for discussing the issues and developing support for the Greek Cypriots. In recent years, however, it has begun to forge stronger links to the Greek-American community; many Greek-Americans have become members, and the club now enters into those church activities that relate to Hellenic culture. For example, the Professional Society sponsors the March 25 celebration at the church, since this furthers awareness of the Greek war of independence. The Hellenic Professional Society thus offers understanding and preserving Hellenic heritage as a common ground between Greek-

Americans and new immigrants. Obviously, this group does not reach all segments of either Greek group, but it shows the beginning of more cooperation and understanding between the two groups.

The annual Greek Festival is also a unifying feature of the community. The festival was begun in 1967 as an outgrowth of Annunciation's fiftieth anniversary celebration. The general format of the festival—Greek food and dancing, church tours, and lectures—as well as its goal of raising money for the church while familiarizing non-Greeks with Hellenic culture and the Orthodox religion, have remained constant throughout the years. But the scope of the event has grown each year as more and more Houstonians come to enjoy the festivities. Many community members work for months in advance of the event, cooking thousands of servings of *pastitsio* and *spanakopitakia,* practicing many hours for the dance programs, and importing thousands of Greek items for the gift shop and *agora.* Others offer their support by working during the three days of the festival, serving traditional foods and wines, cleaning up, and so on. By the time the festival has ended each year, all kinds of Greeks—old-timers and newcomers, recent immigrants and third- and fourth-generation Greek-Americans, regular church attendees and those who come only at Easter—have taken part and have shown Houston a little of what the Greek spirit is.

The Future of the Greek Community

The Houston Greek community has undergone several changes in the postwar period. These might be taken as evidence that assimilation is occurring among Houston's Greek-Americans, but a distinction must be made between cultural changes—alterations in patterns of family life, language, friendship, and so on—and the disappearance of a group. A group can undergo many changes and still continue to maintain its identity. Indeed, one might make a strong case that a group *must* undergo changes if it is to survive; it must be flexible enough to be responsive to the needs and capabilities of its members. If speaking the Greek language were a requirement for membership in the

Greek community, a large part of its current members would be excluded. Alterations in many traditional patterns have been very positive for the community. For example, the traditional patriarchal family in which the father was the only breadwinner and also the unquestioned head of the house, while the mother took sole responsibility for the housework and raising the children, has given way to a more egalitarian family in which the mother as well as the father may work outside the home. The father, as well as the mother, may change diapers and cook dinner. Few young couples today would care, or even find it possible, to fit into the traditional pattern. Such changes thus enable an individual to be an American, to participate in American society, and yet remain Greek. It is precisely because of such changes that the Greeks of Houston have such a strong, vibrant, and progressive community.

What characteristics separate Greeks from non-Greeks, then? As long as some distinguishing features remain, it probably matters little what they are; these unique characteristics vary from one ethnic group to another, and perhaps even from one Greek community to another. For Greek-Americans, the fundamental feature seems to be the Greek Orthodox church. The fact that Eastern Orthodox churches are all national churches binds each of them very closely to an ethnic community, with no need for apologies. Religious affiliation is a very common and acceptable feature of American life, and being associated with a national church gives Orthodox people a very strong basis for their communities that many other ethnic groups do not have. The Catholic church is composed of Italians, Germans, Irish, and Mexicans; Judaism encompasses people of many nationalities; but the Greek Orthodox church is made up of Greeks, the Russian Orthodox church of Russians, and so on. When people's ethnic heritage and their religion reinforce each other in this way, it provides a very strong basis for the continued existence of the group.

There are two foreseeable areas of difficulty for the continued existence of the Greek community in Houston and in America. First is the fact that younger church members want the Greek Orthodox church to "spread the good word" and make itself more available to outsiders. If this happens and non-Greeks enter the church on a large scale, the tie between ethnicity and religion that undergirds the Greek community might begin to break down. The second challenge to the continuation of Greek identity is the possibility of American Orthodoxy, in which each of the ethnic Orthodox churches would give up its separate congregations and hierarchy, its unique identity, and merge into one "American" Orthodox church. This would represent the ultimate in separating the Greeks' religion from their ethnicity, which would threaten this community far more than high rates of intermarriage or loss of the Greek language. Although American Orthodoxy is not likely any time soon, quite a number of younger Orthdox people are heading toward this arrangement. The attitude that it is Orthodoxy that matters, not ethnicity, is not unusual, and many would like to remove the ethnic traditions from the Orthodox church. Consequently, one sees increasing interaction between various Orthodox churches. In Houston the Greek church, Annunciation, and the Syrian church, St. George, exchange services on occasion; their members have retreats together, and their priests address members of one another's congregations. Also, a choral group, St. Romanos Chorale, is made up of people from all Orthodox churches in the area.

Before American Orthodoxy becomes a reality in the United States, ethnicity among Orthodox people will necessarily have declined considerably; but there are no signs that this is going to happen any time soon. Certainly, as long as the older generation is living, it will not occur. Orthodox people have too much respect for their elders to change the familiar churches. And as long as immigration continues from Orthodox countries, at least some part of each national church will be made up of people who want to hear the liturgy in their native language, in a familiar setting, among their own people. For these reasons, among others, the Houston Greeks will probably maintain a strong community for several generations to come. One of the advantages for all Houstonians will be that the highly successful, colorful, and authentic Greek Festival will probably continue to grow each year. During those days in October, there are many who claim the Greek food, dancing, games, and heritage as their own; and since it has become such a happy experience for all, everyone is "a little Greek" at that time.

Jews

Elaine H. Maas

Scribe working on Torah scroll. The text of the Torah (the handwritten scroll of the five books of Moses) is drafted in a Hebrew unchanged through countless generations, and must be letter-perfect. A Torah containing two scribal errors may not be used in worship. Photograph by Gay Block; reprinted by permission.

ike the majority of Houston's residents in general, most of the 30,000 to 35,000 Jews in the city today are newcomers. But just as something of Houston's historically developed ethos or tone still affects the current city, so, too, the current Houston Jewish community is still affected by the historical ethos of the early Houston Jews. The following brief historical survey of Jews in America and of Jews in Texas and Houston in particular will give a background for understanding the Jews in Houston today. The larger population tends to view all Jews as being alike, as having the same religious views and practices and the same attitudes and way of life; however, Jews differ in all of these aspects.

First, though, who are the "Jews"? There are two ways in which Jews in any American city are generally viewed. One view, that of many of the larger, Gentile (non-Jewish) population, is that all people of Jewish descent are Jews and are part of "a Jewish community." Among the Jews themselves the matter is more complex, for the definition of who is a Jew has yet to be formulated. Jews perceive themselves as being Jews in different ways and to different degrees, and some of Jewish descent do not think of themselves as Jews at all. There is no central organization to which all Jews belong; there is no one ideological view that all Jews hold; and many calling themselves Jews belong to no religious congregation of Judaism.

To point to this problem of definition is merely to emphasize that there is not one, unvaried, distinctive group of Jews. Rather there is a Jewish population that embraces Jews of many different types.

The Jews in America

Jews have been closely associated with the beginnings of America, Texas, and Houston. Jews were present from the very first moment of the discovery of the New World, for five Jewish Marranos[1] were in Christopher Columbus's crew. Because the Jews were expelled from Spain

---

1. Jews who were forced to convert to Christianity during the Spanish Inquisition.

in the same year that America was discovered, Spanish (or Sephardic) Jewish refugees—many of whom had initially gone to various other countries—were among the first settlers to come to the United States. They constituted the first of three main Jewish waves of immigration to the United States, though this first wave was more of a steady trickle.

The Sephardic Wave

Individual Jews settled in Virginia as early as 1621, but the first recorded Jewish group settlement was in 1654 in New Amsterdam (later called New York). They were allowed to stay there "providing the poor among them shall be supported by their own nation." The Jews have attempted to honor this stipulation throughout their history in America. By and large, they settled in all of the thirteen colonies, but primarily on the seacoast and in a few leading cities, where their mercantile talent and connections with other parts of the world could be utilized for developing the trade of the colonies, a type of work that fulfilled an important need for America and for which the Jews were particularly well suited. Initially, Jews in America were not allowed to engage in retail trade. This resulted in their engaging in the kinds of economic activities open to them—foreign and intercolonial trade.

In Europe the Sephardic Jews had chiefly been merchants, and many were from wealthy, aristocratic families. They practiced a traditional Judaism. Upon coming to this country, they founded institutions like those they had known in the Old World—a cemetery (which always came first), a synagogue, and the school that usually went with it—and they organized to assist the needy and helpless among them. Being few in number, they needed no other institutions. By the time of the Revolution, there were about 2,500 to 3,000 Jews in the colonies, with five congregations. They fought in the Revolution both as officers and soldiers and contributed their full share of patriots off the battlefield as well as on it. One of the most important was Haym Solomon of Philadelphia, who helped finance the Revolution, lending his entire fortune to the government. When he died, his family was left destitute, for none of the money was ever repaid. Jews participated in the growth of the colonies in many ways: for example, they introduced the whale-oil industry and helped develop others, such as the indigo trade.

While the direct influence of Jews on America was exerted chiefly through their activity in trade and commerce, their vastly greater influence was indirect, through the Old Testament. The Puritans, who were great students of the Bible, carried Jewish ideas into the founding of their colonies and, through the colonies, into the life of America. The Mayflower Compact was based on the laws of Moses. The arguments and inspiration for the Revolution itself were drawn largely from Hebrew history: such basic Jewish and American values as love of freedom and equality stem from the same source.

By and large, the Sephardic Jews, who lived side by side with their Gentile neighbors, discovered that America was a nation in which there was freedom of religion for the most part, a separation of religion and state, and a plurality of religions. They themselves contributed to the diversity of the religious scene, helping to create a milieu in which no single religion dominated but in which belonging to *a* religion was important. In short, the Jews were accepted as part of the American scene. Although few in number (by 1820 they probably totalled no more than 5,000), they were well established and respected. They formed a secure foundation for the Jews who were to come. Two of the notable Jews of this period were Judah Touro, merchant and philanthropist of New Orleans, who during his lifetime and upon his death gave money to numerous non-Jewish and Jewish charities of every kind, and for whom Touro Park and Touro Hospital are named; and Uriah P. Levy, a United States Navy Commander, who abolished the practice of corporal punishment in the Navy.

The German Wave

The majority of Jews who migrated in the second wave (from about 1815 until the 1890s) were part of a larger German group that came to America. Of the 5 million Germans of all religions who fled to the New World during this period, about 200,000 were Jews. The German Jews went mostly to the same places as the non-Jewish Germans. The United States was an expanding frontier at

this time, and the immigrants scattered thinly throughout the nation, including the Alaskan territory. Most of the Jewish communities of our country, including the one in Houston, were founded during this period.

The German Jews, in contrast to the proud and cultured Sephardics, were mainly poor and uneducated (with the exception of the "forty-eighters," a group that included many of Germany's most educated and wealthy citizens). Usually they began work in the new land as peddlers, providing services that the expanding frontier needed. Similar to the Sephardics, they came with a traditional Judaism. Initially they joined the existing Sephardic synagogues, but they soon withdrew to form their own, both because they were more comfortable with their own ritual and people and because very soon they desired "reforms" in the Orthodox ritual. This desire for religious reforms (modernization) became a growing movement that ultimately produced Reform Judaism, one of the three main branches in American Judaism today. The German Jews, reflecting the German temperament and love for "organization," were also responsible for taking Jewish activities out of the synagogue and creating instead the multiple secular institutions (such as charity organizations, child-welfare agencies, lodges, and brotherhoods) around which Jewish communities revolve today.

The German Jews, like the Sephardics, became part of the American mainstream and contributed to the civic, cultural, and economic life of the country. Because Jews lived in both the north and south, there were Jews fighting on both sides of the 1861 Civil War. Jews who rose to prominence in various fields during the nineteenth century in America are too numerous to mention, but one of the most interesting was the poet Emma Lazarus, whose words at the base of the Statue of Liberty are known to almost every school child: "Give me your tired, your poor, your huddled masses yearning to breathe free."

The Russian Wave

The Russian influx was the most massive of all the Jewish immigration waves. Whereas in 1840 there were about 15,000 Jews in America, mostly of Sephardic descent, and in 1880 there were about 250,000, mostly of German background, by 1928 there were 4.2 million Jews, fully 3.5 million of whom were of East European birth or descent. To escape the legalized tyranny enacted under the czar, entire communities of Jews, both rich and poor, educated and ignorant, fled from Russia, principally to the United States. Of the 2 million Jews who entered the United States between 1881 and 1920, 70 percent came from Russia and 25 percent from Austria-Hungary and Romania.

When they arrived, America no longer afforded the same opportunities for independent traders. The time of the expanding frontier had ended, and the industrialization period had begun. The available jobs were in the large cities. For various reasons most of the immigrants settled in New York City, and it became the city with the largest Jewish concentration. Jews soon represented 25 percent of the city's total population, a proportion they have maintained ever since. Because of the abject poverty and living conditions of the Jews in New York, the established Jewish community attempted to redirect immigration into the more sparsely settled communities of the southern and western United States. The port of Galveston, Texas, was one of those to which the immigrants were directed.

The Russians, similar to the German Jews before them, wanted to form their own synagogues and charities; they founded their own distinctive institutions, which stressed education and Jewish culture. In contrast to the German Jews, who considered themselves a religious group only, the Russian Jews also wanted to maintain their Jewish cultural life. In Russia they had been accustomed to living as one nationality among many, a Jewish nationality that differed from the others in its culture; they had not experienced the period of Enlightenment and the emancipation that the Jews in Germany and France had. Their lives were even more secularized than those of the German Jews, but it was a Jewish secularism, not German or American.

The majority of the Russian immigrants took their religion for granted, just as their predecessors had, and their multitudes of tiny synagogues were strictly Orthodox. With the passage of time, however, Russian Jews began to fill the ranks of Conservative Judaism,

the second branch of Judaism that developed in America. Conservative Judaism was more modern than traditional Orthodoxy but more traditional than Reform. (For instance, the Conservatives introduced an English sermon and relaxed some of the rigid regulations concerning personal life, but insisted on keeping the dietary laws and preserving the traditional Sabbath.) It appealed to the new East European immigrants, who wanted to retain their rituals and traditions but also wanted to become "Americanized."

By 1920 three branches—Reform, Conservative, and Orthodox—existed within American Judaism, each representing a greater (Reform) or lesser (Orthodox) degree of change from ancient forms, induced by conditions in the United States. (These three main divisions still exist in American Judaism, and they continue to be affected by the conditions surrounding them.)

The Russians, like the Jewish groups before them, became part of mainstream America. The contributions of Russian Jews and their descendants are probably better known to us, since they came to America in more recent times. Most of us are familiar with names such as Eddie Cantor, Al Jolson, Harry Houdini, and the Marx Brothers (in the field of entertainment); George Gershwin, Leonard Bernstein, and Irving Berlin (composers); Beverly Sills (opera singer); J. D. Salinger and Leon Uris (authors); Joseph Pulitzer (founder of the School of Journalism at Columbia University and the Pulitzer Prizes in journalism, letters, and music); Al Capp (creator of "Li'l Abner"); Sandy Koufax and Mark Spitz (athletes). Less well known is the contribution that Jews of this period made to the labor movement in America. One of the most outstanding figures in this sphere was Samuel Gompers, who was the American Federation of Labor president for forty years and a major leader of American workmen for a generation or more.

The first World War interrupted the flow of Jewish immigration to America, and it was never fully resumed. The quota systems of 1921 and 1924 virtually closed the gate.

The historical pattern of immigration, then, accounted for the religious development that divided a

Tombstone in Strangers' Row, Beth Israel Cemetery.

*Texas' first Jewish house of worship,
Congregation Beth Israel, Franklin Avenue at
Crawford (1870–1908).*

single tradition into three branches. It also accounted in part for the multiplicity of philanthropies and communal organizations that developed as Jews "took care of their own." Immigration created diversity among Jews, just as it did in the American society at large.

The Jews in Texas and Houston

Jews were also in Texas from its earliest days. The colonization of Texas by Americans did not begin until 1821, long after the initial spread in the nation of the Sephardic wave of Jews. Texas was part of the expanding frontier that existed when Germans came to this country during the mid-nineteenth century, and the first substantial number of Jewish settlers in the state were immigrants from Germany. However, a few Jews from various places in this country and abroad found

their way to Texas earlier. One, Samuel Isaacks, was among Stephen F. Austin's "Old Three Hundred," the first group of colonists, who came in 1821 when Texas was still a part of Mexico.

By 1831 there were Jews living in Velasco, and then, following this settlement, in Nacogdoches, San Antonio, and Bolivar. A particularly prominent Jew was Henry Castro, a French Jew from a Marrano family, who between 1843 and 1846 brought between 4,000 and 5,000 people from the Alsace-Lorraine region to colonize what is now Medina County (southwest of San Antonio), and for whom Castro County and Castroville are named. In general, Jews settled throughout Texas, both in the large cities and in the small towns and rural areas, many becoming prominent citizens in their communities. They fought in the various battles: some with Sam Houston at San Jacinto, some with Fannin at Goliad.

*Zacharias Emmich, first ordained rabbi of
Congregation Beth Israel.*

*Drawing of Congregation Beth Israel,
Lamar at Crawford (1908–1925).*

Beginnings

Jews were in Houston from its beginning. Houston was founded four months after Texas won her independence from Mexico at the battle of San Jacinto in 1836. Eugene Chimene, a Jew from France who fought in that battle, is considered to have been the first Jewish settler in Houston. Records show that several Jews owned stores as early as 1839.

The most prominent early Jewish settler was Jacob de Cordova, a Sephardic Jew who came to Philadelphia from Jamaica as a young boy. He came to Galveston in 1837 from New Orleans and later moved to Houston. Cordova was an alderman of Houston and a representative in the Texas legislature; in 1849 he helped lay out the city of Waco, setting aside a parcel of land for each church. He introduced the Order of Odd Fellows into Texas and founded a chapter in Houston.

An original member of the Houston Chamber of Commerce when it was formed in 1840, he was one of a committee of three appointed to draft its constitution. He became a prominent land merchant, published books on Texas, and in 1858 toured the eastern United States and England to publicize Texas as a place to settle.

In 1850 there were possibly seventeen Jewish adults (eleven men, six women) in a total Houston white population of 1,863. They came from a variety of places, including Germany, Jamaica, Holland, Louisiana, and Ohio; they represented a mixture of Sephardic and German backgrounds. By 1860, at which time there were sixty-eight Jewish adults (plus forty children), the Jews in Houston were established both as a Jewish community and as part of the larger, general community. The typical Jewish institutions had been formed: the cemetery (in 1844); the Hebrew Benevolent Society, to take care of the needy (in 1855); and in 1859, the Hebrew Congregation Beth Israel, the first Jewish congregation in Texas (today known as Congregation Beth Israel).

Typical of German Jewish communities in the United States a this time, Beth Israel began as a traditional (Orthodox) congregation; and also typically, a trend toward "reforms" soon became apparent. There were also the usual conflicts between those who wanted the reforms and those who did not. For instance, when the Reform prayer book was finally voted in, the books "mysteriously" disappeared!

The Jews took part in aspects of the social life of Houston, including being active in both the Independent Order of Odd Fellows and the Masonic lodges. Several Jews served as officers in these two societies; and just as today many of those active in the larger community are also active in the Jewish community, so these same men were also the leaders in the first Jewish society, the Hebrew Benevolent Association. While Jews were accepted in the civic and social life of the community, none in Houston achieved the political prominence that some did in Galveston and other Texas cities as early as 1853.

By 1877 the Jewish population in Houston had grown to 461. (Galveston's Jewish population was 1,000.) As Houston grew as an economic community, the participation of Jews in that community, as well as within their own Jewish community, also grew. In 1868 Morris A. Levy and Henry S. Fox were part of the group that organized the Houston Ship Channel Company for the purpose of dredging Buffalo Bayou to accommodate ocean-going vessels. J. Reichman was an alderman of the city, and Henry S. Fox was one of the original directors of the Houston Board of Trade and Cotton Exchange.

In 1886–87, as the influx of the Russian immigrants was beginning, many more Jews held positions in the business and civic spheres. One was a director of the Houston Gaslight Company; another was president of the Houston Electric Light and Power Company (in later years Jews would be conspicuously absent from the management of utility companies); one was city secretary and treasurer. Thus, similar to the Russian Jewish experience elsewhere in America, the Russian

immigrants found upon their arrival in Houston an entrenched and prosperous German-Jewish community. During this German period, Beth Israel completed its transition to classical, or pure, Reform Judaism. This early dominance of the classical Reform branch of Judaism contributed to the tone, or ethos, of the Houston Jewish community for years to come.

During the wave of Russian immigration, which began in approximately 1880, many newcomers found their way to Houston directly from Europe. Others came as a result of the "Galveston Plan," an attempt to redirect Jews from the crowded slum conditions of New York to less populated areas of the country. The Russian immigration period seems to be the one in which differences were sharpened between Houston Jews (and southern Jews in general) and the Jews of the large cities, particularly those of New York City. Instead of the Russians stamping their ethos on the Jews already in Houston, as they did in New York and other large cities, they were absorbed by the ethos or style of those who were here. This resulted partly from their accommodation to the majority Houston Jewish population, but also from their response to the same milieu that had produced the Houston Jewish community's character in the first place. That is, their experience was not like that of the Russian Jews arriving in New York. That immigrant population found industrialization in full swing; they had to find work in sweat shops, were forced to live in crowded conditions, settled in exclusively Jewish areas with a distinctive Jewish way of life that retained many Old World customs, and came to exhibit the competitive aggressiveness that crowded conditions in large cities tend to promote in all their populace. The East Europeans who came to Houston and other places in Texas found a pioneer country where there was still plenty of room for expansion and opportunities for the peddler. They still formed a small minority (less than 2 percent) of the city's population, and while they tended to settle in the same areas as other Jews of their socioeconomic level, they still lived in blocks that were predominantly Gentile and thus were in daily contact with Gentiles. They maintained the traits of courtesy and friendliness that southern and suburban milieux tend to evoke.

Relations between Jews and Gentiles in Houston

and Galveston had always been very good; Jews had mingled with the community at large, many having prominent positions. With the influx of the Russian Jews, this tendency toward integration continued. As before, many Jews joined the Masonic order, the Eastern Star, and the Rotary Club, and had Gentile friends. Among those who had always participated in the larger community's cultural and civic endeavors were some of the rabbis. Rabbi Henry Barnston of Beth Israel was part of a nucleus that helped form the Houston Symphony Society and the Museum of Fine Arts. Rabbi Henry Cohen of Galveston, esteemed by Jew and Gentile alike, achieved a national reputation for philanthropic and humanitarian endeavors that served Jew and Gentile, black and white, indiscriminately.

Although the Jews continued to lead a life that was for the most part integrated with that of the Gentile community, they also continued to maintain their Jewish communal life and practice their religion. As the East European influx grew, additional associations and organizations appeared, reflecting the needs of the newcomers. Several small Orthodox synagogues were formed to serve them. In 1924, typical of the pattern in Jewish communities at this period elsewhere in the United States, a Conservative congregation, Beth El, was formed, appealing primarily to the new East Europeans for whom the Orthodox was "too" Orthodox.

The Houston Jewish community's distinguishing character was probably set by 1924, when immigration virtually stopped in the United States. Contributing to this tone was the fact that while anti-Semitism existed in Houston, it was always perceived by most Houston Jews as being of a milder form than that often found in other cities. They attributed this in part to the relatively higher prosperity in Houston. In essence, the Houston Jewish group was one that felt comfortable living as Jews in a Gentile community. It was not a particularly noticeable or vocal group, but it was a viable one; and just as Houston was both different from and similar to other cities in America, so, too, the Houston Jewish community was both different from and similar to other Jewish communities.

The community received its share of refugees from Germany in the 1930s, but this influx did not disturb the basic structure of the Jewish community. It did, however, bring to the fore the problem of where Jews were to go and the issue of Zionism, an issue that divided the community. Later, with the passage of time and the establishment of Israel, the problem ceased to exist. Israel became, in fact, a unifying force. Because Israel has become the haven for more than a million Jews since the Nazi era and is the ancestral home of the Jewish people as well as the birthplace of the Jewish faith and Bible, it is not surprising that for many Jews Israel has special meaning. But spiritual bonds and emotional ties are quite different from political loyalty. Just as many Americans retain strong attachment to the country of their ancestors, so many Jews feel attachment to Israel.

As in Jewish communities elsewhere, the Jewish immigrants who have moved to Houston since 1945 have come from all parts of the world and from all socio-economic backgrounds. But they have been few in number and have been easily absorbed into the community. Houston has continued to be a "boom town" offering each new immigrant economic opportunities.

Historical Residential Patterns in Houston

With some simplification, one can designate four major Jewish residential areas in Houston during the last 130 years. It should be remembered that "Jewish areas" in Houston have always been predominantly Gentile, with perhaps only one to three Jewish families on a block. Why have many Jews tended to live near one another in the same geographical areas? One reason is to be near the Jewish institutions they use, primarily the synagogue. Another stems from the desire to be near the people they know (from their congregation, for example). Then, too, certain residential areas have in the past been closed to Jews.

The early business district of Houston was centered around Buffalo Bayou, Main Street, Franklin, and Congress, with residences dispersed around it. In 1913 no one lived much farther south than McGowan Street. In 1925 Rice Institute (as Rice University was then called), which had opened in 1912, was considered "the end of town." When Congregation Beth Israel was first formed (in 1859), its services were held in a frame building on LaBranch and Prairie. It grew and in 1870

Adath Yeshurun Synagogue, Walker at Jackson (1908–1945).

moved to Franklin and Crawford, where it completed its transition to Reform Judaism. A minority opposed to reforms broke away and in 1889 formed a traditional (Orthodox) synagogue, Adath Yeshurun, composed mainly of the new East European immigrants who were just beginning to arrive. Beth Israel, still growing, moved farther south in 1908 to Lamar Street.

Initially, most of the Jews lived in and around the First and Second Wards and then the Third Ward, near the first locations of Congregation Beth Israel. (The new Orthodox synagogue was also located there.) As the East Europeans began moving into Houston, they tended to settle in the Fifth Ward (around Franklin and

Navigation) and in the Sixth Ward (around Houston and Washington Avenues). Jews were, therefore, somewhat dispersed over the city, although practically none lived in the Heights. Two additional small Orthodox synagogues were formed to serve the Jewish population living in these new areas. (Orthodox Jews must be within walking distance of their synagogues, because they are forbidden to ride on the Sabbath. Reform Jews do not observe this restriction.)

The second area of Jewish residences began to take shape between 1920 and 1924 when Jews, along with the Gentile population, began moving first to Washington Terrace (a new subdivision bounded by Almeda on the west, Alabama on the north, and Blodgett on the south) and then, in 1924, also to Riverside Terrace (a newer subdivision extending farther south from Blodgett to North and South MacGregor). This southeastern section of the city remained the second major Jewish residential area until the end of the 1950s. During this period, the existing congregations relocated there. Also, the other two of today's three main congregations were formed: the Reform Congregation Emanu El in 1943 (by members who withdrew from Beth Israel in conflict over a variety of issues, including Zionism) and the Conservative Congregation Beth Yeshurun (formed in 1945 by a merger, due to financial difficulties, of the Conservative Congregation Beth El and the Orthodox Congregation Adath Yeshurun, from which the members of Beth El had originally withdrawn).

The third major shift began during the mid-1950s. Houston was expanding as a result of the population explosion that had taken place after World War II. There was a general trend of residential movement from the southeastern sections of the city to the southwest; and by the mid-1950s, the Jewish population (which in 1955 was approximately 13,500 to 14,800), along with the Gentile population, began moving across Main Street southwestward, especially to the areas around Braeswood Boulevard.

By 1963 the center of gravity of the Houston Jewish community had shifted to Meyerland. Once more the Jewish institutions—the congregations and the Jewish Community Center—moved to the "new Jewish area." The three Orthodox synagogues merged to form one United Orthodox Synagogue and erected a new building on South Braeswood between Stella Link and Post Oak. Beth Israel built on North Braeswood near Hillcroft. Emanu El, already located on Sunset Boulevard across from Rice University, did not have to move, nor did the two small splinter congregations formed in the 1950s (one classical Reform and the other Conservative), for they, too, had built in the southwest.

By 1972 some Jews had moved farther southwest into the new Fondren Southwest area and also into the Memorial-Spring Branch area. For the first time, several "clusters" of so-called Jewish areas were discernible.

A fourth pattern of Jewish residential locations is now apparent in Houston, with an explosion of locations as well as several "clusters." This development will be discussed in subsequent sections.

The Jews of Houston Today

In looking at Jews in Houston today, one should begin by examining the new general environment to which Jews, as well as other Americans, are now adapting. Since the early 1970s the general environment has been one in which there has been increased regard for ethnic identity and diversity. Economic and social discrimination has diminished for all groups. Women have gained rights and sought equality. Youth who were hippies have become respectable; the drug culture has spread; families are less stable. In American society in general, the trend toward increasing bureaucracy, complexity, impersonality, and secularism has continued unabated. The Jewish community in Houston has mirrored all of these trends.

In 1983 the vast majority of Jews in Houston (whose population is estimated to be between 30,000 and 40,000) are neither native-born Houstonians nor Texan. Houston has experienced a great influx of newcomers in recent years, and the Houston Jewish community has received its share. However, the Jewish population still represents but a small minority, about 1.6 percent, of the total Houston population, the same percentage it has maintained throughout the city's history. The newcomers have migrated from all over the world, but the most significant numbers have been from Russia (since 1973 about five hundred families have come to Houston), South Africa, Canada, and other parts of the United States.

There are now eighteen religious congregations serving Greater Houston, ten of which are new. Locations include Missouri City (in Fort Bend County), The Woodlands, and the north Harris County and south Montgomery County areas; two congregations serve the far west Memorial area. And reflecting the variety of types of new Jews in Houston, there is now a

Confirmation class of 1917, Adath Yeshurun.

Chabad Lubavitch Center (a Hasidic sect), a Sephardic congregation, and even a gay congregation.

The majority of Jews still live in the southwest area of the city, but as the new synagogue locations reflect, they are also moving into many of the outlying areas. Generally it is the newcomers who have settled in the new areas. It is estimated that 28 percent of the Jewish population, or 800 to 1,000 families, live in the Memorial area between Gessner and the Katy Freeway. Other newcomers have helped swell the Fondren Southwest area; the Sephardic congregation is located there as well as the Lubavitch Center. Meyerland still has a large concentration of Jewish families, however. Almost all of the major Jewish institutions, including the Jewish Community Center and the Jewish Home for the Aged, are located between Meyerland and Fondren Southwest. The trend toward several "clusters" of Jewish concentration, first noted in the early 1970s, is now confirmed.

Occupational Patterns

One aspect of the Houston Jewish community upon which the newcomers have had an impact has been its socioeconomic pattern. Since the early days in Houston, up until the 1970s at least, most Houston Jews have been merchants. (Historically, economic discrimination made it necessary for Jews to engage in

Confirmation class of 1910, Beth Israel.

occupations in which they could work for themselves.) Even though Jews became involved in real estate development and building and other diversified areas, the Houston Jewish community in general earned its income, according to a survey in 1975, primarily in direct retail business or in activities supportive of such business, and secondarily through the major professions. It was primarily a white-collar community by occupational and educational level. (The pursuit of learning, which stems from the Torah's emphasis on education, has generally characterized Jews, regardless of social and economic background.) This pattern was similar to that of Jewish groups elsewhere who lived in small cities where they were a minority. In contrast, many Jews in New York are taxicab drivers, waiters, barbers, and so on.

By 1983, however, because of the diversified backgrounds of the Jewish newcomers, the proportion of Jewish blue-collar workers in Houston had risen. Jewish women have entered the work force in greater numbers, mirroring the general trend among women in America. With the decline in economic discrimination, many Jews now work for large corporations that in former years did not usually hire Jews. It may well be that now the majority of Houston Jews are no longer engaged in mercantile activities.

While studies generally confirm that American Jews are financially prosperous as a *group,* not all Jews are wealthy, and there are also a considerable number of poor ones. Houston Jews are no exception, according to a 1975 survey. Moreover, most are not in the financial bracket of the wealthiest Gentiles. The majority, like the larger population, fall between the two ends of the financial spectrum.

The Jewish Family

Jews have enjoyed a reputation for stable families. In recent years, however, Jewish families in America, including those in Houston, have been following the demographic patterns of the larger society. The divorce rate has increased among Jews, even among the Orthodox, the most traditional branch. Studies have indicated, nevertheless, that over time, despite the increase of divorce, Jewish rates have remained proportionately the same relative to those of other religious groups. That is, while Jews are divorcing more frequently than they did in the past, they are still divorcing less often than their non-Jewish counterparts.

As is true of the larger society, Jews in Houston and America are marrying at a later age than in the past; married couples are having fewer children (the Jewish birthrate has declined below the replacement rate); and both the number of single-person households and the number of households without children have risen sharply. A major concern of the formal Jewish community is stemming the possible erosion of Jewish identification that might be caused by Jewish family change, for numerous studies have shown that the family is the primary source for Jewish identification. Organizations and synagogues are attempting to respond creatively to the needs of the new types of alternative households—the singles, the divorced, the childless couples.

Regarding families and Jewish identification, there has been an increase in the numbers of Jews marrying non-Jews. "Intermarriage" is the term now used by rabbis to refer to marriages where the non-Jewish mate converts to Judaism. When the mate does not convert, the term "mixed marriage" is used. The rates of both mixed marriages and intermarriages have risen sharply in the past ten years. But the proportion of non-Jewish mates who convert to Judaism is about the same as the number who do not, so the result is neither a net gain nor a loss of members to Judaism.

In the past, most Jewish parents would have been devastated if their child had married a non-Jew. Since the 1970s, with the change in youth's views and the rise in such marriages, most parents simply *prefer* a similar-religion marriage for their child to aid in family and couple compatibility. At the level of the formal Jewish community there is concern because Jews are not reproducing themselves, and it is felt that mixed marriages can ultimately lead to the dissolution of the Jewish people.

The Formal or Organized Jewish Community

Since, behaviorally, Jews are similar to other Americans, how do they maintain their Jewishness? One way is in having their separate organizations and institutions. In addition to religious congregations, a myriad of formal organizations exist in the city for Jews to participate in if they wish. Many Jews active in the formal communal life have come to refer to these organizations and associations (including the religious congregations) and the events and activities associated with them as the "formal" or "organized" Jewish community. In looking at the organized community, however, it is important to remember that it does not include all Jews. Many Jews do not belong to any of the religious congregations or other formal Jewish associations, and among those who do, not all participate in them or psychologically identify with them to the same degree. It cannot be said too often that there is not one unvaried distinctive group of Jews who are all alike.

Since the synagogue, or temple, is the primary Jewish institution, the following brief survey of the different branches of Judaism, drawing in part on *What Is a Jew?* by Rabbi Morris N. Kertzer, will also shed light on one basis for differences among Jews. As noted earlier, in American Judaism, there are essentially three major religious groupings: the Orthodox, the Conservative, and the Reform. To call them sects or denominations would be inaccurate, says Rabbi Kertzer, because it

"Mock Trial," 1915, presented by the Jewish Literary Society.

would imply sharper differences than really exist. The underlying basis of Jewish belief is the same for all three—the differences are in interpretations and emphasis. This difference is expressed both in the synagogue worship and in the daily life of the people.

Orthodox Jews believe that the traditional law contained in the Bible and in the Talmud—the oral law—is divine in origin and not subject to modification. They practice a traditional Judaism. They are the strictest observers of the Sabbath. (Between sundown on Friday and sundown on Saturday they engage in no work of any kind, no travel, writing, or business deal-ings, no carrying of money or even discussion of weekday affairs.) They follow the dietary laws in detail, use only Hebrew for prayer and ceremonial services, and maintain a separate section for women in the synagogue. Men (and, among the ultra-Orthodox, also the women) keep their heads covered at all times. Orthodoxy is not completely unyielding to the chance conditions of life. For example, although it is forbidden to eat on the Day of Atonement, it is also forbidden not to do so if it endangers life. For those in military service, some latitude in dietary observance is also permitted.

Reform Jews view the Bible not as a divinely dic-

Congregation Emanu El, formed in 1943.

United Orthodox Synagogue, formed in the mid-1960s.

tated book, but as an inspired record written by men. Religious laws are seen as functions of their particular time and therefore subject to modification. For example, just as animal sacrifice gave way to prayer when man and his social conditions changed, so other biblical injunctions—such as dietary laws—can be viewed as functions of their time and modified or discarded. Thus, if Reform Jews observe any customs, it is because they choose to do so, not because the observance is required by religious law. The permanent elements of Judaism are seen to be not the forms of religious worship or ritual (the ceremonial laws) but rather the underlying moral and ethical laws of the Bible. In the Reform temple—as the Reform house of worship is generally called—men and women sit together; prayer is largely in English or any vernacular; instrumental music is used; male worshipers do not wear head coverings or prayer shawls. The High Holy Days are observed less traditionally, as is the Sabbath. The Reform is always the branch most amenable to change. It was the first branch to ordain women as rabbis.

Conservative Jews follow the pattern of traditional Judaism, by and large, but feel that Jewish law must of necessity grow if it is to remain alive, and that hence *some* change is natural. Conservative Jews adhere to the dietary laws, with some minor relaxation, and observe the Sabbath, High Holy Days, and festivals traditionally. But in the synagogue they have instituted many of the forms of Reform Judaism, such as the late Friday evening service, responsive readings, fixed hours of worship, a more extensive use of English in prayers, and the sitting together of men and women. Head coverings are worn by men only when in the synagogue or during acts of worship.

Although these are the basic differences between the three branches in America, there has always been a wide range of diversity within each of the three groups, Rabbi Kertzer notes, for there is no element of compulsion in the American synagogue. Some Conservative congregations are indistinguishable from Orthodox; some Orthodox congregations allow men and women to sit together; and some Reform congregations pray with covered heads and wear prayer shawls.

Congregation Beth Yeshurun, formed in 1945.

Moreover, the branches differ from one geographic area to another. Congregations called Reform in one part of the country might be considered Conservative in another. For example, the Conservative congregations in Houston would be considered Reform in the large eastern cities; most of the Orthodox congregations would be considered Conservative; and to many, the Reform congregations would be considered so "reformed" as to have lost all essence of Judaism. The more recent congregations of each branch, started by newcomers, tend to be more traditional than the established ones in Houston.

The three largest religious congregations in Houston today, as in the 1940s, are the two Reform congregations, Beth Israel and Emanu El, and the Conservative congregation, Beth Yeshurun. But typical of the general pattern in Jewish communities, the Orthodox branch has grown in number of members and prestige; some feel this has come as a result of the renewed respect for tradition since the 1960s and the attraction of the Orthodox for Jewish youth seeking relevance and "real" Judaism. However, in terms of membership size, the Orthodox branch remains the smallest of the three branches in Houston. As in other American Jewish communities, all three branches of Judaism in Houston have become more alike. Because of the new pride in Judaism and respect for its traditions, the two major Reform congregations in Houston have become more traditional, reinstating some customs once discarded, such as having a cantor and introducing more Hebrew in the service, and in general celebrating Jewish culture and history in their congregational life. Partly as a result of the impact of secularization, the Orthodox has moved toward the Conservative position.

In regard to congregational affiliation, Houston is still unlike the large eastern cities but is similar to the smaller or southern communities in that most Jews feel it important to belong to a synagogue or temple. This circumstance may perhaps be explained by their proportionately smaller numbers and their desire to affiliate for the sake of identity. To belong to a synagogue or temple, however, does not necessarily mean active participation. Many Jews attend the synagogue only on the High Holy Days and/or some Friday nights on special occasions, such as a Bar or Bat Mitzvah, or to say prayers on Yarzheit (the anniversary of the death of a relative).

Studies show that Jews in Houston probably follow the national trend of Jews in America concerning religious observance in the home. That is, while more Jews are returning to traditional practices, they are generally selective: they may light the Sabbath candles, but they are not strict observers of the Sabbath; they may celebrate the festivals of Chanukah and Succoth, but they do not follow dietary laws. It is interesting to note that in the extreme Orthodox Lubavitch Center, where the Sabbath and dietary laws are kept strictly, the bulk of the membership is young couples, many of them the youth of the 1960s.

Religious customs and practices have always played an important role in strengthening family and group bonds. It is true that in recent years, particularly for Reform Jews, there has been renewed interest in traditional holidays and customs. But even before this time, most Jews—even the peripheral ones—participated in certain holidays and customs: the family Passover

A bride and groom stand beneath the chuppah *(marriage canopy) at their wedding. The association of the* chuppah, *usually consisting of four poles and a canopy, with the wedding rite can be traced to the Bible. The physical appearance and religious significance of it, however, have undergone many changes.*

Seder, the High Holidays, and, less often, the yearly memorial services that take place at the synagogue and the cemetery. These occasions provide opportunities for Jews to meet relatives and friends whom they may not otherwise see during the year. It is one means whereby even peripheral Jews can maintain ties with other Jews. With the large memberships of the synagogues today, with diminishing extended family closeness, and with the greater number of single and other alternative types of households, such integrating forces are becoming weaker.

It is not necessary for a Jew to belong to a congregation to practice the religion of Judaism. Saying prayers, keeping the Sabbath, and participating in rites and rituals can all be done at home. Nor, for some, is it necessary to belong to a synagogue or be ritually observant in order to feel that they are "good" Jews. Some Jews participate only in the secular organizations of the community—the "secular Jew" versus the "religious Jew." Some participate in neither religious nor secular activities and yet consider themselves "good" Jews if they practice the moral precepts of Judaism in their

Rabbi Roy Walter of Congregation Emanu El with his son Benjamin cradling the Torah.
Photograph by Gay Block; reprinted by permission.

daily lives—i.e., "Do unto others as you would have them do unto you"; "Act justly, love mercy, and walk humbly with your God." For many Jews, one of the positive aspects of the Jewish religion is that it is a religion from which one can take as much or as little of it as one wishes. The rules of worship are far less exacting than the rules of conduct. For Orthodox Jews, of course, to be not only a good person but also an authentic Jew, one must observe all of the more than 613 commandments. Other characteristics of the Jewish religion are that it has no dogma and no hierarchy (a rabbi is not a priest), and that it is open to differences of opinion. These aspects seem to account for the trait of Jews epitomized by the saying that "if you have two Jews, you have three opinions."

A basic value in the Jewish religion is "Tzedakah." Its closest English translation would be "just" or "righteous" giving, for there is no Hebrew word for "charity." True charity is anonymous and stems from the heart. Its highest form to Jews is helping people to help themselves. Giving (or philanthropy), in the sense of Tzedakah, is a biblical injunction. Tzedakah knows no racial or religious boundaries, and many Jews have been raised to think that they must help their fellow human beings. According to many Jews, however, history has taught them that the only person who will help a Jew is a second Jew. Hence, the Jews—in Houston as elsewhere—view themselves as people with a special burden to bear. That is, while they participate in the life of the community at large, giving time and money to charitable endeavors of a nonsectarian nature, they must also give to Jews who are in trouble and need help, because "if a Jew won't help a fellow Jew, who else will?" Jews appear to have helped fellow Jews in the United States ever since they first arrived in 1654 and promised the Dutch government they "would take care of their own." Their methods for doing so, however, have changed over the years. What were once small volunteer groups are today large organizations run by professionals. The present-day system of fund raising—utilizing data processing, scientific surveys, and the like—mirrors the complexity and bureaucracy of the larger world; but the value on which it is based is still the old one of Tzedakah.

"Giving" is a thread that runs throughout the fabric of the Jewish community. It penetrates organization and synagogue life, for Jews are constantly either taking part in fund raising or being asked to give. Jews have a reputation for being very successful fund raisers. It is all the more remarkable because they contribute their time and money generously not only to Jewish organizations but to non-Jewish ones as well. In the general community, for example, Jews have always participated in various civic groups, particularly charitable ones. Jews have served and continue to serve on the boards of many Houston hospitals, universities, and foundations—including Methodist Hospital, Texas Children's Hospital, Baylor College of Medicine, the University of Houston, and heart and cancer research foundations. They have been large contributors to groups such as the Houston Ballet Foundation, Channel 8 (KUHT-TV), the Houston Symphony, the Houston Museum of Fine Arts, and the United Fund. The Jewish Institute for Medical Research, a division of the Baylor College of Medicine located in the Medical Center, was built with money donated by Houston Jews. Ben Taub General Hospital was named for its greatest benefac-

tor, a Jew, as was Cohen House, the faculty club at Rice University. Most recently, two new wings of the architecture building at Rice University were named in honor of their donors, Isaac S. and Mildred D. Brochstein and Kenneth Schnitzer. Because anonymity is valued by many Jews, there are numerous works of philanthropy by Houston Jews that will never be known by the general public.

In addition to religious congregations, the formal Jewish community includes more than eighty organizations or common-interest associations to which men, women, youth, singles, and older adults may belong. Included among these are the sisterhoods and brotherhoods of the religious congregations; various women's groups such as the National Council of Jewish Women and Hadassah; men's organizations such as B'nai B'rith and Jewish War Veterans; the American Jewish Committee; City of Hope, a national organization that supports a free, nonsectarian medical and research center in Duarte, California; and the Jewish Community Center, which is actually nonsectarian. There are also various service agencies, such as the Jewish Family Service, and Seven Acres, the Jewish home for the aged. While it is not an organization, an integral part of the Jewish formal community is the weekly newspaper, the *Jewish-Herald Voice,* published since 1908.

As in the past, the various organizations and groups tend to attract different segments of the Jewish population; but today, because Jews are more homogeneous, the appeal is based mainly on differences in interests and age rather than on deeply felt ideologies. In general, women participate in their organizations more than men do, probably reflecting the fact that more women have the time to volunteer. Particularly in the past, participation served as a career substitute for many women by providing a stimulus and an outlet for their energies and giving them a sense of accomplishment. There are "career ladders" in the organizations and leadership training sessions, seminars, and the like. Some of the organizations are primarily involved in community-at-large service projects; some in aid to Israel; some in fostering community relations and combating anti-Semitism.

The formal Jewish community has not been without

Rabbi blowing shofar *(usually a ram's horn). Blasts of the* shofar *announce the beginning and conclusion of the High Holy Days, Rosh Hashana and Yom Kippur. Photograph by Gay Block; reprinted by permission.*

criticism from some members of the Jewish population, particularly the older generation of long-time Houstonians. The comments are typical of those to be heard from the rank and file of a population anywhere today: the congregations are too large; there is too much impersonality and materialism in the large organizations and associations; people no longer have the same values—people used to have time to have tea and chat; there used to be more understanding among people; giving today is a commercial process—it's not from the heart anymore.

Discrimination and Anti-Semitism

Any discussion of Jews must include the subject of discrimination and anti-Semitism. Even though Houston Jews have always perceived Houston as having a relatively low level of anti-Semitism, most adult Jews feel that it exists as a latent possibility. Scholars have noted that a rise in tensions is often accompanied by an increase in prejudice towards Jews as the proverbial scapegoat; thus, many Jews remain wary. Recent upheavals in the world have produced anti-Zionism and anti-Israel feelings that Jews have equated with a broader anti-Jewish sentiment. Indeed, some of the national New Right and New Left movements have seemed to display anti-Jewish attitudes, a cause of concern to Jews in Houston and elsewhere.

In Houston, as elsewhere in the United States, economic and social discrimination against Jews has generally declined in recent years. For example, by the early 1970s there were no longer quotas for Jewish or other minority medical students at Baylor College of Medicine. On the other hand, even in 1983 many companies that conduct business in the Middle East have occupational discriminatory policies in regard to Jews. These companies—not only oil companies but also architectural and construction firms—will not hire Jews, or if they do, will not send them abroad or allow them to work on projects for Arab clients. Officers in many of these firms have signed agreements with Middle East companies saying, in effect, that Jews are not involved in any of their business dealings—even though such discrimination is against federal law.

Historically, anti-Semitism in the United States has been different from the European variety. In Europe it has often been a state policy; in America, it has never had any legal status and has never been governmentally sanctioned. When anti-Semitic incidents have occurred, they have been sporadic and usually impulsive. Most often hostility towards Jews has taken the form of social and economic discrimination. As important as the documentation of any anti-Semitism that may exist is how the Jewish people perceive the anti-Semitic climate, whatever it is in fact, and how they are affected by it. Among the deplorable results of prejudice and discrimination for any group are the psychological scars, the certain sensitivities and anxieties engendered in the victims. For example, some adult Houston Jews in the early 1970s had the attitude that Jews should display higher standards than Gentiles, "because we are a minority and hence must be on our best behavior." Sometimes this sensitivity is referred to as having to be the "good" representative. Others feared that the behavior of one Jew would cause repercussions for other Jews—a kind of sensitivity that has been called a sense of "collective accountability" or "interdependence of fate." By the late 1970s, though, because of the decline in perceived hostility, such scars were becoming less evident among Jewish adults in Houston, and, most significantly, they were almost nonexistent among the youth.

The Future

Newcomers have had an impact on the Jewish fabric of Houston in several respects. What their ultimate effect will be is too early to tell—just as predicting the future of Houston is difficult. But certainly the addition of such groups as the Lubavitcher and the Sephardic has made for a richer texture, providing a variety of ways of being Jewish, some new to the Houston Jewish community. The community's overall profile, however, remains much the same. There have always been Jews in Houston who were religious and those who were not; those who participated and identified with the Jewish formal and informal life and those who did not. As another saying goes, "Jews are like everyone else, only more so." There have always been, and still are, both internal and external forces—in Houston and elsewhere—favoring and discouraging the survival of the Jews as a distinctive group. At present, their existence as a distinguishable group seems assured for an indefinite period. And, as in the past, they will continue to contribute to the religious, civic, cultural, and business life of Houston.

Germans

Theodore G. Gish

Grand officers of the Sons of Hermann, April 28, 1921. Photograph from the Bank of the Southwest/Frank J. Schlueter Collection, Houston Public Library Metropolitan Research Center.

Germans and German-Americans have played and continue to play a surprisingly pervasive, sometimes colorful, and frequently important role in many aspects of Houston's development. Even before the Allen brothers advertised Houston as a city in the summer of 1836, the very first settlement within the present city limits, in an area south of Buffalo Bayou and west of Highway 59, became generally known as Germantown because of the predominantly German inhabitants of the area in subsequent years. It is for this reason that Canal Street was once known as German Street.

The city's present mayor is a German-American whose maiden name is Niederhofer. Kathy Whitmire is the second German-American in this high office (Fred Hofheinz was the first) in the last decade. Yet, because of the invisibility of German-Americans as an ethnic minority (in part self-imposed, to be sure, by the experience of the two world wars), the average Houstonian is unaware of these and other more significant German-American contributions in the past and present economic, political, religious, and cultural life of Houston.

In order to understand the role of German-Americans in Houston, it is necessary first to examine briefly their role in the history of the United States and, in particular, in the development of Texas. Statistically, German-Americans in the United States are more numerous than their low visibility might suggest. An Associated Press article, appearing in both daily papers in Houston in May 1982, pointed out that "more Americans can trace their ancestry to Germany than to any other country." The article referred to a 1979 study of the Census Bureau that indicated that "28.8 percent of Americans reported themselves at least partly of German ancestry." The article indicated that this "would mean that about 52 million Americans consider themselves at least partly German."

That more than one-fourth of the American population may have some claim to German-Americanism no doubt has news value, partly because of the growing importance of ethnicity in America. In addition, such information also reflects the fact that in 1983 the United States and the Federal Republic of Germany celebrated the 300th anniversary of the arrival of the first German settlers in America. On October 6, 1683, the pastor

Francis Daniel Pastorius arrived in the present harbor of Philadelphia on the *Concordia,* the Mayflower of German immigration, with thirteen Mennonite families from Krefeld, Germany. After a sea voyage of ten weeks, these families founded Germantown as part of Penn's colony. The arrival of these first German colonists in America was observed in the United States and in the Federal Republic of Germany with a variety of public and private celebrations. Both countries, for example, issued commemorative postage stamps, and there was a ceremonial meeting between President Reagan and Bundespräsident Karl Carstens in Philadelphia, where the original Germantown is now a suburb. In addition to the historical importance of these events, both nations are aware of the ways in which these commemorative activities can also strengthen the cultural bonds, and with them the political ties, between the two countries.

In *The Germans in America,* Carl Wittke states that during the American colonial period, "crop failures, famine, heavy taxes, the misrule of petty princes, the burden of military service, and the persecution of religious groups . . . were the main reasons why German farmers and burghers turned to the new land across the Atlantic." For those Germans who, like the Krefeld Mennonites, were members of Protestant sects (German Quakers, Dunkards, Moravians), religion was a major reason for their immigrating to America in the eighteenth century. There was no real "Germany" in a political sense at that time; but in the numerous German states, these religious sects were declared illegal, since only Catholic, Lutheran, and Reformed (Calvinist) faiths were allowed.

By the time of the American Revolution, more than 100,000 Germans had immigrated to Pennsylvania, and eventually that state became one-third German. While most of the Germans who came to America at this time settled in either Pennsylvania or New York, in the early part of the century more than 30,000 Protestants were expelled from Salzburg; many of them immigrated to Georgia. Like these Salzburg refugees, thousands of Protestant Palatinate Rhinelanders came to America for the same reasons. The Rockefeller family, for example, immigrated in 1733, while Peter Zenger, the champion of American freedom of the press, came to the colonies as an orphan from the Palatinate region.

During the Revolutionary War, German-Americans fought on both sides, although for the most part their sympathies were with the colonists. Many of the nearly 30,000 German mercenaries who bore the collective designation "Hessians" (since the Hessian princes had most abused this practice of contracting their countrymen into military service) elected to stay in America after the war, and they too helped to populate the new nation, particularly the remaining unsettled areas of Pennsylvania.

Since the next important period of German immigration to the United States coincides with the formative period of the German presence in Texas, we may now focus attention on these conditions in the Lone Star State.

The Germans in Texas

The important period of the immigration of Germans to Texas is the nineteenth century, particularly the period 1830 to 1860, and then the two decades after the Civil War. Of particular importance during the middle of the century was the immigration of nearly 15,000 Germans to Texas (approximately 8,000 in the year 1847 alone) under the grandiose colonial schemes of the Adelsverein (Society of Noblemen), which called itself, grandiloquently, the Society for the Protection of German Immigrants in Texas (Gesellschaft zum Schutz deutscher Einwanderer in Texas). Actually, more Germans came to Texas after the Civil War (during the period 1865 to 1890), but the prewar immigration is more important because of the concentration of relatively high numbers of immigrants in a few key years and the selected sites of their settlement. This pre–Civil War immigration not only led to the development of the German Hill Country communities, particularly New Braunfels and Fredericksburg, but also contributed materially, during formatively important years, to the development of Galveston, San Antonio, and Houston. During certain periods of the nineteenth century, consequently, the populations of Galveston and San Antonio were estimated to be between one-third to one-half German, while the population of Houston (less "German" than the other two cities) was similarly estimated to be between 20 and 45 percent German.

The social conditions of Germany, described earlier by Wittke, had improved only slightly by the beginning of the nineteenth century. A few of the reigning princes had become "enlightened" in at least some aspects of their leadership. In the main, however, these princes remained a conservative lot, and personal liberties, as are known today, were very limited. Moreover, the standard of living remained low. While the first half of the century was also a period of considerable political turmoil, in the long run few political improvements for the individual citizen resulted. Napoleon's rise to power and his defeat of the Prussian army in 1806 put an end to the Holy Roman Empire, an unwieldy confederation of many small and a few large German states whose demise was long overdue. These states did unite themselves, however, in a way they had never done while members of the Empire, during the Wars of Liberation against Napoleon. After Napoleon's defeat at Waterloo in 1815, the Congress of Vienna, under the leadership of the arch-conservative prime minister of Austria, Prince Metternich, created the German Federation (Deutsche Bund) of thirty-nine states from the old Empire. This Bund maintained peace in central Europe and political harmony among the member states until the revolution of 1848. It did so, however, by severely limiting the civil rights of the German population.

During the 1830s there were minor uprisings in the German states, frequently led by students. These disturbances occasioned even more repressive measures by Metternich, who controlled German political life during this period. During the revolution of 1848 street fighting erupted in Prussia and Bavaria. Metternich fled to England, and the ruling princes agreed to certain concessions, in particular the convening of a convention in Frankfurt for the purpose of drafting a democratic constitution for a new Germany. The constitution was duly drafted, but with the revolutionary spirit now dissipated, none of the German princes would agree to become the head of the new government, nor would the states ratify the constitution. Consequently, the political life of Germany reverted to the way it had been in 1815, except that the middle class, now a political reality, was taken somewhat more seriously. The German lands did not really become united until the period of Bismarck and the creation of the second Empire, after the Franco-Prussian war of 1870–71.

If Germany's political revolution was unsuccessful, the same cannot be said for the revolution in Germany's cultural life. With the writings of Goethe (1749–1832), Schiller (1759–1805), and the Romanticists, German literature came of age. While in former times German writers had imitated the literary conventions of France and England, now the writings of Goethe (particularly his drama, *Faust,* and his novel, *The Sorrows of Young Werther*), the freedom dramas of Schiller, and the poetry of the German Romanticists were praised and emulated in those countries. Moreover, the superiority of German letters in what is often called the Age of Goethe was matched by German achievements in music, philosophy, and science.

The nineteenth-century German immigrants to Texas, consequently, grew up in a homeland of cultural riches and political restrictions. While the Texas immigrants shared with earlier German immigrants to America a desire for social and economic betterment, only the Wends, the Slavic Germans from Saxony and Prussia, came as a group to Texas for reasons of religious freedom. Additionally, many of those involved in the uprisings of the 1830s and in the revolution of 1848 (the Forty-Eighters) came to Texas because they were attracted initially to the republican form of government and later, once Texas joined the Union, to the freedom they perceived in the United States.

Some of the German immigrants, imbued with the spirit of the Romantic age, also came to Texas because of an idealized view of America and the American West that they obtained from the travel books and fictional accounts written about America and particularly about Texas and its Republic at that time. Between 1815 and 1850 more than fifty books were published by Germans who had visited America. In these books, Texas was better discussed and advertised than any other state in America. Most of the accounts extolled life in America, and occasionally the writers also took the opportunity to criticize living conditions in Germany. Hermann Ehrenbert's *Texas und seine Revolution* (*Texas and Its Revolution,* 1843) was widely read, because in addition to being a guide to Texas it also described his experiences as a "citizen of the Republic" and as a soldier in the War of Independence.

The fictional accounts by writers and poets who had never visited Texas and consequently whose fantasy could have free rein in proclaiming its wonder were, in some ways, more important than the guidebooks. Hoffmann von Fallersleben, the author of Germany's national anthem ("Deutschland, Deutschland über alles") was so taken by the stories of Texas told to him by Gustav Dresel, who spent the years 1838 to 1840 in Texas and mostly in Houston, that he seriously considered immigrating himself. Von Fallersleben was unable to take this step, however, so he wrote poetry about Texas instead. Verses like the following from his *Texanische Lieder* (*Texas Songs,* 1846), with "San Felipe" given as the fictional place of publication, were no doubt encouraging to the immigrant bound for Texas:

Der Stern von Texas
Hin nach Texas! Hin nach Texas!
Wo der Stern im blauen Felde
Eine neue Welt verkundet,
Jedes Herz für Recht und Freiheit
Und für Wahrheit froh entzundet—
Dahin sehnt mein Herz sich ganz.
The Star of Texas
On to Texas! On to Texas!
Where the star in the blue field
A new world indicates,
Every heart for right and freedom
And for truth it animates—
There my spirit yearns to go.

Another extremely influential writer was Charles Sealsfied, an Austrian, whose real name was Carl Anton Postl. Sealsfied also never visited Texas, but in his extensive travels throughout the United States he did come as far west as New Orleans. His many novels and travel accounts, some of which he wrote in English, were extremely popular both in Germany and in the United States. In books such as *Nathan der Squatter Regulator, oder der erste Amerikaner in Texas* (*Nathan the Squatter Overseer, or the First American in Texas,* 1837) or *Das Kajutenbuch oder Schilderungen aus dem Leben in Texas* (*The Cabin-Book or Descriptions of Life in Texas,* 1841) Sealsfied not only idealized American frontier life and American democracy, but he also fictionalized as no other writer had done before the romantic life of the settler within the veritable paradise of Texas. The following, for example, is the description of a settlement not too far from Houston:

A more beautiful or more favorable settlement you could not imagine. On one side lay what are called clearing lands, from which the primitive forest had just been removed; on the other, immense prairies with the tall grass waving about the heads of the browsing cattle, and horses that were pulling and tumbling against each other like rolling stones; the sound of tinkling cowbells came to our ears in the gentle breeze, and in the far blue distance a thick fog was seen glimmering in the sunbeams through every opening of the vast forest. There was something charming and irresistible in the landscape.

I found the rudiments—the A B C of squatter life— in the clearings, in the woodland and in the live oaks; the spelling book in the rude and artless dwellings, in the horses and in the corn stubbles. I saw plainly that I had only to do as the squatters had done to accomplish the same ends. He only, who has to solve the difficult problem of getting along in the backwoods, can form any idea of the childish haste with which I pounced on every object. The log house had irresistible charms. I was in an ecstasy at the thought of the time when my beloved family, in their plain and simple robes, would come to meet me at the cabin door, as I returned from the field.

What immigrant living a politically and physically confined existence in Germany could resist such descriptions that abound in Sealsfied's novels about Texas?

During the Spanish and Mexican period, there were a number of colonial plans, some of them very elaborate, that would involve bringing large groups of Germans to Texas. Austin wanted to bring Germans into his colony because he admired their character, their industry, and their opposition to slavery. Austin also shrewdly felt that Germans did not have the mania for speculation that possessed the English and the North Americans. But, because of the climate, he was only able to recruit five Germans for his colony.

The first settlement of Germans in Texas was Industry, in Austin County, founded by Friedrich Ernst in 1831. Ernst, who had been the gardener for the Duke of Oldenburg, had read the popular guidebook to America, Gottfried Duden's *Bericht über eine Reise nach den westlichen Staaten Nordamerikas* (*Report of a Trip to the Western States of North America*, 1829) before he left for the United States. Ernst spent a year in New York with his family before coming to Texas, where he obtained a league of land from the Mexican government. In a letter home in 1832, Ernst lavishly praised the settler's life in Texas and compared the climate of Texas favorably to Italy. This letter was reprinted in German newspapers and also in Detlev Dunt's guidebook, *Reise nach Texas* (*Journey to Texas*, 1834). Published in this fashion, Ernst's letter was an authenticated inducement in encouraging other Germans to come to Texas. In 1838 Ernst plotted the town of Industry and advertised town lots for sale (50' x 150', $20) in the Houston newspaper. Mrs. Ernst, the first German woman in Texas, opened a hotel in Industry in 1840, which many prominent Germans, including members of the Adelsverein, visited and which they called an "oasis in the desert."

In the decade after the founding of Industry, a number of nearby German settlements were established in what is known as the eastern German belt of Texas. In 1834 members of the von Roeder family and Robert Justus Kleberg (who was married to one of the von Roeder daughters) came to Texas, in part influenced by Ernst's letter, and founded the settlement of Cat Spring. The von Roeders were cultivated people and purportedly brought the first piano to Texas. This piano was, unfortunately, lost along with other valuable household possessions when Mexican soldiers burned down Harrisburg during the War of Independence. Robert Justus Kleberg became a renowned Texas rancher, and his son, by marrying a King daughter, helped to found the dynasty of the King Ranch. Other German settlements, such as Frelsburg, Roedersmühle (now Shelby), Mühlheim (now Millheim), and New Ulm, developed in the late 1830s and the 1840s, much as did Industry and Cat Spring, around the farm of an original settler.

The greatest immigration to Texas by Germans occurred, as has been mentioned, under the auspices of the Adelsverein. In 1842 a group of German noblemen

An early photograph of Hermann Hospital. Photograph from the Bank of the Southwest/Frank J. Schlueter Collection, Houston Public Library Metropolitan Research Center.

met in Biebrich on the Rhine to formulate colonization plans for Texas. The possibility of financial gain and vague dreams of an overseas empire for Germany doubtlessly motivated these noblemen as much as a genuine wish to help their subjects find a better life in the New World. The next year, two members of the society visited Texas and returned with differing views regarding the possible success of the society's proposed undertaking. The Adelsverein, nevertheless, proceeded with its plans. In 1844 newspaper articles announced the society's willingness to assist Germans who wanted to immigrate to Texas under its program. Upon the payment of a specified amount, the society would provide passage to Texas, convey land to the colonists (320 acres for a family, 160 acres for a single male), and assist materially in the establishment of permanent colonies.

In 1844 the society also appointed Carl, Prince of Solms-Braunfels, its commissioner-general and dispatched him to Texas. The Adelsverein's concession rights to one grant expired while Solms was on his way to Texas. The prince, furthermore, did not wish to use the Fayette County plantation, Nassau Farm, which the society had already bought, since Solms felt it was too close to Anglo settlers for whom he had little regard. Instead, the society entered into a land grant partnership with Henry Francis Fisher (Heinrich Franz Fischer) and Burchard Miller (Burkard Müller), recently arrived Germans who were now Houston land investors. The Fisher-Miller Grant consisted of more than three million acres, which alone greatly impressed the Adelsverein since it was nearly ten times the size of the Dukedom of Nassau where the society had been incorporated. But there were also severe disadvantages to the grant. Located near the present city of Mason in West Texas, it was too far from the

Laying of the cornerstone, First Evangelical Church, January 30, 1927. Dr. D. Baltzer, pastor. Photograph from the Bank of the Southwest/Frank J. Schlueter Collection, Houston Public Library Metropolitan Research Center.

seacoast to make trade profitable. Moreover, half the land was unsuitable for any sort of agriculture. Fisher and Miller were, to be sure, unaware of this, for they had never set foot in the region. Few white men had, since the area was under the control of the Comanches.

By the summer of 1844 the first immigrants began to arrive in Galveston after an arduous two-month sea voyage, usually from Bremen. Solms' aristocratic bearing was unsuited to frontier Texas. He also possessed few managerial skills and no understanding whatsoever of the complex business affairs of the society. Nevertheless, Solms did what he could in his short stay in Texas to initiate the society's colonization plans. To provide access to the grant area, he established the port of Carlshafen (later called Indianola), where the immigrants were brought by packet boat after their arrival in Galveston. Since the grant was so far inland,

Solms planned to establish several colonial stations on the way to the grant site. With this in mind and on land purchased from the Veramendi family in San Antonio, Solms and several hundred colonists founded the first settlement in May 1845, suitably named New Braunfels.

The colonists suffered greatly during this time. Shelter was inadequate in Carlshafen and the immigrants, already weakened by the sea voyage, were exposed to the rigors of Texas coastal climate (including an unusually wet and cold winter) and were ravaged by cholera and yellow fever. The war between Mexico and the United States, which broke out in 1845, made providing for the colonists even more difficult.

Solms returned to Germany soon after the founding of New Braunfels. By this time, the operations of the Adelsverein in Texas were in organizational and financial disarray, and more immigrants were arriving in Galveston. Solms' successor, however, the very capable Baron Ottfried Hans von Meusebach (who called himself "John Meusebach" as soon as he arrived in Texas), was able to bring some order into the operations of the society. In 1846 Meusebach founded Fredericksburg as the second settlement site. A year later, shortly before he resigned his position, Meusebach successfully concluded a peace treaty with the Comanches, thus finally opening the vast grant area for settlement.

By this time, however, the Adelsverein was virtually bankrupt in Texas, and it ended its existence in the state courts of law. Some settlers did take possession of their land in the Fisher-Miller Grant, and a few small settlements were established, only to die out a short time later. But the Adelsverein had opened the great expanse of West Texas to the white man and had bestowed upon the Texas Hill Country its unique and abiding German quality. Many of the immigrants, of course, hearing in Galveston of the society's problems, did not continue their relationship with the Adelsverein. They either remained in Galveston, went to Houston, or settled in the eastern German belt in Austin, Fayette, and Lee counties.

The society's demise had little effect on the continuation of German immigration to Texas. German immigrants, in fact, were particularly attracted to the growing towns of Fredericksburg and New Braunfels (which by mid-century had become the state's fourth-largest city) and to nearby San Antonio, which became very German at this time. Particularly after the revolution of 1848, German liberals came to Texas as political refugees. Many of them became civic and business leaders in their new homeland. Some of these Forty-Eighters also helped establish unique intellectually oriented communities, such as Sisterdale and Comfort. These communities were often derisively called Latin Settlements by Anglo neighbors who felt their inhabitants were better speakers of Latin than they were farmers!

In 1854 the Wends, the only German group to immigrate to Texas primarily for religious reasons, founded the community of Serbin in Lee County. Under the leadership of their pastor, Johann Kilian, several hundred Wends came to Texas on the *Ben Nevis* to avoid the continuing religious and ethnic persecution they felt in their ancestral homes in Saxony and Prussia. Since these Wends were already established as a congregation in Germany, and since they spoke the Slavic Wendish language in addition to German, they formed a uniquely independent (and somewhat parochial and clannish) group of German immigrants to Texas.

The Civil War brought all immigration to Texas to a temporary standstill, but after the war Germans continued to arrive in greater numbers than before. Because of their Union sentiments, German-Americans often acquired important political positions in the larger Texas cities during the Reconstruction period. Artisans and professional people continued to immigrate to these cities, particularly in the last quarter of the nineteenth century. With the arrival of the windmill and the railroads, German settlements were established in the Panhandle, where farming communities such as Muenster still flourish.

The Mennonites, finally, were the last group of Germans (although they were actually Swiss-German in origin and many of them had lived for centuries outside of Europe) to arrive in Texas. They have been coming to Texas in small congregataions since 1905, virtually to the present time.

During the Second World War (when, in fact, thousands of German prisoners-of-war were temporary immigrants to Texas) and in the decade after the war, German immigration to Texas briefly underwent an upsurge, although it was nothing compared to the experience in the nineteenth century. Among the tremendous influx of newcomers to Harris County, there are still many German immigrants arriving; so one can say they continue to influence the development of Houston in ways that will be described in the next three sections.

Germans in Houston: The Beginnings

Most historical accounts of Houston mention the importance of people of German descent in the town's formative years. This is particularly true of descriptions of Houston by German-Americans themselves.

But even a contemporary Anglo historian such as David McComb in his *Houston: The Bayou City* (1969; revised edition, 1981) mentions the strong German element among the predominantly southern population during the city's early years. Remnants of this historical German presence remain in street names, such as Binz, Studemont, or Usener; in municipal designations (primarily Hermann Park); and in the names of families still active in Houston's civic, cultural, and business life, such as Settegast, Bering, or Hofheinz. But such family designations are only the most obvious indicators, an ethnic substratum, in effect, of the considerable German-American participation in the city's development. Moreover, Houston still has a significant German element. The nature and impact of the more recently arrived Germans upon Houston is different, of course, from those immigrants who helped to found the Magnolia City.

It is surprising, consequently, that there has been no formal or even informal general accounting of the importance of the German element in Houston's past and present development. This study represents only a beginning and is necessarily both incomplete and sketchy in many respects. Nevertheless, it should convey some idea of the magnitude of the German presence in Houston: how persons of German descent have helped, and continue to help, this southern and Texan metropolis, and at the same time, how they have preserved their own German heritage.

Germans were among Houston's earliest settlers. Even before the Allen brothers designated Houston as a town, a settlement grew up around the farmstead of Mary Wilkins, her two daughters, and a son-in-law. This farm was situated on the south bank of Buffalo Bayou, below its large horseshoe curve, in an area that is now bounded on the east by Highway 59. By 1826 the area had twenty inhabitants, and in 1835 the Allen brothers moved to the area from Nacogdoches. At this time, the settlement began to be called Germantown, because the majority of its inhabitants were German. The Frost family bought land in the area and began to develop it. By the late 1840s the official designation Frost Town became interchangeable with the unofficial Germantown. Frost Town was a small municipality,

only four blocks long and two blocks wide, with its main street being Spruce. Frost Town lasted as an independent city until the 1870s, when it was taken over municipally by Houston. There was actually a second location, situated in the present area of the Heights, north of White Oak Park, and bounded on the east by Interstate 45, that was officially surveyed and deeded as Germantown. Very little information exists on this Germantown. Purportedly it was developed in the 1840s by Elizabeth E. Parrott, who had sold the original land to the Allen brothers for Houston as a site north of the bayou in competition with the new city of Houston.

The designation Germantown for the Frost Town area persisted from the beginnings of Houston until the turn of the century. The area exhibited many German characteristics. Jesse Ziegler, in his book *Wave of the Gulf,* recalls playing in Germantown as a child in the 1870s. He remembers fondly the homes of prominent Germans such as F. W. Heitmann, H. F. Fisher (the major partner of the Fisher-Miller grant), John F. Usener, and Ignaz Veith. Concerning the area, Ziegler reported: "The homes all had beautiful flower gardens and well kept vegetable plots which helped to sustain them. There were small goats which roamed the hills by the dozens. . . . The Swiss and the Germans knew the value of goat's milk and all kinds of food were made out of the milk." According to Ziegler, "one reason Frost Town was settled so quickly was the fact that the German colonists came and, finding friends or relatives who they had known in the old country, they remained instead of going on into the interior." Mary Lee Phelps, in *A History of Early Houston,* also writes about the Germans in Frost Town. She mentions the Settegast family and Charles Schrimpf, who raised cattle on his field and was prosperous enough to send his son to school in Germany. Phelps also describes the dances held on Saturday night in Clopper's barn, and the sad occasion when Martin Floeck opened a brewery and offered free beer to his guests. The party was a great success until one of the celebrants accidentally kicked over a lantern that caused the brewery to burn to the ground on its first night of business.

Many of the Germans who settled in early Houston

came directly from Germany. One group, however—members of the Germania Society—came in 1839 from New York. The society was organized in 1838 by Germans who had immigrated to New York in 1835. In its printed constitution, the society described its goals: "To unite more closely the Germans living in the United States, in order to maintain and promote a vigorous German character, good German customs, and German culture; to support the principles of a pure Democracy in the new home." The society reflected the interest in Europe and America at that time in utopian communal living experiments, such as Brook Farm in Massachusetts. It planned to establish a colony either in Wisconsin, Oregon, or Texas, and finally chose Texas. Early in November 1839, 130 members set sail from New York on the brig *North.* They arrived in Galveston on Christmas Day, only to learn that a yellow-fever epidemic was raging and that its latest victim, a German, had just been buried in Houston. Most of the colonists stayed on the boat and returned to New York. The Usener, Schweickart, Habermehl, Bottler, and Karcher families, and a single man named Schnell, however, settled in Houston.

Just what percentage of Houston's early population was German is a matter of some conjecture. One estimate in 1840 was 400 out of a total population of 1,500 or 2,000. From all evidence, these early German immigrants were well liked by the other settlers. As the Houston *Morning Star* stated on December 17, 1839:

Amongst the newcomers we are delighted to see the florid-complexioned and blue-eyed sons and daughters of Germany. To those people we extend the hand of welcome. A large number of these hardy and industrious persons are now in our place, seeking for employment and an honest livelihood. Amongst them are farmers, mechanics, and persons of almost every trade and vocation. They are ready and anxious for work. Whoever wants assistance to cultivate his soil, servants for his house, artisans to work in the shop, day-laborers, shoemakers, and so forth, can find in the honest Germans, who now have possession of the Capitol [the former government building of the Republic, where the city then allowed German immi-

grants to stay], the very persons who will suit him. They will add to the wealth, the physical power, and the numerical force of our infant nation; they will be good citizens in time of peace and invaluable soldiers in the hour of war.

By 1840 in any case, the number of Germans arriving in Houston was such that those who were already established in Houston founded the German Society of Texas (Der deutsche Verein für Texas). Its bylaws stated its main purposes as: "1. To promote the prosperity of our German fellow-citizens to the best of our means; 2. to assist the stranger with counsel and action; 3. to minister the necessaries to the sick and needy; 4. to inspire confidence to the immigrants and to encourage them." The Republic of Texas granted the society a charter in 1841, and it began its activities with fifty-three members. The Verein was defunct during the Civil War. After the war, it became the Deutsche Gesellschaft (the German Society) and lasted until the end of the nineteenth century.

By the mid-nineteenth century, there was a considerable latitude of opinion concerning the percentage of Germans in Houston's total population. Estimates at that time vary from 20 percent to one suggesting that more than half of the inhabitants of the city were German. There are also several estimates of 40 to 45 percent. More recent evaluations place the figure at approximately 20 percent. There is, no doubt, a lack of consistency in these statistics between native-born Germans and first-generation German-Americans.

In any event, Germans—in addition to those settling in the Germantown area—influenced early Houston in a variety of ways. One of the best accounts of this influence and of early Houston in general is Gustav Dresel's *Houston Journal.* Dresel was a perceptive and well-educated young businessman from Mainz who lived in Texas during the years 1838 to 1840, and particularly in Houston, where he also worked. Dresel's *Journal* is a primary historical document for Houston during these years, and it is also a unique and well-balanced source of information about Germans and the German element in the city at that time.

Not all Germans who visited Houston in the early years (or in the years since, for that matter) have written positively about the city. Prince Solms of the Adelsverein, for example, had the following to say about Houston in his guidebook to Texas, which he published when he returned to Germany in 1846:

Houston on the Buffalo Bayou has more houses than citizens. . . . Since the Brazos is navigable from here, the farmers bring their cotton there and sell it to the native businessmen, who in turn transport it by water to Galveston. This alone affords the town some life. Otherwise it would be only a gathering place for loafers of the surrounding bottom lands, who go there mainly to gamble and to trade horses with the hope of defrauding someone.

Similarly, Victor Bracht, an officer of the Adelsverein when it was virtually bankrupt, wrote adversely in his *Texas in 1848* that some "immigrants will not take advice—seem to prefer the marsh prairies along the Buffalo Bayou near Houston where all of them will soon perish like flies." Of course, Bracht was trying to encourage immigrants to settle in the society's colonies in the Hill Country.

Dresel was in Houston much longer than Solms or Bracht. He also was not aloof like Solms. His friendliness was often reciprocated, and on one occasion it was amusingly equated with his nationality when a Coushatta Indian friend of his, old Timby, was moved to say, "You good man, you good *papeshillo*,[1] you Dutchman." Since Dresel was not a member of the aristocracy but was a political liberal, the truly democratic social process of the young Texas Republic interested him as much as did Houston's rustic physical appearance. Consequently, he emphasized this process in his initial description of Houston:

The front of our house was provided with a porch, that is a gallery, which furnished shade and served the neighborhood as a happy gathering place in the evening. At that time, as seen from here, the gay-colored, wild, and interesting city of Houston looked very picturesque. The few cabins, the numerous tents, the Capitol, the President's Mansion, and the many camps of recently arrived immigrants offered a novel and peculiar sight. The streets and squares that had been laid out were still covered with trees and stumps that obstructed the way, especially at nighttime.

At that time fifteen hundred to two thousand people, mostly men, were living together in Houston in the most dissimilar manner. The President, the whole personnel of the government, many lawyers who found ample means of support in those new regions, a large number of gamblers, tradesmen, artisans, former soldiers, adventurers, curious travelers from the United States, about a hundred Mexican prisoners who made suitable servants, daily new troops of Indians—all associated like chums on an equal footing.

Crimes, the desire for adventure, unfortunate circumstances of all sorts, love of freedom, and the fair prospect of gain had formed this quaint gathering. It was everyone's wish to be somebody in the general deeds. Everyone stood on his own merit. No family connections, former fortune, rank, or claims had any influence on present civic position. The constitution of Texas, which is purely republican and is taken from the Code Napoleon and the constitution of Mexico, and particularly the constitution of Louisiana, grants everyone who distinguishes himself for the general welfare the opportunity to attain the highest offices of the country by means of elections. Only talent, or rather its useful application, is taken into account. Not birth nor a bold front, but the vote of the people, turns the scale.

By the 1850s a visitor to Houston, such as the New York journalist Frederick Law Olmsted, could report in his *A Journey through Texas* that the "greater part of the small tradesmen and the mechanics are German." In his *Journal* of a decade earlier, Dresel also describes a number of important German businessmen and civic leaders. He talks about the Gerlach and Levenhagen families, whose members became aldermen and school trustees in the 1840s. Dresel also worked for George Fisher. Fisher had been elected

---

1. *Papeshillo* is Coushatta for "man," possibly like the German-Jewish usage of *Mensch.*

mayor in 1839. The election was contested, however; and in a second vote, Fisher lost to George Lively. Fisher was nevertheless involved in a number of other civic activities. He was an alderman and an associate justice of the Harris County Commissioners Court, and he helped to found the Chamber of Commerce. The country of Fisher's birth, even the accuracy of his surname, is uncertain; but it is believed that he was German, since he spoke excellent German and was the first president of the German immigrant aid society, the Deutscher Verein für Texas. Dresel also described the importance of the saloon, the Round Tent, run by Henry Kessler, a Silesian. An even more important gathering place than the Round Tent was Kessler's Arcade, where the City Council itself occasionally met. The Arcade's atmosphere, as Dresel described it, was quite German: "In the evening we betook ourselves to Kessler's Arcade, where the notables of the city would take a drink and where we Germans regularly congregated. The *Augsburger Allgemeine* and two American German newspapers were kept. Mr. Kessler often organized musical soirees of amateurs, too, which honest Planter Ernst of Mill Creek frequently attended."[2]

It is impossible to list all the German individuals and, particularly, German-American families who have contributed to Houston's development since its early years (and still do so). Any listing would also omit many important names. Nevertheless, no German history of Houston would be complete without a brief survey provided, for the most part, by Houston German-American Karl Micklitz:

1. *Bering*—a large family with many branches, involved in manufacturing and the hardware business.

2. *Binz*—Jakob Binz, a German-American from Chicago, built Houston's first skyscraper (six stories). Binz married Pauline Schweikart, and their son was in real estate and the cattle business with a Settegast.

3. *Heitmann*—leaders in the hardware business, and later in oil-field supplies, and other activities.

4. *Henke*—Henry Henke was one of the founders

of Henke & Pillot (later sold to become part of the Kroger grocery chain).

5. *Hermann*—George Hermann (actually a Swiss-German) was one of the city's leading early philanthropists.

6. *Holtkamp*—tin and sheet metal works.

7. *Keller*—a large family involved in the wholesale grocery business, cotton, carriages.

8. *Koehler*—C. J. Koehler operated an early variety store.

9. *Kuhlmann*—family active in many fields of business.

10. *Meyer*—Joseph F. Meyer and Co. was for many years an important hardware business.

11. *Priester*—one family member was a prominent physician. The family also had important property holdings in lower downtown Houston.

12. *Sauter*—Sauter's delicatessen was once very popular with Houston's businessmen.

13. *Schweikart*—arrived with the Germania Society in 1839; involved in the insurance business.

14. *Settegast*—a Settegast was an agent-general in Germany for the Adelsverein; a large family active in real estate, cattle raising, livery stable operations, and undertaking.

15. *Stude*—Stude's was once the city's leading bakery.

16. *Rudersdorf*—builder of many of the turn-of-the-century homes in the city.

17. *Usener*—arrived with the Germania Society in 1839. This family's involvement with Houston's history has been well researched. (See Dorothy E. Justman, *German Colonists and Their Descendants in Houston*.)

Germans also contributed to the cultural life of early Houston in several primary ways. Dresel reported that Houstonians "love German singing very much," while much later McComb wrote similarly that in Houston "those with the greatest interest in music were German immigrants." The city's first musical concert in May 1840, with solos on piano, violin, and French horn, was, in fact, under the direction of Emil Heerbrugger, a German. Concerning Mr. Heerbrug-

2. Ernst was the founder of Industry, the first German settlement in Texas.

Schott's Bakery. Photograph courtesy of the San Jacinto Museum of History Association.

ger, the Houston *Morning Star* wrote in October 1840, "a serenade by some Germans under the direction of Mr. Heerbrugger, the most accomplished musician that has ever visited the country" was "as sweet and delightful music as ever broke the slumber of mortals." Houston's two German singing societies, the Sängerbund and the Liederkranz, are still in existence today. The Sängerbund was founded in 1883 and the Liederkranz in 1925. In the decades around the turn of the century, the Sängerbund played a major role in Houston's cultural life. Houston was often the host city for the state's convention of German singing societies, the annual and later semiannual Sängerfest. These conventions were elaborate affairs, lasting several days and involving as many as two dozen singing groups. Host cities vied with each other in arranging for a number of spectacular public concerts for which, eventually, the local singing groups engaged professional talent from outside of Texas. In 1903, for ex-

ample, the entire St. Louis Symphony Orchestra as well as singers from the Metropolitan Opera in New York were brought to Houston to augment the performances of the Texas singing societies. There is still a state Sängerfest convention in Texas, although it is not nearly as elaborate as it once was. Its last meeting, in fact, was in Houston in May 1981 at the Liederkranz Hall. On that occasion, the two Houston singing societies were joined by six other groups from Austin, Dallas, and San Antonio.

A German actress performed during Houston's first theater season, organized in 1838 by John Carlos and Henry Corri. Madam Louise Thielmann came to Houston briefly from the St. Charles Theater in New Orleans. In the 1850s she acted in the German theater of New Orleans, playing, for example, in Schiller's *Die Räuber*; Madam Thielmann also translated English plays into German for the New Orleans German Theater. In 1840 the initial production of an amateur act-

Postcard of Turner Hall and Garden, Houston, postmarked 1913. The Turnverein was founded in 1854 and was located at this time on Prairie and Caroline Streets.

ing group, the Houston Dramatic Society, was the English translation of a play entitled *Pizarro or the Death of Rolla* by the popular German dramatist Kotzebue. In the 1850s the German Opera Troupe was also reported to be performing in Houston.

Houston's most important German society, at least in its formative years, was the Turnverein. Athletic organizations under this name (*turnen* literally means "to do gymnastics") developed in Germany during the early part of the nineteenth century, along with German singing societies, as part of the liberal student movement during the Romantic era and the repressive Metternich period. The Turner clubs, along with the singing societies, were quickly established in America by immigrants as twin focal points of German ethnic and cultural identity. The Houston Turnverein was established in 1854, and it is still in existence today. Although the Cincinnati Turnverein was established a few years earlier, Houston's club is reputedly the

oldest in terms of the years of continuous existence. The Houston Turnverein was established when ten young men met at the home of Peter Gabel on Preston. At one point there were nearly 1,400 members, and the organization had a Turner Hall on its property of the entire city block (bounded by Prairie, Caroline, Texas, and Austin).

Houston Turners were involved in a variety of civic activities. In the club's founding year, it established the city's first fire-fighting company. Shortly thereafter, the Verein organized the Turner Rifles, which helped to quell civil disturbances and occasionally guarded the city's jail. They also established a German-American school that only lasted a short time, and they participated in the local Howard Association chapter.[3] During the Civil War, the Houston Turners formed militia units that fought in skirmishes in Galveston and else-

3. A forerunner of the Red Cross.

*First German Evangelical Lutheran Church. Photograph from the Houston Public Library
Metropolitan Research Center.*

where. Captain E.B.H. Schneider, a legendary founding member of the Turnverein who was still engaging in gymnastic exercises in his seventies, lost an eye during the fighting in Galveston.

Much in the same spirit as the Sängerfest, the Turnverein in Houston organized elaborate festivities involving not only athletic and military drill events, but also balls, concerts, and banquets. Ziegler's description of one such festival, in which he himself participated, gives the modern reader some sense of this important German event in Houston now unfortunately long gone:

At break of day, the Turner flag was raised on top of the building, the band played the national anthem, and the old cannon was carried to the banks of the bayou where salutes were fired. At eight-thirty o'clock the military commenced their program. The command "Fall in" was given; they marched several times around the hall, put through their drills and then faced in single file toward the athletic equipment. Here each member of the company went through the particular act in which he excelled. I recall that my contribution had to do with the rapid scaling of a swinging ladder, an act that I performed in those days with cat-like ease, but that I would scarcely relish at my present age.

After so vigorous a program, we were delighted at noon to sit down at the annual stag-feast, a meal that left nothing to be desired. For a week the hunters would scour the woods and prairie for the choicest game to be had. It was not unusual to see upon the heavy laden board a wild black bear, sixteen point buck, wild turkeys, squirrels, opossums and rabbits. Too, there were several roast pigs with apples in their mouths. The salads, pies and cakes were prepared ahead of time by the members' wives. Tax on imported wines was slight and the table presented an array of German wines, sparkling Burgundy, Moselle, Mumm's, and Louis Roeders, sufficient to warm the cockles of the heart of a connoisseur.

Outside in the "garden" the members dined al fresco amidst rose and grape arbors and the wisteria vines that grew in abundance. Occasionally, one would observe three or four generations of a given family at one of the tables. Wines flowed freely, folksongs of the fatherland were sung, while the younger children performed the rustic dances of the old country.

The Balls that brought a close to the day's celebration were brilliant and colorful affairs, the beautiful women in satin, silks and velvets. True enough, all did not possess these luxuries of dress, for as the wife of one member told me, many of the wives would meet for nights previous and create their tarleton dresses by candlelight and oil lamp and under the soft light of candelabra in the hall, these dresses shone with a brilliance that suffered little by comparison with the more expensive garbs.

The suppers at these annual dances were another outstanding feature; I have never seen more appetizing delicacies nor more delicious wines.

Beginning in 1889, the Turnverein also organized the annual German Day in Houston. This event, which also entailed many festivities and parades, was part of a national celebration among German populations, held yearly on October 6 to commemorate the arrival of the first German colonists in America on that date in 1683. According to Moritz Tiling, the German Days were still magnificent affairs when he wrote his book, *German Element in Texas*, in 1913. The following, for example, is Tiling's account of the 1909 and 1910 events (the last two that Tiling describes in his book):

German Day celebration in 1909 was the first since many years in which the German-American citizens of Houston went prominently before the public, and under the direction of President A. Hellberg and Grand Marshal Wm. Bottler, proved conclusively that the spirit of former years had only been dormant, but not extinct. The splendor of the great street parade, the "clou" of carnival celebration, is still fresh in the memory of all who saw, applauded and admired it, and does not need to be extolled.

Extensive preparations had been made for the celebration in 1910, which exceeded in its scope and the magnificence of its parade any previous festival. The orators on this occasion were Governor-elect O. B. Colquitt, and J. C. von Rosenberg, Grand President of the Order of the Sons of Hermann in Texas. The greatest pageant was again under the command of Grand Marshal Wm. Bottler, while Messrs. V. Juenger, C. Stock and C. W. Hille, with a strong corps of assistants had for two months been industriously engaged in planning, building and decorating twelve gorgeous and artistically finished floats that in beauty of conception and elegance of execution, eclipsed anything heretofore seen in Houston.

Beginning in 1869, the Turnverein also organized the city's annual Volksfest. It continued the direction of this event, until the festival became a state affair in 1897. For the Volksfest in Houston, the Germans had their own festival grounds. The following is McComb's description of the Volksfest:

Sporting events were often a part of the fairs sponsored by Houstonians. The Germans, from 1869 to the mid-1870s, presented an annual late-spring celebration called Volksfest, which attracted thousands of visitors from south Texas. A parade featuring floats and King Gambrinus, the German Baccus, usually led the way to the fairgrounds. Here, on an acre of land decorated with flags and evergeens, would be swings, dancing circles, seats, benches, and booths for the sale of lemonade, ice cream sherbet, venison, beer, pies and perhaps "solid shot" for the older people. The Germans offered speeches, gymnastics, music, dancing, and baseball contests for entertainment. At an elaborate, two-day Volksfest, in 1874, a group dressed in armor and helmets and equipped with swords presented a sham battle.

Mention should be made, finally, of a German organization of rather recent vintage in Houston. With the encouragement of the German Consulate, the Deutsch-Amerikanischer Club Houston (DACH) was established in the mid-1960s. While DACH has attempted to be both cultural (in a "high-brow" sense with lectures, discussions, the showing of German films) and social, it is now primarily a social club where members, vir-

tually all of whom are postwar German immigrants, dine and dance especially during traditional German festive occasions (at Fasching, the German Mardi Gras celebration, during the Oktoberfest period, at Christmas and New Year's). The distinctive German aspects of these celebrations are also, in effect, cultural in nature.

It is a popular belief among German-Americans that more people spoke German than any other European language, except English, in Houston during its formative years. There are also two indices of the extent of the German reading public in these years. From 1859 and the beginning of Houston's first German-language newspaper, *Der Texas Democrat*, until 1917 and the First World War, which brought an end to the *Texas deutsche Zeitung*, fifteen such newspapers existed in Houston. The majority of these papers were weeklies, and none of them, except the *Texas deutsche Zeitung* (1873–1917), lasted very long. One of the most interesting of these papers was the *Deutsche Post* (1881–1885). It was edited by Charles Medlucka, whose unusual and ungrammatical Bohemian German was eagerly awaited by its subscribers. Unfortunately, the paper itself literally died a linguistic death with the editor's own death in 1885. Since the demise of the *Texas deutsche Zeitung* in 1917, Houston has not had a German-language newspaper until recently. In September 1979, Liselotte Babin began a bilingual monthly paper, *Deutsche Welt-USA* (*German World-USA*). Mrs. Babin has also had a Sunday morning musical radio program, with German commentary, for many years. At the present writing, it is not known what other German-language radio programs, if any, have served Houston in the past.

The second indicator of the German reading public in early Houston concerns the Houston City Library, a subscription library that was in George Baldwin's bookstore from 1870 until the 1890s. The advertisement announcing this library in 1870 states, "2000 volumes English and German." It has not been possible to ascertain what percentage of these volumes were in each language, but the advertisement does, at any rate, entice one to speculate on the strength of such a library and its German reading public at that time.

The Dentist, *a ship owned by Dr. J. Fred Usener, Jr., on Buffalo Bayou around 1910, before the ship channel was built. Dr. Usener is second from left; the ship was docked at the Broadway and Harrisburg dock. Photograph courtesy of Mrs. Dorothy E. Justman and the Museum of American Architecture and Decorative Art, Houston Baptist University.*

For the average immigrant and the immigrant family (particularly women, children, and the older generation), the church was a far more important source of ethnic identity than were the singing societies or the Turnverein. It persevered over the years, along with the family, as a focal point of this identity, even when the church's Germanness, with the passage of time, began to diminish. For these reasons, the Lutheran and the Catholic churches (and to a lesser extent, the Methodist church) evidence a strong German history in Houston's early years.

Biesele, in his excellent *History of the German*

Settlements in Texas, 1831–1861, gives the following account of the first Protestant religious services in Houston:

The earliest record of religious services among the Germans in Texas is found in the Morning Star *of December 24, 1839, which stated that two days earlier a German minister had preached to a congregation of immigrants in Houston. The same paper two weeks later announced regular services of the German Protestant congregation every Sunday morning at the home of Mr. Thiel. Although the name of the minister is not given, the writer believes that it was L. C. Ervendberg, who came to Houston from Illinois in 1839.*

The first German Lutheran Church was not established, however, until 1851. It was organized by Pastor Caspar Braun of Württemberg, one of several Lutheran missionaries sent to Texas in the 1850s by the St. Chrischona Seminary in Switzerland. The first church services were held in a schoolhouse on Texas Avenue until the congregation could build its first church, in 1854, on the south side of Texas Avenue facing west on Milam Street. Behind the church was a school building where pastor Braun also served as a schoolteacher. The continuation of this congregation exists as the First Evangelical Church of Houston and through a separation that occurred in 1879 (one year before Braun's death) in the Trinity Lutheran Church.

Many of the Lutheran churches in Houston, as elsewhere, had church schools for grades one through eight in which the language of instruction initially was German. This instructional language and the German church services were severely affected by anti-German feeling, particularly strong in large cities such as Houston, that erupted in the United States during the First World War. After the war, a few of the Houston Lutheran churches revived their German services. Some, such as Trinity, stopped their German services during the Second World War. During the postwar period, one or two churches had one German service each month. Now only three Lutheran churches have a German church service—one each year at Christmas.

Although a majority of at least the original German immigrants to Texas came from the Protestant areas of Germany, many Catholics were also among the settlers. Bishop Odin of the Diocese of Texas, in fact, in soliciting missionaries for the state, reported in 1850 that 5,000 German Catholics were without spiritual ministrations because of the lack of German-speaking priests. Some American orders, especially in Pennsylvania, sent fathers to work directly with the German Catholics in Texas, but in some instances they left because of the climate and the problems of the Civil War. Other orders arrived, however, such as the Franciscans, who began working among the German immigrants in Houston in the 1860s.

The first Catholic church in Houston, St. Vincent de Paul, was built in 1842 at the corner of Franklin Avenue and Caroline Street. A majority of the parishioners at this church were German Catholics, and many of them spoke no English. Unfortunately, their pastor, Father Querat, spoke French but not German. With the building of the next Catholic house of worship, the Church of the Annunciation in 1870, St. Vincent's became known as the German church, until St. Vincent's was sold a few years later and its congregation merged with that of Annunciation. When Father Querat left his charges at St. Vincent's, he issued the following acknowledgment to his former German parishioners:

Permit me . . . to express my sincere regret at parting with the German Catholics of Houston. For five years I have counted among them many friends, and I am sorry that my ignorance of their language prevented me from working for them as much as a pastor should. . . . I can at least say: Germans, you have now a church of your own, where you can hear the language and hymns of the fatherland; you have a pastor German by birth and education. It affords me the greatest pleasure to announce to you that Rev. J. Blum, the new pastor of St. Vincent is a gentleman.

While German Methodists have not been as numerically strong in Texas as the Lutherans and the Catholics, they too have had their distinctive ethnic presence in Houston. H. P. Young (or Heinrich Jung), who had been appointed as a missionary in Texas by the Methodist Episcopal Church Society, began to work in Houston in 1847. A few years earlier, Young had become a very popular missionary among the Germans in Galveston where on one occasion, it is reported, he held over a thousand spellbound when he preached in German at the beach. Carl Gold, a Jewish convert, took over from Young in Houston and organized a German Methodist congregation in 1848. In 1858 a church was built on the corner of Milam and McKinney. This church was replaced by a new one in 1876, and it became known as the German Methodist Church and, eventually, the Bering Memorial Church.

No account of the German aspects of early Houston would be complete without a final remark about Houston's German cemetery. The present Washington Cemetery was founded in 1887 by the Deutsche Gesellschaft. From the time of its opening until 1901, all cemetery records were kept in German. It was known officially as the German Society Cemetery until 1918, when anti-German sentiment necessitated the name change to Washington Cemetery. Many well-known German-Americans from Houston are buried in the cemetery, including Captain E.B.H. Schneider of the Houston Turnverein, discussed earlier. One of the most interesting graves, however, is not of a German, but of Emma Seeyle who acquired national fame for being the only woman to fight (masquerading as a man) for the Union Army during the Civil War. To avoid detection while sick, Mrs. Seeyle finally deserted, but continued to serve as a nurse. Her book about these exploits, *The Nurse and the Spy*, was widely read after the war.

Germans in Houston: The Aftermath

Apart from the importance of Germans in the establishment of Houston in its early years, the heyday of German cultural life in Houston—as elsewhere in the United States—was the period from 1870 to the outbreak of the First World War. In part, these halcyon days reflected the established importance (and affluence) of Houston business and civic leaders of German descent. German-American families, in successive generations, were able to enjoy the fruits of their labor as respected citizens and, in some cases, as founding members of Houston's young society. During this period, more Germans immigrated to Texas and particularly to Houston, with its burgeoning economy, than had before the Civil War.

Much of this pattern changed with the emergence of anti-German feelings accompanying the outbreak of the First World War in the United States. While this animosity may not have been as pronounced as in Chicago, New York, or Philadelphia, where ethnic minorities have always lived more uneasily with each other

(and with the Anglo majority) than in Houston, the results were every bit as devastating. Mention has already been made of the impact of this prejudice upon German religious services, the German-language newspaper, the *Texas deutsche Zeitung,* and the designation of the German Society Cemetery. It was at this time also that German Street became Canal Street. It is impossible, of course, to evaluate with any precision the effect of this anti-German feeling on the overall state of the German element in Houston. Many of the German businesses in Houston were so Americanized that the effect on them was, for the most part, nil. Still, some Germans at this time also "Americanized" their German names for business (as well as other) reasons. Of course, legions of Houston Germans before them had also done this in times of ethnic neutrality. German cultural events, being directly and ostentatiously ethnic, demonstrably suffered during this period. Most devastating was the direct impact of this discrimination against some individual German-Americans. Such anti-German feeling was not as prevalent during the Second World War, but there were still some instances of it.

Apart from the negative consequences of the First World War, the German element in Houston was also being assimilated and acculturated, even during the years of its cultural heyday. The fact that the German Society Cemetery, for example, kept its minutes in German until 1901 illustrates this process and serves as a benchmark of sorts. So, too, does the amount of German used in religious services, in church schools and most importantly in homes and among extended German-American families. The First World War, of course, accelerated this process and was destructive for language usage, both formal (church, newspapers, German language instruction in schools) and informal (family, friends, business).

Between the two world wars and in the nearly three decades since the end of the Second World War, there were influxes of German immigrants to the South and especially to Houston. Particularly interesting in the oral histories of these immigrants since the First World War are the ways in which they have accommodated themselves to Houston and America and at the same time the ways in which they have preserved their ethnic identities or have wanted to preserve them.

What about the German element in the Houston of the 1980s? While the present study is only a preliminary examination, some observations may be made at this point:

1. Because of the recent resurgence of interest in ethnic origins, the German background of many and particularly older German-American families are now more visible than they were, at least in some instances, earlier. Many members of these older German-American families, for example, are active in the state organization, The German-Texas Heritage Society (founded in 1978), where they are engaged in genealogical and other kinds of ethnic research. More recently arrived German immigrants are less concerned about certain aspects of their ethnic background (genealogy, for example), partly because they are still in the process of becoming Americans, and because their own German past is still a very vivid, and not always positive memory for them. While these more recently arrived immigrants come from all walks of life and represent a great diversity of professions, many of them are involved in the hotel and restaurant business, while a number of Germans now are scientists or are involved in the steel or in the oil industry.

2. Many German-Americans celebrate Christmas with at least some vestiges of German tradition (German food and baked goods; emphasis upon the evening of the 24th; the singing of German Christmas carols). Otherwise, traditional German-American cultural life has in many cases died out or has diminished greatly. Interestingly, however, organizations like the two singing societies still operate as ethnic focal points, both for the German-Americans from older immigrant families as well as for more recently arrived immigrants. For similar reasons, DACH is also able to sustain its own membership.

3. Although the primary (i.e., linguistic) Germanness of Houston's Lutheran churches is greatly reduced (if not, effectively, lost), a latent ethnic quality is still in evidence, and this factor continues to attract both multigeneration German-Americans and recent immigrants to these churches. It is estimated, for example, that approximately 10 percent of the congregation of Christ the King Lutheran Church is able to read and speak German (and this percentage, at least at this church, has been on the increase in the last few years).

4. While it has been estimated that at least 50,000 people can speak German in Houston, they do so only in very specific, controlled situations such as at some functions at some of the German clubs, during certain infrequent church occasions, at certain German businesses, and within some recently arrived German families.

5. The German-American Chamber of Commerce believes that the German heritage in Texas provides, along with other factors, a positive climate for German business in Texas. Be that as it may, German business has energetically shared in Houston's postwar economic boom. The number of German petrochemical companies, steel processors, financial concerns, land developers, and Germans in the hotel and restaurant business in Houston is very significant. As a reflection of this, during the last ten years the Houston Consulate of the Federal Republic of Germany has been elevated to a Consulate-General (and the Consulate-General's office in New Orleans eliminated); the South-Central United States headquarters of the Goethe Institute (the major West German cultural organization) was placed in Houston; and the German business community designated Houston as the site for the southern branch of its German-American Chamber of Commerce.

Houston continues to be a city rich in its German heritage and presence. At the same time, it is a city proud of and accommodating to the varied ethnicity of its citizens. This is especially true of the Houstonians of German descent.

Scandinavians

Louis J. Marchiafava and Charlotte Peltier

Norway pioneers from Hedemarken, Arendel, and Kopervik districts who came to Bosque County, Texas, in 1854. Photograph from the Institute of Texan Cultures.

The opening of the Americas created a tremendous frontier that was to attract some thirty-five million Europeans. Long before planned settlements began in the seventeenth century, the Vikings from Greenland established fishing and trading posts along the coasts of Labrador and Newfoundland named Vinland, or "fruitful land," by the Norsemen. The Viking period, 800–1050 A.D., was a time of widespread expansion of Scandinavian culture. As a kingdom, Denmark included most of present-day Scandinavia as well as colonial holdings. In the late ninth and tenth centuries, the Vikings of Denmark colonized and ruled parts of England. There is even evidence that they knew of the Gulf of Mexico.

In 1619 Jens Munk, a Norwegian, explored the Hudson Bay area and took possession of the surrounding country in the name of King Christian, calling the area Nova Dania. The first Scandinavians to colonize America arrived in 1624 at the site of present-day Bergen, New Jersey. In March 1638, led by Dutchman Peter Minuit, twenty-six Finnish and Swedish crew members built Fort Christina at what is now Wilmington, Delaware, and called the colony "New Sweden." Danes, Swedes, Norwegians, and Finns settled in the Delaware River Valley and Dutch New Amsterdam colony in the 1640s and 1650s. Throughout the rest of the seventeenth century and the early eighteenth, Scandinavians continued to risk the Atlantic crossing to try to create a new life for themselves in the Americas.

The greatest migration of Scandinavians to America occurred in three waves in the latter part of the nineteenth and early twentieth centuries. The first wave occurred between 1865 and 1873. Throughout the Scandinavian countries, population changes and economic factors stimulated mass emigration from the countryside to urban areas. A population boom as a result of high birth rates and changes in the size of landholdings created a growing number of landless farm hands, farm workers, small cottagers, and free lodgers. Insufficient farm acreage and depreciated wages forced farm workers and small-scale farmers to choose between migrating to Scandinavian urban areas or to America. Crop failures in Sweden between 1866 and 1868 made matters even worse. In Norway, where three-fourths of the land could not be cultivated, the growing population could no longer

be sustained with small areas suited for agriculture and limited opportunities in trading and fishing. In relation to per-capita population, more Norwegians left their homeland to immigrate to America than from any other other European group.

The second wave of immigration occurred in the 1880s and 1890s and constituted more of an industrial and urban movement. While some migrants still came from rural areas, increasing numbers were workers in urban industry, crafts, and domestic service. The last great wave came in the first decade of the twentieth century, followed by a drop in the 1920s, when the quota system limited the number of Scandinavians entering the country. Once in America in the early nineteenth century, Scandinavians settled in the middle states of New York, Pennsylvania, New Jersey, and Delaware. The migration west by the 1840s centered in the states of Illinois, Wisconsin, Michigan, and Minnesota. The attraction of owning and farming one's own land was the most common incentive for moving west. American letters sent back to the homeland and extensive campaigns by agents for the transcontinental railroads persuaded Scandinavians to come to America.

Scandinavians in Texas

Both individual immigrants and groups of Scandinavians have played an important role in Texas history. Charles Zanco, a twenty-eight-year-old Danish painter, influenced the design of one of the early Texas "independence" flags. Christian Hillebrandt established large holdings in cattle and acreage near the present site of Beaumont. Descendants of the George Henry Trube family influenced the development of Galveston in the late 1800s. Advertisements by the Norwegians Johan Reinert Reiersen, Elise Waerenskjold, Ole Canuteson, and Cleng Peerson created significant attention to attract fellow countrymen to Texas from the Lake Michigan area, which Norwegians generally preferred—partly because of its geographic similarity to their homeland. Various newspapers and letters written by Reiersen publicized Texas and attracted immigrants to the colony of Brownsboro in Henderson County. Elise Waerenskjold figured prominently in the development of the Four Mile Prairie settlement southwest of Dallas. In 1853 Ole Canuteson, from the Fox River settlement in Illinois, went to Bosque County and founded the principal Norwegian settlement. Cleng Peerson continued to attract Norwegian settlers to the Dallas County area through his communications with various Norwegians in the Midwest and in Norway. Calling Peerson the pioneer of Norse emigration to America, fellow Texans later erected a monument to his memory in Stavanger, Norway.

In the nineteenth century in Texas, the main influx of Scandinavians occurred primarily in the last decade. Scandinavian communities such as the Norwegian settlements in Bosque County and "Little Denmark" in Lee County had been founded in the first half of the nineteenth century; but Norwegian communities remained small, with the 1860 census listing only 326 native-born Norwegians in Texas. By 1900 the census showed the number had increased to 1,356, but in the 1940 census the number had dropped to 1,169. Like other Scandinavian groups, the Norwegians came to Texas to improve their economic and social position. Economic considerations in post–World War II Houston likewise proved to be responsible for attracting the largest number of Norwegians of any city in Texas.

The first Danish settlement that could be called a colony was begun by the Danish People's Society in 1894. The society's land committee investigated possibilities in Texas and found a tract of 25,000 acres for sale by the Texas Land and Cattle Company. Danes who settled Danevang, as the community was called, originally came from the Slesvig, Funen, and Zealand provinces of Denmark and had settled in the Midwest earlier. Faced with crop failure from storms and heavy rains and the loss of horses in 1897 from anthrax, the colony suffered and struggled throughout the early years. Thrift, hard work, raising southern crops such as cotton and rice, and using southern farming techniques all demonstrated the Danes' commitment to their community and sufficiently impressed the bank agents to extend payments due on the land.

One of the distinctive features of the Danish community, and an example of the impact of Scandinavian native traditions on American life, was the use by the Danes of cooperatives. Previous experience in the midwestern states with the cooperative movement led to the organization of a Danevang mutual fire insurance company in 1897, a telephone company in 1913, and a Farmers' Cooperative Society in 1920—which purchased such items as gasoline, fertilizer, and insecticides and established service facilities such as a cotton gin, a welding shop, and a grain drier. In the twentieth century, the economic alternatives offered by urban growth, as opposed to those of a rural agricultural life, have reduced the number of Danes living in Danevang from one hundred families in 1934 to sixty persons in 1971. Today Danes in Texas seek to take advantage of the commercial opportunities in an urban center like Houston, where a high standard of living attracts businessmen and entrepreneurs.

Arriving in Galveston and Port Lavaca, Swedes appeared in Texas as early as 1838 and then generally moved inland away from the "unhealthy" coastal areas. The settlement of Swedes in Houston and Galveston generally occurred later, between 1890 and 1900, when the greatest number of Swedes immigrated to Texas from the north- central states. They established the earliest and largest settlements in Travis and Williamson counties, most notably in the towns of Austin and Brushy, which today still reveal a strong Swedish influence; in fact, the state's only Swedish language newspaper, the *Texas Posten,* is published in Austin. By 1918 approximately a thousand Swedes had settled in Travis County. Other significant early Swedish colonies included Palm Valley, New Sweden, Georgetown, Taylor, and Hutto. Farming in this area became the most frequent occupation of these early Scandinavian arrivals. Others ventured into the business world as small merchants or shopkeepers, as evidenced by businesses with such names as Sellstrom Hardware Company, Sponberg and Bengtson Grocery, and Arthur Morell Automobile Repair Shop.

Statistics clearly indicate the pace of Swedish immigration into the state. In 1850 Swedes in Texas numbered only 48. The number increased to 364 in 1870 and to 4,388 by 1900. By 1910 approximately ten thousand first- and second-generation Swedes had made Texas their home.

The immigration of Scandinavians to Texas from other states leveled off during the depression years of the 1930s. Emigration from Sweden by 1910 had virtually ceased, and by 1940 the census showed 3,046 foreign-born Swedes in Texas. After World War II, however, Swedes and other Scandinavians again began to find their way to Texas because of growing economic possibilities and increasing commercial activities in the Galveston-Houston area. Many of the new arrivals were not rural-oriented settlers like the Scandinavians of prior migrations. Instead, the Swedes came to advance their own business or professional interests. Some immigrated because they had married American citizens. During the same period, Norwegians and Danes were also especially influenced by economic considerations. The Finns in Texas are the most recent arrivals, and their roles are described in the sections that deal specifically with Houston.

Scandinavians in Houston

Scandinavians were in Houston during the early years of the city's founding but for the most part only as travelers making their way to the Texas hinterland. With Galveston as the primary port of entry in Texas, most Scandinavian immigrants during the 1840s followed passage on steamboats along Buffalo Bayou, where they continued their journey on foot or on horseback. The coming of railroads during the next decade, before the Civil War, made travel more comfortable and faster. The earliest recorded Scandinavian in Houston was a Swede named Sven Magnus Swenson. He settled first in Brazoria County, but in 1838 he moved to Houston—two years after the Allen brothers founded the city. Swenson entered into business with a partner but remained in the city for only a year. He then moved to Austin, where he became a successful businessman. Later, during the 1850s, he encouraged other Swedes to leave their homeland for the economic promises that Texas offered. Another early Swedish settler who remained in Houston was August Forsgard. He arrived in Houston in 1848 and immediately entered the mainstream of business life to become a successful merchant.

Scandinavians have never composed a large segment of Houston's population. The migration waves to Houston and its environs followed the general pattern of Scandinavian migration to Texas, with the flow increasing in the twentieth century, especially following World War II. Swedes have had the largest number of settlers, with Norwegians and Danes following. The arrival of Finns has been recent and their number so minor that they do not appear in the 1970 census report. As the economic expectations of Houston increase and its network of international markets multiplies, the number of business-minded Finns is likely to grow. According to the 1970 United States census statistics, 2,118 Swedes, 1,180 Norwegians, and 1,229 Danes, either foreign-born or of mixed parentage, resided in Houston. While these numbers reflect first-generation Scandinavians, they do not include second- and third-generation Scandinavians born in Texas who still claim a strong native heritage.

No enclaves of Scandinavians exist in Houston. Their residences are scattered throughout middle-class housing areas of Houston. The only hint of an enclave was one consisting of several Swedish families living in a neighborhood once referred to as the "Florentine" settlement, located near the city boundaries separating Houston and Pasadena. No trace of this settlement exists today. Similarly, no particular residential areas of Scandinavians are to be found in any of the communities between Houston and Galveston, although several hundred persons of Swedish or Norwegian descent, including those of first-generation status, can be found scattered throughout the various small towns and suburbs.

People have settled in the Houston-Galveston area because of the diverse economic opportunities offered in the region, ranging from truck farming in the early twentieth century to shipping, industry, and the expanding professional fields of the mid- and later decades of the century. As an industrious people, Scandinavians have found the competitive spirit of Houston's commercial environment compatible with their talents and with their desire for life's material comforts and the good life represented by middle-class status. The attraction of Houston's material advantages remains as strong today as it was when Sven Swenson and August Forsgard first settled in the Bayou City.

The Augustana Lutheran Church was founded in Houston in 1928 and was the first Lutheran church organized by Scandinavians. Most of its members were Swedish.

Language

In addition to geographic proximity and a similar historical experience, Scandinavians also share a common linguistic heritage. Language presents no serious barrier to understanding in the Scandinavian countries, with the exception of Finland, and even there special circumstances permit communication. Swedish, Danish, and Norwegian, while distinctive national languages, nevertheless possess sufficient similarity to allow educated adults to understand the spoken and written languages of their neighbors. This is particularly true between Norwegians and Swedes. Danish is more difficult for Swedes and Norwegians to understand as a spoken language, but with care and a minimum of preparation, both groups can do well with it.

Reading Danish is an easier task. The Finnish language does provide a barrier, since it is unrelated to any of the languages of its Scandinavian kin, but a common heritage has mitigated the difference. As a consequence of the centuries of Swedish rule and settlement, the Swedish language is still officially accepted as Finland's second language. Approximately 7 percent of the population today speaks Swedish and, in many instances, only Swedish. A language network has therefore resulted from a common shared historical background that in turn imparts to the Scandinavians a sense of community.

Scandinavians as an immigrant group have generally found no serious obstacles to coping with the English language. Their ability to adapt to the new language has coincided with their desire to assimilate into American society and culture. Reinforced by a respect for education, as evidenced by traditionally high levels of literacy in their home countries, they have viewed fluent English as a prerequisite for good citizenship and economic success. Consequently, loss of the language heritage occurs quickly. As one Swedish-American writer noted in 1904, "The more progressive element of the first generation speak English from choice, the second from necessity, and the third knows little about the language of their grandparents."[1]

Religious Heritage

Religion has been the primary integrating cultural element in the history of the Scandinavian nations. Toward the close of the Middle Ages, Denmark, Norway, and Sweden were drawn loosely together into a union under the leadership of the Danish king, Eric of Pomerania. The Scandinavian union lasted until the early 1500s when Sweden, under its national hero, Gustavus Vasa, won independence from Danish rule. The movement for independence coincided with the spread of Protestantism. With the Reformation movement underway throughout Europe, Swedish and Danish students returning from Germany spread the Lutheran doctrine in their respective countries. The royal heads embraced the new teachings and established Lutheran national churches as a means of strengthening their own positions as rulers of sovereign states.

Lutheranism became Sweden's official state religion in 1527. In the succeeding decade, Denmark, with its Norwegian dependent, also accepted the new faith. Sweden introduced Lutheranism to the Finns. Despite its status as a grand duchy of the Russian empire, Finland maintained Lutheranism.

Today Lutheranism is the official state religion in all the Scandinavian countries, although all religious sects are free to follow their beliefs. In Sweden approximately 98 percent of the people are members of the Lutheran Church. Finland has a membership of 95 percent, with 1 percent of the population belonging to the Finnish Orthodox Church and the remainder divided among Jews, Moslems, and Roman Catholics. In Denmark 97 percent of the people belong to the country's Lutheran state church and 3 percent to the Roman Catholic church. Similarly, 97 percent of the Norwegians are Lutherans, with four other denominations composing the remainder.

Most Scandinavians in Houston, as well as in the rest of the United States, are predominantly Lutheran, thereby following the precedent of their European religious experience. But other denominations have also been founded in Houston by Scandinavians. Swedish Methodists founded congregations and became active in community life. In Galveston, the Reverend P. A. Juhlin directed the first Methodist church in 1885, while in 1917 H. A. Peterson organized the first Methodist congregation in Houston. The newly formed congregation was the city's first Swedish church. The church's minister, O. E. Linstrum, became well known in Houston for his work among soldiers encamped at Camp Logan during 1917 and 1918. Without a church building of its own, the congregation held services at the Bering Memorial Methodist Church.

For nearly all immigrant groups, the church has traditionally provided a center for meeting friends and socializing as well as worshipping. However, the church has played a less significant role for Houston's Scandinavians than for other immigrants, because of the ease with which they have assimilated into their adopted homeland and joined activities, whether of a business, social, or religious nature. Moreover, religion is a very personal experience for Scandinavians, a characteristic that is not always manifested in regular church attendance—as can be noted from statistics gathered through the state church organizations of their native countries. Nevertheless, the church provided a convenient focal point for some Houston-area Scandinavians during the early twentieth century and presently serves nonresident Scandinavians such as Norwegian and Swedish seamen who seek spiritual or social companionship in the course of their visits to Houston. For most second-generation or newly arrived Scandinavians, however, the church as a "social

---

1. Nelson, Olof N. *History of the Scandinavians and Successful Scandinavians in the United States.* Minneapolis: O. N. Nelson & Co., 2nd Rev. Ed., 1904.

center" has been replaced by clubs or culturally oriented organizations. As one early member of the Augustana Evangelical Lutheran Church's congregation commented, "The older generations really established the churches and now they are gone, most of them. They were the ones who were so interested in keeping up the traditions."

Two churches have most prominently served the Scandinavian community in Houston. The first, the Augustana Evangelical Lutheran Church, was organized on March 28, 1928, in Houston's YMCA building, just five months after its first worship service was conducted in October 1927. Charter members with names like Gustav Johansen, Hans C. Christensen, Sven Rudd, Gust Edming, C. O. Carlson, and John Bjork reveal the Scandinavian and, for the most part, Swedish lineage of the church's founders.

Through the missionary zeal of the church's first pastor, Emil Johnson, a church building was constructed on donated land at Wheeler and Chartres Streets. Completion of the church required a congregational effort, with members contributing their labor and skills as well as money. In 1937 a parsonage was built, thus providing the pastor with living quarters on the church grounds. A parish hall was added in 1949. Under the guidance of Johnson and succeeding pastors—Eric N. Hawkins, James M. Anderson, Paul T. Seastrand—the parish grew by 1953 into a congregation of more than 250 members. By January 1945, a daughter congregation, Christ the King Lutheran Church, was organized by a group of Augustana's members.

The course of the Augustana Lutheran Church is a microcosm of the Scandinavian experience in Houston and the ease with which Scandinavians have assimilated into the community. From the beginning, the church membership was never wholly drawn from the Scandinavian community, but instead reflected the ethnic composition of the church's neighbors. The evangelical nature of Scandinavian Lutheranism and the desire of the church's members to become an integral part of the community demanded that parishioners be welcomed from whatever groups there were who joined in worship. The church's organiza-

tions, including a Women's Missionary Society, a Missionary Guild, and a Lutheran Brotherhood Chapter, best reflect the spirit of the pastors and their flock. At a time of racial tension in 1956 over the earlier United States Supreme Court's integration order, the church's Board of Trustees signed a manifesto that read in part that "no local church has any more right to decide to be racially or culturally exclusive than it has to modify or abandon any article of faith." The humaneness that has traditionally characterized the Scandinavian lifestyle remained an active part of the church's activities when Pastor John P. Murray became the executive director of the Houston Council on Human Relations in 1967.

The second church and the one that continues to exemplify the Scandinavian presence in Houston is the Norwegian Seamen's Church. Established in 1969, the church today fulfills dual religious and social purposes. As its name implies, the church's primary purpose is to serve the religious needs of Norwegian seamen visiting Houston. The pastor and his staff also provide assistance to seamen in practical matters, providing transportation and guiding them to agencies such as the Norwegian Government Seamen Service, the International Seamen Welfare Center, and the Norwegian Consul-General's office, where they can be helped with specific problems. Service is not restricted to Norwegian nationals. Aid is also given to Swedish and Danish seamen, and for that reason, the church receives cooperation from officials of both countries, as evidenced by the participation of the Danish Consul-General on the church board. The Norwegian Seamen's Church has become a focal point, therefore, for social activity and Scandinavian cooperation, as well as religious communion.

Festivals

Scandinavians who have decided to make their homes in Houston generally carry on some of the traditional celebrations associated with their native festivals and holidays. The one holiday widely celebrated among Scandinavians in Houston as a time of family-related

Gulf Coast Scandinavian Club members wear their authentic folk dress at a public program. The clothes are handmade in the tradition of Swedish craftsmanship.

activities is Christmas. For all Scandinavians, Christmas Eve is the high point for the celebration. Each group has its own variation of a special food to mark the occasion. Swedes, for example, serve a variety of dishes, including broiled ham, marinated herring, and rice grits with almonds or rice porridge with butter and cinnamon. In many homes, *lutfisk* with melted butter and boiled potatoes is essential to a proper Christmas dinner. Among the delicacies served by Norwegians are batches of cookies called *fattigmand* and a special pudding containing a hidden almond. Like the Swedes and Danes, the Norwegians believe that whoever receives the almond will be married next. Finns serve a special Christmas Eve dinner consisting of a fish called *lipeäkala,* baked ham, mashed turnips, and a dessert of rice porridge.

Special celebrations mark the arrival of Christmas, which for Norwegians begins on Saint Thomas Day, December 21. A Norwegian custom, *ringe in Julen* or "ringing in Christmas," calls for the ringing of church bells at 4 P.M. on Christmas Eve. Perhaps the most charming Christmas custom still celebrated among Houston Swedes is on December 13—Santa Lucia Day or the Festival of Light. The celebration, which is traced to a medieval Italian legend, is highlighted by a procession led by a young girl dressed in a white gown and crowned with evergreen leaves and seven candles, symbolizing Santa Lucia as the symbol of light and hope in the world. Following the procession, the participants enjoy a punch called *glögg,* which is accompanied by specially prepared ginger cookies. Presents are often distributed to the children at this festival. Another festive holiday still popular among Houston Swedes is Midsummer. The Midsummer Eve celebration is held on the Friday that falls between June 19 and June 26. Friends gather at night to celebrate with food, drink, and music to welcome the longest day of summer. The highlight of the celebration is the singing of folk songs and dancing around the Maypole, gaily decorated with seasonal flowers and greenery. A less frequently celebrated occasion is Walpurgis Night, which is held on the last day of April or on May Day Eve. Walpurgis Night represents a mixture of an ancient heathen festival and a later celebration dedicated to Saint Walpurgis, an eighth-century saint. The festival is now a means of meeting friends and singing songs outdoors and culminates in a bonfire around which the celebrants dance to the accompaniment of accordion music.

National holidays are also observed among the official representatives of the Scandinavian nations stationed in Houston. Norwegians honor Constitution Day on May 17. Swedish representatives acknowledge June 6 as Flag Day, while the Danes remember June 5 as Constitution Day. The Danes are exceptional in that they also recognize July 4, American Independence Day, which is traditionally celebrated by Danish members of the Rebild Society, a group organized some seventy-five years ago to promote friendship between Danes and Americans.

Organizations

Scandinavians, while one of the most thoroughly assimilated groups in Houston's international community, have nevertheless attempted through clubs and organizations to preserve the cultural heritage of their native countries. Some organizations have also been created to strengthen trade ties between Houston and the Scandinavian interests represented in the city. Regardless of the focus of the organizations, they all serve to enrich the cultural diversity of Houston as well as sustain its economic vitality.

Since the late 1940s, individuals of Scandinavian ancestry have formed social organizations, but it was not until 1951 that Houston's oldest Swedish group was founded. Mrs. Gunnar Dryselius, wife of the then–Swedish Consul-General in Houston, formed the Linneas of Texas Society. The objective of the Linneas, which consists of women of Swedish descent, is to "provide a mutual cultural enrichment and understanding of the peoples of Texas and Sweden" through education, literature, and art. Their programs include scholarship grants to encourage Scandinavian studies, sponsorship of cultural events, donations of books to hospitals and educational institutions, and public demonstrations of Swedish handicraft.

The Gulf Coast Scandinavian Club had its first meeting in the fall of 1967. In 1968 the club received its state charter. Attracting members primarily from the Dickinson-Galveston area, the club is one of the most active in Texas. It cooperates with Swedish organizations in Houston and throughout Texas. More than a social group, the club actively seeks "to preserve, perpetuate, and educate in things Scandinavian." The club sponsors a troupe of Scandinavian folk dancers who appear at functions and festivals around the state. All members of the dance group perform attired in original folk dress, reflecting the different provinces of Sweden. Language courses are offered to interested members and the general public. Like the Linneas, the

The Santa Lucia Christmas celebration is re-created by members of SVEA, a Swedish women's organization in Houston.

Gulf Coast Scandinavian Club cooperates with the Texas Swedish Cultural Foundation, Inc., to promote scholarships for the study of Scandinavian topics.

SVEA is the most recent Swedish organization to appear in Houston. Founded in April 1980, this new group was organized by Swedish women as a nonprofit society to maintain ties between Sweden and Swedes living in Texas. SVEA also provides a valuable service by dispensing information of a practical nature to newly arrived Scandinavians in Houston. In addition, the organization sponsors scholarships, disseminates information about cultural events, and encourages the preservation of Swedish customs by hosting cultural activities for its members. Membership in

SVEA is open to women sixteen years or older who have at least one Swedish parent. All members are required to speak Swedish fluently.

The Danes and Norwegians have several social groups that promote understanding of various facets of Danish and Norwegian culture, such as the Danish Rebild Society. Another similar group is the Norwegian Society of Texas, founded in March 1975, with chapters in selected cities, that honors the Norwegian heritage in Texas and seeks to advance good will among Norwegians and Americans in general. The society also sponsors Norwegian-language courses to preserve the Scandinavian heritage and to offer opportunities to individuals who require a knowledge of the language for either business or travel purposes. Most recently, a new organization, the Sons of Norway, was founded primarily to expand interest in Norwegian culture.

Government representatives and business organizations advance the commercial interests of Scandinavians in Houston. Two commercial organizations are the Norwegian-American Chamber of Commerce, created in 1973, and the Export Council of Norway, established in 1979 as a quasi-official agency under the Norwegian Ministry of Foreign Affairs. Both the chamber and the council are housed in the offices of the Norwegian Consul-General. The Export Council concerns itself with strengthening Norwegian business interests in Houston, while the Chamber of Commerce assists Houston firms that wish to enter Norway's business markets. Together, the agencies provide an aggressive, well-coordinated commercial approach.

The Danish Consul-General and the Swedish Trade Office represent the business interests of their respective countries in Houston. In addition to commercial interests, however, the Danish Consul-General's office is responsible for matters of a diplomatic nature involving local issues. The office also provides assistance to Danes visiting Houston. As the official representative of the Danish government, the Consul-General's office seeks to cooperate in sponsoring cultural programs to foster a better understanding between Danes and the Houston community.

Since 1973 the official organization that represents Finnish interests in Houston has been the Consul-General's office, under which two specialized agencies function. The first is the Trade Office, and the other is the Office of Science and Technology. As the titles indicate, both offices are involved with trade and the rapidly developing area of high technology. At this time, no group in Houston, either governmental or private, is promoting Finnish culture.

Shipping and Business

One of the main reasons that Scandinavians have continued to be attracted to the Houston area has been

their association with shipping-related industries. Danish influence in shipping and freight forwarding and the number of Danish seamen on ocean-going vessels led to the establishment of the Danish consulate in Houston in 1979. Similarly, the combination of Norwegian shipping and oil-related interests led to the creation of the Export Council in 1979 and a Norwegian commercial officer post in February 1980.

Of all the Scandinavian countries, Norway has the most significant shipping interest in Houston. More than 400 Norwegian ships pass through the Port of Houston every year. Because the Vikings of the twentieth century continue to supply a large number of seamen on ocean-going vessels, Scandinavian governments have been interested in seamen's facilities in major world ports. The International Seamen's Center, which was founded in 1962, and the Norwegian Seamen's Church indicate the importance of Houston as a frequent port of call for Norwegian sailors. Trade between Norway and Houston is most obvious in its statistical evidence. In 1978 imports from Norway totaled $37.3 million but increased by 142 percent to $90.1 million in 1981. Exports to Norway also climbed by 128 percent between 1978 and 1981, from $43.4 million to $99.0 million.

The growth of Scandinavian trade is also evident in the importation of such traditional Swedish products as furniture, machinery, high-quality steel tools and instruments, automobiles, crystal, and other similar merchandise. Denmark has likewise offered products ranging from foodstuffs to furniture and household articles. Perhaps Houstonians are best acquainted with Swedish automobile dealerships. One-half of the cars produced in Sweden are imported into the United States, with Houston as an important outlet for their sale.

Norway, Finland, and to a lesser degree Denmark are represented by businesses in the petroleum and high-technology industries. Houston's status as an international energy capital influences Norway's own economic development, especially since the discovery and exploration of Norway's offshore oil resources. Houston provides Norway with consumer and industrial outlets to explore on a worldwide scale, including geographical proximity to emerging third-world markets. More than fifty Norwegian companies are represented in Houston, thereby making Norway the fifth-largest foreign business community in the city. During the last twelve years, sixty-three foreign banks have become active in Houston. Included in this figure are three Norwegian banks, one of which, the Bergen Bank, focuses on worldwide trade and shipping activities. The business interest is reciprocal, however, with nearly forty Houston-based investment companies with commercial ties to Norway. Norway's investment in Houston's future is large, and its size is likely to increase as the interest of Norwegian companies shifts from the northeastern United States to the international and commercial network that has developed in the Houston Gulf Coast area.

The commercial advantages so attractive to the Danes and Norwegians have also brought the Finns to Houston. For years Finnish consumer goods have been accessible to the public in retail establishments. Three major Finnish companies operate in Houston. Two—a shipping firm and an oil-related equipment company —have prospered in Houston since the mid-1970s. Finnish ships, for example, now carry 50 percent of the imports from Scandinavia and 14 percent from Europe. More recently, an oil refinery company has been operating in cooperation with a locally based firm. From Houston the Finns have access to major industrial development in the Middle East and Asia, where subcontracting opportunities in the areas of electrical mechanical installation, construction, and mining exist. Similar possibilities exist in South America. From Houston the Finns also have access to technical knowledge and can import high-technology products for Finnish companies.

The Scandinavian Legacy in Houston

The number of Scandinavians in Houston is small when compared to other groups, such as the Germans or even the Greeks, so that their presence is not obvious to the casual observer. The opportunities that originally brought Swedes, Norwegians, and Danes to the area in the nineteenth century continue to attract modern-day Vikings, adding Finns to their number. As people known for their shipping and commercial enterprises as well as business talents and manufacturing skills, Scandinavians are increasingly finding Houston an international city and reservoir of economic opportunity. Scandinavians are one of the most successfully assimilated groups in American society, and their presence in Houston is no exception. Because of their adaptability within the community, the visibility of the Scandinavian element is not at first apparent, except in terms of names, well-known products, business establishments, or visits by foreign dignitaries.

Despite their assimilation, Scandinavians have always maintained a link with their heritage. First-generation Swedes and Norwegians have been particularly active in preserving some of the more culturally meaningful traditions and customs, and as a result their children have remained aware of their roots. These cultural ties are reinforced as new arrivals become residents and strive to instill in their children a respect for their Scandinavian heritage. The various organizations and groups previously discussed serve as a focal point for maintaining a Scandinavian identity or awareness through their sponsorship of festivals and celebrations. It is an effort that benefits the community as a whole, for it adds richness to Houston's ethnic diversity and cosmopolitan complexion.

Acknowledgments

A number of organizations and individuals provided invaluable assistance in this enterprise, including the Gulf Coast Scandinavian Club, the Linneas of Texas, SVEA, Nilsdotters Scandinavian Folk Dancers, Norwegian Vice-Consul Guro Vikor, Norwegian Export Officer Charles Baldwin, Finnish Consul-General Kimmo J. Sahramma, the Reverend Georg Borresen of the Norwegian Seamen's Church, and the Center for Public Policy, University of Houston. Also, special thanks are extended to Danish Consul-General Kaj Hansen and his wife, Ingrid, and to Inga-Lisa Calissendorff, Gudren Merrill, and Ingrid Werler.

French

John S. Ambler

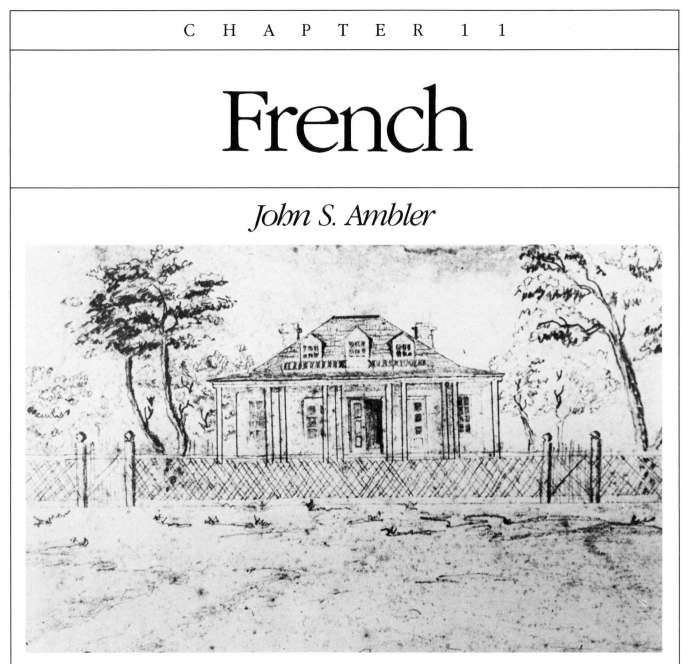

Austin home of the French Legation to the Republic of Texas. Sketch by Dr. A. Lee. Photograph courtesy of the Institute of Texan Cultures.

Although less numerous than several other national and ethnic groups in Houston, the French have made contributions out of proportion to their numbers to the cultural, economic, and culinary life of the city. In order to place their contribution in perspective, we begin with an examination of the historical role of France in America, then narrow the focus progressively to the French experience in Texas and Houston.

The French In America

The history of European exploration and settlement in North America is largely a tale of three empires: the English, the Spanish, and the French. In the seventeenth century, while the English explored and settled the Eastern seaboard of what is now the United States, and the Spanish extended their conquest of treasures and souls to Florida, Mexico, and the southwestern United States, the French were opening up Canada, the Great Lakes, and the vast Mississippi Valley. Numerous French place names, from Marquette to Saint Louis to New Orleans, bear historical witness to the breadth of New France. Had the French, rather than the English, prevailed in the French and Indian War from 1754 to 1763, or had Napoleon chosen to put his enormous energies into colonizing Louisiana, rather than selling it to help support his European wars, much of middle America might still speak French.

Although France once controlled more of North America than did England, her settlers were always less numerous. By 1750 there were some 80,000 French colonists in America, mostly concentrated in Quebec, compared to 1.5 million English colonists. Among the earliest colonists in America were those hardy French who settled in Acadia, Nova Scotia, beginning in 1604. Repeatedly caught up in the fighting between the French and the British, they finally were forced into exile by a British governor in 1755. Many ultimately made their way to the bayous of southwest Louisiana, where they have maintained elements of their language and culture to the present day.

The French In Texas

The French first arrived in Texas by accident. In August 1684, Robert Cavelier, titled Sieur de la Salle by King Louis XIV, set sail from France with four ships and 300 people to establish a colony at the mouth of the Mississippi River. Victims of bad weather and poor navigation, they landed instead on the Texas coast near Sabine Pass. After futile exploration for the Mississippi, La Salle established Fort Saint Louis on Garcitas Creek some five miles inland from Matagorda Bay. Within four years La Salle was dead, murdered by his own men, and all but a few of the colonists had fallen victim to famine, disease, or Indian raids.

In the course of the eighteenth and early nineteenth centuries, hundreds of French explorers, missionaries, traders, retired officers of Napoleon's army, adventurers, and pirates ventured into Texas. They established no permanent French settlements comparable to those in Louisiana, but left colorful legends, like that of the Lafitte brothers and their pirate republic on Galveston Island from 1817 to 1820. Spain looked with hostility upon any French designs on territory that she claimed as her own.

The independence of Texas, declared in 1836, attracted new European settlers, including two curious groups of French utopian socialists. The first of these communities was created in 1848 by members of the Icarian Society, led by Etienne Cabet. It lasted only one year in its original location near present-day Denton in North Texas before being forced by crop failure to move to Illinois. Six years later, Victor Considérant arrived at a 57,000-acre site near Dallas with some 350 French socialists. Their goal was to create at La Reunion a society guided by the teachings of the French philosopher Charles Fourier and based upon the ideals of cooperation and equality, rather than upon individualism and competition. Like the Icarians before them, they were unskilled at agriculture, unaccustomed to the rigors of pioneer life, and, under pressure, still all too vulnerable to the bourgeois maladies of jealousy and individualism. La Reunion dissolved after four years, leaving its well-educated citizens to return to Europe or, in many cases, to enrich Texas society with their talents in medicine, botany, music, banking, and manufacturing. A few years ago, a multimillion-dollar complex was completed in downtown Dallas called Reunion Plaza, harking back to this early French settlement in the city's history.

The most durable implantation of French colonists and culture took place at Castroville, west of San Antonio. Under contract from the Texas government, between 1843 and 1847, Henri Castro brought a total of 2,134 colonists, mostly from French Alsace, to farm the 640-acre plots reserved for each family. They survived epidemics, drought, and Indian raids to build a community that in its language, stone architecture, and traditions was a bit of Alsace in Texas. The Franco-Texas Land Company brought another smaller wave of French settlers in the 1870s. These immigrants were among the early settlers in such West Texas towns as Mineral Wells, Baird, and Sweetwater. Like most French immigrants outside Castroville, they and their children soon blended into the melting pot of Texas society.

The French In Houston

The first recorded commentary by a Frenchman about Houston was offered by Father Emmanuel Domenech, who passed through the young town in the late 1840s en route to San Antonio and Castroville, where he worked as a Catholic missionary. "Houston," he wrote in his journal, "is a wretched little town composed of about twenty shops, and a hundred huts, dispersed here and there, among trunks of fallen trees. It is infested with Methodists and ants." Even in the present day, one can find at least a few French people who essentially share Domenech's opinion of Houston. There have been many others, however, who have found it to be a land of opportunity. Among the 613 foreign-born residents who made up a third of Houston's population in 1850, there were 48 French people. In 1860 there were 60, making them the fourth-largest group of foreigners after the Germans (768), the Irish (240), and the British (159). These early French Houstonians, like those who came during the next century, were too few in number and too easily assimilated into American society to form a permanent and distinct French community.

In the 1920s there were fewer than fifty French-born people living in Houston: a few university teachers, a part-time consular agent, and a smattering of World War I war brides, some of whom worked as beauticians and waitresses. Professor Jules A. Verne, chairman of the Department of French at the University of Houston, founded a French review entitled *Le Bayou,* which was published from 1936 to 1961. In the depths of the depression, he and André Bourgeois, professor of French at Rice University, organized a French theater, Le Petit Théâtre Français, which functioned from 1932 to 1937. By the outbreak of World War II, the small French community had been supplemented by the arrival of dozens of French engineers employed by the Schlumberger brothers, Conrad and Marcel.

The Schlumberger story is the unlikely tale of a French physicist from a country that has no oil, who came to Texas to show Americans how to find it. A professor at the famed School of Mines in Paris, Conrad Schlumberger conceived the idea of plotting subsurface strata by passing an electrical current through them and measuring the extent of resistance. In June 1925 Conrad's brother, Marcel Schlumberger, arrived in Houston and soon negotiated a contract with Royal Dutch Shell, acting for its Texas affiliate Roxana Petroleum. Paul Charrin, E. G. Léonardon, and a team of young French engineers were hauling trucks, generators, and electrical cable around the Gulf Coast conducting surface electrical logging. This work was initially judged to be unsuccessful. When its American contracts were not renewed, Schlumberger withdrew most of its engineers in the late 1920s to take up major exploratory work in Romania, the Soviet Union, and Venezuela. By 1933 Schlumberger's improved techniques had been fully proven. Its teams were called back to Texas. An American branch, the Schlumberger Well Surveying Corporation, was established in 1934 with its headquarters in Houston. Schlumberger was on its way to becoming one of Houston's major firms and a giant in the well-surveying field. Although the technical and managerial work was shifted progressively to Americans within the American branch of Schlumberger, several of the original French team of engineers became national and international authorities on various geophysical techniques.

World War II contributed substantially to the expan-

cinquième jour du mois de Septembre de l'an de grâce mil huit cent trente neuf.

twenty fifth day of September in the year of Our Lord One thousand eight hundred and thirty Nine.

(L. S.) – Mal. Duc de Dalmatie.

(L. S.) – J. Pinckney Henderson.

Nous, ayant agréable le susdit Traité en toutes et chacune des dispositions qui y sont contenues, ainsi que les Articles additionnels qui le suivent, Déclarons, tant pour Nous que pour nos héritiers et Successeurs, qu'ils sont approuvés, acceptés, ratifiés et confirmés, et par ces présentes signées de notre main, Nous les approuvons, acceptons, ratifions et confirmons, Promettant, en foi et parole de Roi, de les observer et de les faire observer inviolablement sans jamais y contrevenir, ni permettre qu'il y soit contrevenu directement ni indirectement pour quelque cause et sous quelque prétexte que ce soit. En foi de quoi, Nous avons fait mettre notre sceau à ces présentes. Donné en notre Palais de Fontainebleau, le deuxième jour du mois d'Octobre de l'an de grâce mil huit cent trente neuf.

Louis Philippe

Par le Roi :

Mal. Duc de Dalmatie

With the Franco-Texian Treaty, signed on September 25, 1839, France became the first nation to recognize the Republic of Texas. Photograph courtesy of the Institute of Texan Cultures, from the Texas State Archives.

sion of Houston's French population. With Paris under Nazi control, many Schlumberger people made Houston their permanent home, including Conrad Schlumberger's daughter, Dominique, and her husband, Jean de Menil. The de Menils became leading patrons of the arts, making major contributions to the Museum of Fine Arts, the University of Saint Thomas, and Rice University. They built the Rothko Chapel, a jewel of modern architecture; and a new Menil Museum is being constructed to house their outstanding collection of works of art.

In the 1960s and 1970s, French commercial interests in Houston expanded dramatically. By 1980 six French banks had established offices in Houston, drawn by rapid economic growth in the area and the presence of investment opportunities. In that same year, more than thirty French firms in Houston were providing the oil and gas industry with services ranging from exploration to equipment to construction. In 1981 the French oil company, Elf Acquitaine, acquired Texas Gulf, a large American oil and minerals company with major offices in Houston. Several French real estate developers have provided the capital and the plans for townhouses, apartment complexes, and office buildings. The Meridien Hotel, owned by Air France, the Sofitel Hotel, and the Versailles, an apartment complex, are among recent French ventures in Houston real estate development.

In many of these French-owned firms, the majority of personnel—even the manager—is American. But established firms, heavy on French capital and light on French personnel, were not the only French participants in Houston's economic growth. Reports in the French press of the Houston boom helped to lure dozens of bakers, chefs, hairdressers, and other private entrepreneurs. By 1980 they had helped to swell the population of French-born Houstonians to about three thousand, although some of them are not planning to stay in Houston throughout their careers.

In Search of a French Community

Organizations

There are growing numbers of French people in Houston, but is there a French community? All but a few of the two dozen French people who were interviewed in 1981 felt that there is neither a general sense of community nor a network of organizations to which most French people belong. French people in Houston do not live in a concentrated area. Although most remain at least nominal Catholics, there is no single common church to bring them together.

The French are not known as joiners; yet significant numbers of them do belong to organizations that are exclusively or partially French. The largest of these is the Alliance Française, which was formed in the 1920s by the American wife of the first president of Rice University. The majority of its more than 400 members are still American, although a number of the Alliance's cultural programs are conducted in French and draw dozens of French participants. Its Bastille Day party, with a usual attendance of 200 to 400, is one of the social highlights of the year. A small French veterans' association, the Association des Anciens Combattants et Militaires, was founded in 1979 and now displays the French tricolor flag alongside the United States' own red, white, and blue for Memorial Day ceremonies. Its two dozen members gather for meetings three or four times each year. Houston also has a chapter of the Union of French Abroad, which meets every few months. For the business community, there is the Franco-American Chamber of Commerce. The Chamber's membership of 125 is evenly divided between Americans with business interests in France and French businessmen with interests or operations in the United States. It holds monthly meetings and publishes a quarterly newsletter on the activities of its members.

At least three hundred French women married United States military personnel during or immediately after World War II and settled in Houston. Many of these newly arrived war brides were discouraged by the unavailability of familiar French foods, by the total unfamiliarity of a sprawling, automobile-based city, and by the Houston climate before the era of air conditioning. Scores of disoriented French war brides found counsel and comfort in the home of Germaine Miller, who was herself the French wife of an American naval officer and who chose to settle in Houston because of its friendliness. By the end of the 1970s, there was a formal organization, Houston Acceuil (Houston

The Leeland Street headquarters of Schlumberger, occupied in December 1935. This structure was destroyed by fire in 1945. Photograph courtesy of Schlumberger.

Welcome), to provide help with problems ranging from finding a French cheese shop to locating a French-speaking physician. More than eighty families—90 percent of these being short-term French residents—belong to this organization. Its women's bridge meetings—like those of expatriates everywhere—offer an occasion to relax in the company of fellow citizens and to share feelings and impressions about such curious American phenomena as the fifteen-minute dinner, prayers before football games, and the use of first names with virtual strangers.

Language

With rare exceptions, the French in Houston are proud of their language and cultural heritage. And yet, after two generations the language is usually lost. The primary cause is intermarriage with Americans who do not speak French. The short-term residents, of course, speak French at home and leave with no more

serious cultural scars than perhaps their children's acquired taste for "junk food" and extracurricular activities. Among permanent residents, again the language survives with the children when both parents are French and speak their native language in the home. When only one parent is French, the dominant language spoken is rarely French. The French parent often speaks to his or her children in French and arranges for them to visit relatives in France. These children usually understand French; but once they begin school, they prefer to speak English to both parents. In an English-speaking society, it is difficult for a single French-speaking parent to overcome the child's desire to talk the way his teachers and friends do. One French woman said of her American husband, wholly without bitterness, "His culture absorbed mine." When the children grow up, they usually marry persons who are not of French descent. Rarely is an active knowledge of the French language passed on to the third generation, although French grandparents sometimes manage to

The Leeland Street office of Schlumberger, completed in 1938. Photograph courtesy of Schlumberger.

teach their grandchildren a little French by speaking to them in that language. Only through a constant influx of French people can the spoken language be kept alive.

Education

The arrival in Houston of many new French businesses in the 1970s led to a growing demand for a French school. The French oil company Acquitaine (later Elf Acquitaine) created a small school, originally for a dozen of the children of its own employees. This school, known as La Petite Ecole Française, offered special late afternoon classes after the children had completed their regular American school day. Then in 1976 three organizations joined forces to create the French School: the French Consulate, a parents' association, and the French Lay Mission (La Mission Laïque Française), which sponsors schools for French children around the world. Under the directorship of Roger Truchi, the school opened in 1976 with 22 pupils, of whom 17 were French, 2 were Swiss, 2 were Lebanese, and 1 was American. In 1978 the school joined the Awty School, of which it now forms the Bilingual Section. By the 1981–82 school year its enrollment had risen to 139, of whom approximately 115 were French. These students take four periods in French and three

Conrad and Marcel Schlumberger. Photograph courtesy of Schlumberger.

in English, preparing for both an American high school diploma and the French *baccalauréat*. Thirteen of the Bilingual Section's fifteen teachers are accredited and tenured in the French national education system. Children of temporary French residents can return to France and re-enter French schools with a minimum of difficulty.

Since there are some six hundred French families in Houston registered with the French consulate, and perhaps as many more who are not registered, the majority of French children obviously are in regular American schools. Approximately three-quarters of the parents of children in the Bilingual Section are employees of banks or oil-related firms that pay the

tuition fees. Yet permanent residents are also represented among these parents, including six bakers, a chef, and other independent entrepreneurs in investment and real estate development.

Education is an area in which the French almost invariably see sharp differences between France and America. French schools are perceived to be more demanding and more highly disciplined, and to offer fewer choices among courses and activities. Those who prefer the French system (and they seem to be in the majority) regret the time that American students spend on relatively frivolous courses and extracurricular activities. Professional people who did well in the French education system are the most likely to take this view. Those who view American schools more favorably are impressed with the schools' flexibility and their interest in social, artistic, and athletic, as well as academic, development. French people who have arrived in Houston recently, or those who frequently go back to France, tend to feel that as the French secondary schools have moved toward mass education and American high schools have expanded honors programs, the gap between the two educational systems has narrowed somewhat.

Links to France

With few exceptions, permanent French residents eventually take out American citizenship and come to think of themselves as American at least as much as French. Yet they normally retain strong ties to France. The frequency of their visits to that country is conditioned by four factors: their profession, their financial resources, the presence of close relatives in France, and their initial reasons for coming to America. One successful French baker returns several times each year to examine new equipment and supplies. Those who can afford to travel typically spend at least part of each summer in France. Others look forward to a return once in a decade or less. Visits become less frequent when parents in France die or move to Houston, as happens occasionally. Finally, there are some in this group, as in any immigrant population, who left France because of unhappy experiences there and who have little desire to return even for an occasional visit.

Divisions Within the French Community

Formal and informal social networks link groups of French people to each other in Houston. Yet there is no general sense of community among them. There are no evident political or religious divisions among French Houstonians. The two most important lines of division seem to be length of residence and level of education.

French employees of French firms, brought to Houston for a residence of only a few years, have relatively little contact with permanent French residents. Their social contacts tend to be with each other and with the American employees who outnumber the French in the local offices of most French firms. Among permanent residents, the majority belong to no group that brings them into association with other French people. The same people tend to see each other at social and cultural functions. Although small entrepreneurs are represented in the Alliance Française membership, organized cultural and social life seems to attract primarily well-educated French people. Hairdressers, restaurant waiters, and less well-educated war brides are more likely to be left out of the social functions of the consulate and of the formal organizations.

The Cajuns

The largest group of Houstonians of French background is not composed of those who frequent the Alliance Française and spend their vacations in France, but rather the Cajuns, thousands of whom have drifted west from Louisiana in this century in search of jobs. The 1981 Houston telephone book included 3,202 listings of 38 common Cajun names. There were 456 listings for Broussard, 229 for Le Blanc, and 143 for Boudreaux. A conservative estimate would number Cajuns in Houston at more than 10,000. The Cajuns are more numerous than the French in Houston, but are they French at all? Some of them claim ancestors who left France for Acadia in the seventeenth and eighteenth centuries. Displaced to southwest Louisiana, these Acadians, or "Cajuns," intermarried with people of other national backgrounds, but preserved their language and culture into the twentieth century when two world wars, urbanization, and then television threatened to draw them into the cultural melting pot.

In the fall of 1981, a random sample of thirty-five Houston Cajuns was interviewed by telephone. Twenty-one were born in southern Louisiana; the remainder —mostly born in Texas—are only one generation removed from New Acadia. Of the thirty-five, thirty-one still have close friends or relatives in Louisiana and twenty-one still visit there at least once a year. The external ties of these Houston Cajuns are to Louisiana

Crawfish races are a favorite festival activity in Texas and Louisiana.

and not to France. Although several members of the sample believe that they must have distant relatives in France, not one is in contact with any family members there. After three centuries in the New World, it is not surprising that the Cajuns have largely lost contact with their original motherland.

The Cajun dialect of French has survived, although it is losing ground to English. Thirteen of the Cajuns reported that they speak some Cajun French; but only three speak it regularly in their families. Two of these three were "black Cajuns" residing in Frenchtown, near Lockwood Drive in East Houston. Even there, where speakers of Cajun French are concentrated more

densely than anywhere else in the city, the younger generation rarely speaks any version of French. Although Houston Cajuns no longer think of themselves as French, almost all are proud of their Cajun background. Bumper stickers such as "Cajun Power" and "Cajuns live better, love better" attest to this pride. When asked what else one should know about the Cajuns, the interviewees responded with comments like these: "I'm proud of what I am." "Cajuns are fun-loving and very family-oriented." "The *camaraderie* of Cajuns is great." "Cajuns have the best parties around." "I'm proud to be a Cajun." Yet, despite their fondness for Cajun company, they have even fewer organizations than the French. Apart from two university alumni clubs (University of Southwest Louisiana and McNeese College) and some groups in Catholic churches, they have few formal institutions to bring them together. Those who maintain active social relations with other Cajuns gather at informal Cajun dinners or a Cajun restaurant like Ragin' Cajun Po-boys. There are few barriers to integration into non-Cajun society. The old stereotype of Cajuns as backward and barefoot, with only a shaky command of English, is badly out of date. Among the Houston Cajuns, for example, are highly successful geologists and petroleum engineers who integrated easily with other Americans. Most now believe that their Cajun background is either insignificant or a positive advantage in their social and professional relations.

For more than a century, isolated in a remote, rural environment, Cajun culture not only survived but absorbed blacks, Spaniards, Italians, and others who settled in New Acadia. Now it is weakening in the Acadian heartland. In Houston what remains is pride of origins—stronger now than twenty years ago—and a love of Cajun food, stories, and music.

Conclusion

Houston's French residents have enriched the life of the city in many ways. They have contributed heavily in leadership and gifts to its art museums and universities. They have been in the forefront of efforts to make Houston a center of petroleum exploration. They have taught French in Houston schools and universities. They have brought French cuisine to add to the city's cosmopolitan flavor. Most recently they have provided capital to help spur Houston's economic growth. But they have not created a permanent and encompassing community comparable, for example, to that of Greek Houstonians.

Why have permanent French residents, and particularly their children, been assimilated so quickly? Marriage to non-French Americans is one primary reason. Permanent French residents, whether the original corps of Schlumberger engineers, the war brides, or the recently arrived bevy of bakers, typically came to Houston relatively young and married American citizens. Even when both parents are French, their children rarely choose marriage partners from among the small number of their age-mates of French descent. As a group, moreover, French Houstonians were and are relatively well-educated and prosperous. They have little in common with the European immigrants who poured into the United States in the nineteenth century, or with most of present-day Houston's large flow of foreign immigrants. And, unlike the poor Castroville farmers who endured great hardships a century ago, those French people who dislike Houston today and who refuse to assimilate usually have the resources to leave.

American society poses few obstacles to the assimilation of immigrants from France, which is generally viewed as a country of sophistication and good taste. Once a French resident learns English, his national background is more often a social and professional advantage than a handicap. If there are obstacles to cultural assimilation—and of course there are—they are often to be found in the individual attitudes of the immigrant. For generations, schools in France have been reaffirming the view that French culture is unsurpassed in the world. While some French immigrants are intrigued by Houston's informality and frontier spirit, it is not surprising that others (along with many native Americans) are critical of undemanding schools, permissive child-rearing, and materialistic values. Forty years ago, Americans tended to assume that immigrants should jump eagerly into the melting pot. Today, many would hope—perhaps vainly in the case of the French—that cultural differences will survive to continue to enliven and enrich a diverse society.

A Mosaic of Culture and Cultures

Mary Schiflett

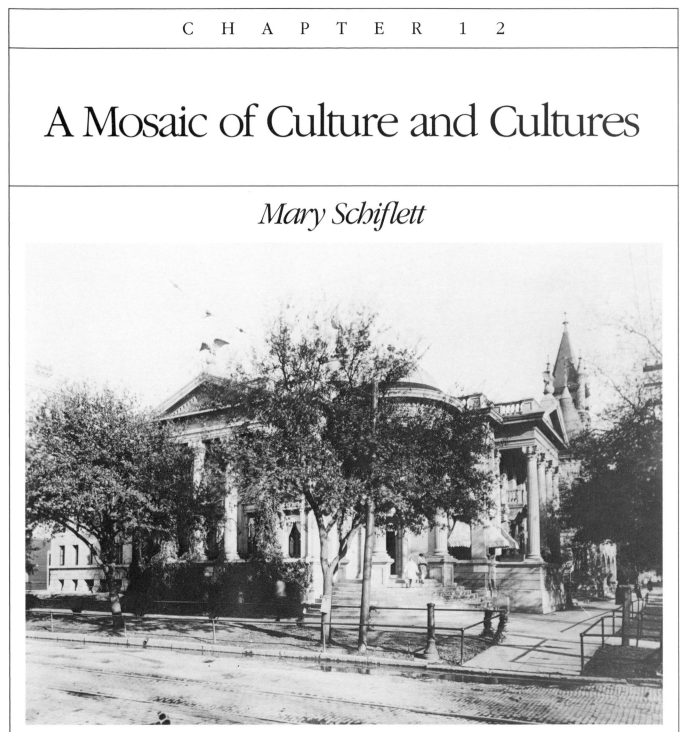

Exterior view of the Houston Lyceum and Carnegie Library, about 1917.

*T*he authors of the preceding chapters have shown that the strength and identity of ten ethnic groups have contributed much to Houston's past growth and to its current vitality. The word *culture* has been used by several of the authors to mean those highly selective values, ideals, symbols, and possessions that give cohesiveness to the group, a sense of identity to the members of the group, and an accumulation of all these qualities as heritage to be passed on to their children.

A second definition for the word *culture* comes at the edge of societal commentary in expressing the level of development and delineation of civilization. Houston's collective culture has been somewhat dominated by the large and strong community of English, Irish, and Scottish descent, and only slightly less, the German community. At the same time, Houston's cultural mosaic has afforded considerable accommodation to many other ethnic groups. Their selection and expression of ways to show enjoyment, the presentations planned for themselves and their new neighbors, the celebrations of civic and religious events, and the varied reminiscences from the "old country" (wherever that may have been and no matter how many generations back) have all been cultural in both senses of the word.

It is probably unnecessary to distinguish between what might be called ethnic culture and the culture more attuned to classic knowledge. Much like the concept given in the word *time*, culture is generally understood in its several meanings while defying a definition about which none would disagree. It has been the interplay of culture and ethnic contribution that has highlighted for outside observers the freshness and dynamic vitality of Houston. Perhaps it would be so for any city that had grown as rapidly and as recently along the open coastal plains of the American Southwest. It seems interesting that, among those who enjoy making comparisons, it is easiest to compare Houston one category at a time, rather than as a whole. (It is like Los Angeles in its sprawl; like St. Louis in its mixture of conservative values; like Atlanta in its heritage but nonreliance on southern heritage; like New Orleans with its port and even with its weather.) The whole of Houston remains varied in social, economic, and even political life; we should not be surprised, therefore, that the city also appears unique in some other aspects.

In this mode, then, is there something unique about Houston in the way in which it entertains and enlightens itself? Are the ornaments of civilization—theater, dance, musical performances, drama, literary readings, and even the more popular pursuits of circuses, parades, folk-play parties, baseball, and the like—any different in this town from those found somewhere else? With these questions in mind, we shall consider the mosaic of culture and cultures in Houston.

Today, the city has a major symphony orchestra, an internationally famous opera company, one of the best regional professional acting groups, a ballet company that has won gold medal awards, and a park program of entertainment that runs free to viewers for almost six months each year. The city is also the site of the first public educational television station in the land. It has kept its small-town air as it celebrates Saint Patrick's Day with a parade that is more all-inclusive than it is Irish. Juneteenth features concerts that draw many who are not black; everyone lines up to cheer the Fiestas Patrias parade; and October is a busy month for all concerned as it includes the Greek Festival, the Ten Ten (October 10th) celebration of the Chinese, and the German Oktoberfests.

For one thing, cultural events that transcend or defy ethnic lines have been evident since the beginning of the city, and this may be different from the experience elsewhere in the nation. Houston culture appears to have been vigorous—even lusty—in its infancy. Early on, the entrepreneurship of those who arrived and quickly dubbed themselves "Houstonians" included traveling and local stage productions, reading societies, and learned lectures, as well as events often associated with frontier towns, river towns, and coastal port towns. Houston culture has always included such memorable occasions as a concert of Chopin's music. Its history also includes a legendary impresario, Edna Woolford Saunders, who was successful in Houston for more than fifty years, and the Majestic Theatre, a building whose design became the prototype for four thousand duplicate structures. Underlying all of this is a tradition of public support from some who had scarcely unpacked their belongings and others who had lived in the town for more than eighty years.

This chapter makes no attempt to be the definitive historic record of Houston's cultural development. To do so would require several volumes, not just a few pages. Rather, it presents the author's own personal memory and some recollections of a few others. Together, these thoughts suggest the mosaic of Houston's public events. That the mosaic has enlarged yet stayed much the same supports the thesis that Houston and its culture are unique.

What is Ethnic Culture in Houston?

In the 1960s, as part of his American tour, an outstanding young Polish pianist was booked for a concert in Houston. He came with the highest artistic credentials and with rave reviews from the international press. He had been the favorite pupil of Ignace Jan Paderewski, the admired Polish senior statesman and world-renowned musician who, even after he had reached his eighties, had continued to perform in the United States to raise money for Polish war refugees. The new musician was Witold Malcuzynski, who had made a sensational debut in Paris and more recently in New York's Carnegie Hall. He had also just been announced as the national touring artist for a trip by the New York Philharmonic. The last grand-prize winner of the International Chopin Competition in Warsaw before World War II, he was also one of the first new recording artists signed after that war by the British Broadcasting Company and the London Philharmonic Orchestra. Here, clearly, was a talented musician whose concert should draw all serious music lovers in the Houston area.

Yet when the Malcuzynski evening is recalled, perhaps the strongest memory is one of the audience itself. They sat proudly cheering after each selection, and they festively greeted one another in the concert hall foyer—a surprisingly large number of them wearing Polish native garments and still more wearing small Polish flags in their lapels or pinned to their blouses. To them, it was definitely an ethnic occasion. As much as they were in-

dulging their interest in one who had achieved celebrity rank with his accomplishments, they were also reaffirming their shared ethnic background. Even those, perhaps especially those, who had assimilated so that neither by surname nor by facial features were they distinguishable as Polish were once again seeking to be singled out by their ethnic origins.

While this phenomenon is certainly not limited to Houston nor concentrated just in the past cultural life of the city, it seems more noticeable when a star is brought to Houston from another country or another environment than it would be in many other American cities of similar size. One might argue that the recentness of the arrival of so many Houstonians at any point in its history—the city has nearly doubled its population every two decades since its founding on August 29, 1836—would logically encourage its citizens to look back to their common heritage. It is only natural that the local ethnic communities would attend such programs to applaud this commonality only a little less than they might attend to enjoy the performance. One might argue that Malcuzynski was a singularly talented man with his own strong nationalistic tradition to uphold, both in his choice of music to perform and in his choice of famous mentor, and that these choices etched deeper such a reaction among Polish Houstonians. The same thing happens, though, when other artists without such strong orientation appear in Houston; and in some instances it has been as difficult for some ethnic audiences to gain acceptance as it was for the talented performers. For example, Paul Robeson and Marian Anderson were among the first blacks to achieve fame as classical musicians, and they both performed concerts in southern and southwestern cities during their long careers. Different locations reacted in different ways to local blacks who wished to buy tickets. Houston, like some other cities, set aside a part of the balcony—a practice that grew as blacks began to attend many cultural events and to lend their presence and support to Houston's larger art scene.

In Houston, integration of the audience came quietly, without much comment or incident. Today many blacks regularly attend art openings, museum lectures, symphony concerts, opera performances, and all of the other cultural events. They purchase tickets to sit wherever they wish, and it is painful to recall they once sat in the back of the hall after perhaps having arrived by riding in the back of the bus. Even today blacks attend in greater numbers, however, when artists such as Leontyne Price, Shirley Verrett, or Andre Watts are booked. For those events, blacks who do not regularly attend the season performances contact the box office for tickets to the show. This growing ethnic pride in black artists and the ability to attend high-cost events are not lost on those art managers who are ever looking for ways to expand the audience. Indeed, by booking a black performer, they know they can often increase the box-office take. It has helped in still another way: more young blacks have been hired in organizations such as the Houston Grand Opera, giving these young apprentices a chance at the small roles and chorus groupings that are so essential for them in developing their potential as future leading singers. This has traditionally been the route to the top for white singers, and now it is rightfully shared.[1]

If blacks have not had many artists as role models until recently, the Jewish community has supplied more than its share. Houston audiences for all cultural events are Jewish to an extent larger than the percentage of Jewish Houstonians, and this has been true throughout the city's history. All of the arts, but music particularly, are such a large part of the Jewish world tradition that any roll call of artists would probably show the final figures as favoring Jews. So, how

1. Historically black singers in the United States have come from a church choir background, with the choir director having served as scout and teacher. The lack of blacks in serious music organizations is not limited to the South and Southwest but has been the case generally throughout the music world. Some blacks achieved fame in vaudeville, in rhythm and blues, and in jazz bands, as well as in solo performances for the nightclub circuits. The recital hall and slots in symphony orchestras or opera companies have been another matter. Some credit television with helping to break this barrier. Blacks were never minstrel singers, incidentally, those "black faces" being achieved by a burnt cork on a white-faced singer. Minstrelry has a stronger historic tie to the European traveling horse-and-cart family acting groups and circuses than to anything that has come down through the American Negro tradition.

does one make a case of ethnic support for a Jewish performer?

There is another factor that is dominant when one considers the differences in how a Jew is defined, even by other Jews. Is the distinction one of a particular ethnic origin, or is it one of a particular religious faith? Non-Jews tend to call people "Jewish" if either relationship is there, yet a large part of the Jewish community recognizes as Jews only those who practice their religion on a regular basis. Included here are some people who, by profession of faith, have embraced the Jewish religion and become Jews with no ancestral ties. Another group are those persons who, as children of intermarriages, are fractionally Jewish by the historic or cultural description if not by the religious one. To identify someone by national origin, race, or religion becomes ambiguous and even undesirable when the person being described thinks it in error. Because it is the Jews whom we are discussing, and because of the history of their persecution in aggressive and passive ways in so many localities throughout history, we must deal with such considerations seriously. On the other hand, evidence exists for the argument that ethnic groups such as Houston Jews do lend healthy support to local events that are not necessarily "ethnic," other than by the accident of birth of the performer. When a relatively unknown violinist came from Israel near the beginning of his career to perform as soloist with the Houston Symphony, the audience had more Jewish patrons in attendance than even usually come. Nor is this support demonstrated only for Israeli talent; no matter which country has fostered the development of a Jewish artist, the Houston audience will generally be augmented disproportionately by Houstonians who share a Jewish heritage—however it may be defined.

An excellent example comes from another culture. This one involves a newcomer to Houston, the contribution he has made to the arts, and the rapid involvement of those whose ancestors came from his homeland. While some ethnic groups are more difficult than others to identify by sight, even a relatively unpracticed eye can discern a performer who is Chinese. Also, Chinese have not dominated the Western arts scene for a reason that has nothing to do with aesthetics or education, but with tradition. There is an older tradition in Oriental music, dance, and graphic arts than in the West, and it is still thriving. In Houston, however, a ballet star whose own meteoric rise has gained him personal fame has contributed to the serious recognition of the entire Houston Ballet around the world. Li Cunxin possesses youth, athletic ability, grace, and whatever extra body chemistry it is that can cause an entire audience to focus on his presence on stage even when there may be others who are dancing the very same steps. He was a dancer in Peking who came to Houston in 1979 at the invitation of Houston Ballet's director and imaginative choreographer, Ben Stevenson. He has quickly become one of the Houston company's leading attractions, contributing far more than just his being a local novelty. When judged against his peers from nineteen countries in the 1982 International Dance Competition, he was given a silver medal in the men's senior division. Unlike many ballet dancers who have left Russia for political reasons as much as for artistic ones, Li Cunxin has stated that he only wants to perfect his knowledge of Western ballet at this time in his career, and that he can do that best in Houston. The Houston Chinese community has supported him and shown an ethnic pride in his achievements. Before his arrival it was rare to see more than a few Chinese in the ballet's audience; now entire families attend, and small children especially are entranced as they watch the accomplishments of one they recognize as being kin. Beyond that, Ben Stevenson has conceived what many consider to be his most beautifully lyric ballet, *Zheng Ban Qiao,* for his handsome young star. This ballet is a perfection of Oriental mystic transparencies and subtleties with Western angularity and dynamism, and Li Cunxin is the single dancer who is most able to convey both vocabularies at the same time with authority and beauty.

There is undoubtedly support or an interest network that comes into play when l'Alliance Française de Houston brings to town someone from France. The audience naturally will be composed of those who feel kinship with that country as well as special interest in the topic. The Alley Theatre's importation of a Russian play sparked interest among Houstonians of Slavic and Russian ancestry. The same was true when the Alley management exchanged actors and scripts with an English theatrical company. *Close Ties,* a successful season opener here, was sent to England, while the English production and acting crew for two Alan Ayckbourn plays traveled to Houston. When these two productions opened, there was an abundance of British accents during the intermission breaks, as might have been expected. The mood of an evening can change, such as when the Ballet Folklórico sets those of Mexican heritage to clapping and cheering in Jones Hall.

It is from the Mexican Houstonians that one finds an exception to the judgment that, while Houston has supported the performing arts for most of its nearly one hundred and fifty years' existence, the city has never developed a star who was internationally known or had a lasting career. The exception is Lydia Mendoza, hailed for more than fifty years as "La Alondra de la Frontera" or "The Meadowlark of the Border." Born in the Houston Heights, she was a local singing favorite by the time she was in her mid-teens. During her long career, she has recorded more than thirty-five albums and hundreds of single records. In addition to performing in auditoriums and halls across North America, she has been given some unusual acclaim by being invited to entertain at the Montreal World's Fair, at folk festivals in the Library of Congress, and at the White House. Lydia Mendoza plays the twelve-string guitar and sings the music that she was taught by her mother. Also a composer, she adds to this Mexican repertoire many songs of her own. She became one of the most popular performers of Mexican music during the 1930s, and fifty years later she is still performing for audiences filled with those who grew up with her music. Although Houston has been her lifetime home, she is not really thought of as a Houston or even a Texas singer. She is an ethnic celebrity, and her ethnic heritage and artistic contribution clearly come from her Mexican parentage and the Mexican culture.[2]

2. For a more complete account of her unusual career, see Carlos B. Gil, "Lydia Mendoza: Houstonian and First Lady of Mexican American Song," *Houston Review,* Summer 1981, Vol. III, No. 2.

The Mainstream of Houston Culture

These examples show that much of Houston's ethnic culture is easy to recognize and that it has been well supported. On the other hand, there always has been a mainstream of culture, in the sense of cultural events that transcend an ethnic identity, and the support for this mainstream has come from all of the groups in the city. If there has been a special emphasis, it has come from Houston's having had a group of wealthy citizens who consistently wanted the best of life, not just for themselves but also for their city. Indeed, starting as early as 1837—less than a year after the Allen Brothers started selling lots along the scant bluffs overlooking Buffalo Bayou—Houston began its tradition of an annual season of well-subscribed public cultural events.[3] On June 11, 1838, Henry Carri brought two plays to Houston: a comedy, *The Hunchback,* by Sheridan Knowles, and Carri's farce entitled *The Dumb Belle— or I'm Perfection.* Historian David McComb has listed the range of entertainment during the first few years as including traveling variety shows, minstrels, singers, comedians, acting companies, a ventriloquist, a phrenologist, professional and amateur performers of musical instruments (including even a band of bell ringers), and a trained animal show.

3. The author acknowledges research work done by Kathy Riola that is used in this section. A longer account of the events of the first few years in Houston may be found in David McComb's excellent book, *Houston: The Bayou City,* University of Texas Press, 1969, pp. 54–57.

Other sources for the history part of this chapter include material at the Houston Metropolitan Research Center and the Texas Room of the Houston Public Library; copies of the *Telegraph and Texas Register* for 1838; scrapbooks compiled by Miss Ima Hogg that are now housed at the University of Houston library; columns written by George Fuermann for the *Houston Post* and material of his that was published as *Houston Recalled: Six Miniatures,* published by Baxter & Korge, 1968; and the *Standard History of Houston, Texas,* edited by Benjamin H. Carroll, published privately in 1912.

For a chronological account of theatrical productions, see Joseph Gallegly, *Footlights on the Border: The Galveston and Houston Stage Before 1900,* The Hague: Mouton & Company, 1962.

Perhaps a more serious kind of culture was extended to the new city settlers by the formation of the Philosophical Society of Texas and the Franklin Debating Society, both groups formed during 1837. Two years later Henry F. Byrne began Houston's first subscription library with his 1,300-volume collection. In 1844 the Sängerbund began its musical life, which continues even today. Then in 1854 the Houston Lyceum began presenting lectures, debates, and musical programs for Houston residents; the Lyceum continued this activity for about forty years. The Lyceum also helped convert the Byrne book collection into Houston's first public library.

With this early enthusiasm evident, Houston became a stopping place for the many entertainers who made their way across the nation. Some of these were in variety shows and family circuses that had in some cases only recently arrived from Europe. Houston was always a good circus town, it seems; and in that history might be the nucleus for the late Judge Roy Hofheinz's having raised $10 million in 1967 to buy into Ringling Brothers, Barnum & Bailey's circus so that, for a time, Houston was its second home.

An interest in the performing arts led to the building of several theaters in the new city. One of the best houses was the Sweeney & Coombs Theater, which boasted of 350 square feet of stage space—enough for the largest productions traveling the circuits at that time. A second important hall was the Opera House, where the first local production of *Carmen* was given. The Opera House burned in 1904, and it was only a short time before Houstonians seriously began planning for a bigger and better replacement—the City Auditorium.

In 1890 the Grace Company's performance of Gilbert and Sullivan's *The Gondoliers* was an occasion for much partying and glittering social dress. One account says that the November 3 opening was attended by 1,700 ladies in Paris creations and homemade gowns, and that all of their gentlemen escorts had donned high-stock collars. Rather than what the audience wore that evening, the more interesting aspect is that *The Gondoliers* had been written less than two years earlier, and it had been performed in England only the season before, in 1889.

Interior of the Houston Lyceum and Carnegie Library, showing the spacious lobby for circulating book service.

The immortal Harry Leighton starred in the Monro & Sage Company production of *The Prisoner of Zenda* in 1901 at the Sweeney & Coombs. Later that year, William A. Brady brought three comedies: *Sorrows of Satan, Foxy Grandpa,* and *Way Down East.* When the Sweeney & Coombs burned—as seemed to happen to many early theaters in the years before electric lights —another "bigger and better" theater was constructed at 320 Fannin. The Fannin location served up such star attractions as Sarah Bernhardt, Maude Adams, James K. Hackett, Blanche Ring, and even a group called the Merry Minstrel Men.

The Metropolitan Opera came to Houston in 1901, bringing three productions: *Lohengrin, Parsifal,* and *La Boheme. Parsifal* was performed in Houston several years before it was given in any European city outside Germany.

All of this is more remarkable when we understand

Early photograph of the Sweeney & Coombs Opera House, built in 1890.

This photograph of the Carter Building in 1915 was circulated widely in the United States to show the phenomenal growth of the new city of Houston. Even at that time, Houston had more skyscrapers than any city in the world of equal population—and was receiving national attention for the rapidity of its growth.

The City Auditorium, also called the Municipal Auditorium, had only the word Auditorium *on its facade. This Greek Revival structure was the largest modern convention hall in the South at the time that it was built, seating 7,000 people. Jesse H. Jones Hall for the Performing Arts is located today on the same site.*

that, at the time, Houston was not even considered the prime dispenser of cultural life in Southeast Texas; Galveston was. From the mid-1840s until the time of the hurricane at the turn of the century, Galveston was Texas's most cosmopolitan and wealthy city. Some of the stars booked into Galveston stage houses did come up to Houston for additional appearances; but more often those Houstonians who could afford it had to travel the fifty miles to the coastal city. Galvestonians still feel the sense of this early importance in culture,

as shown in a recent advertisement for a subscription program series. It urges everyone to come to Galveston's 1894 Grand Opera House and "feel the history: sit in the only remaining historic theatre in the Houston-Galveston area. Many of the greatest performers in history have played the Grand, including: Anna Pavlova, Sarah Bernhardt, George M. Cohan, Lillian Russell, the Stratford-on-Avon Players, John Philip Sousa, Paderewski, Al Jolson, Lionel Barrymore, William Jennings Bryan, Ziegfield Follies, Marx Broth-

This photograph of the Turnverein Club appeared in the Illustrated City Book of Houston, *published in 1915. It was considered at that time to be one of the finest club buildings in the Southwest. The German community in Houston included many of the city's leaders.*

ers, George Burns and Gracie Allen, and even Tex Ritter and his horse."

No discussion of mainstream culture in Houston can exclude mention of the long-time support by one Houstonian, Miss Ima Hogg. Talented as a musician herself, she spent her life bringing music and all the arts to the forefront. Most of her efforts were spent in tireless support for the Houston Symphony Orchestra from its beginning in 1913 until her death just a few years ago. However, an act that she did for her own pleasure has also had significance in helping to recall Houston's early cultural scene. Miss Ima, as everyone called her, saved performance programs, and her scrapbooks for the years 1907 to 1925 are invaluable. Better than the contemporary reviews of those performances—for these often were comments on the social occasion rather than a full account of the performance—her collection of playbills names the sponsoring groups and tells of the selections chosen by the visiting local artists. An important part of Houston's history might be lost but for these programs, which show that the local music clubs gave early sponsorship to many performers, but particularly to musicians. The clubs themselves are an interesting aspect of history in Houston, and they all started at about the same time— although the Sängerbund had a longer history, having started some years earlier in 1844.

The Treble Clef Club was established in 1893, and by 1911 it had 672 members. Its closing concert that year had more than four thousand people attending. At some point it had begun to sponsor visiting artists as well as its own programs, for in 1918 at its 25th Jubilee Concert, Mme. Galli Curci was contracted to give a concert; and in 1919, Jascha Heifetz was the visiting artist. The Houston Quartette Society began in 1900 as a men's English singing society, and it seems to have been the first to establish associate memberships for the purpose of bringing to town outstanding performers. When it was only three years old, in 1903, the Houston Quartette Society extended its influence by creating the Federation of English Singing Societies of Texas. The early organizational meetings were held at the Rice Hotel. One of the more serious groups called itself the Thursday Morning Musical Club. Its entry rules were published in 1908, although the club had been organized earlier. The rules stated that anyone who wished to join would be subjected to a rigorous performance examination.

By 1912 the Houston Sängerbund had 340 at its weekly meetings, and five years later it sponsored a Houston performance by the St. Louis Symphony. In 1914 Houston was on the tour sheet for the National Opera Company of Canada. It brought four productions to town: Saint-Saëns's *Samson et Dalila,* Ponchielli's *La Gioconda,* Massenet's *La Navarraise,* and Leoncavallo's *I Pagliacci.* The Boston National Grand Opera Company brought *Aïda,* and there were a number of less-known companies that either produced operas or presented an evening's entertainment of scenes from operas. Then in 1916, the Rice Hotel contributed to the cultural choices in town by sponsoring a series of matinee concerts and lectures by individual performers.

The year 1910 seems to have been pivotal for Houston's cultural development, and much of the increased activity came from the opening of the new City Auditorium.[4] It was located at the site occupied today by Jones Hall for the Performing Arts. The City Auditorium was used almost every day or every night for some major public event all through its approximately fifty years of existence. In 1910 Houston had a few less than eighty thousand people, but that number was double the population of only ten years before. The city was four miles in diameter, but already the center of town had a skyscraper: the Carter Building at 806 Main, which was sixteen stories high. Several major buildings in addition to the new auditorium were completed in 1910, including the Harris County Court House and the City Hall Market.

Less than a year later, Houston had sixteen symphony concerts in one winter, a record to be envied by much older and larger cities of that era. Even closer at hand, Houston was becoming recognized as the music center for Texas and the Southwest, outstripping Galveston's earlier claim and as yet unchallenged by any other Texas urban settlement. The New York Symphony came in 1910 and again in 1911, the second time under the baton of the much-loved conductor, Walter Damrosch. Efrem Zimbalist appeared in Houston in 1913 for a violin concert.

About this time, one of Houston's young leading citizens moved into a public role that she would occupy for the next half-century. Edna Woolford Saunders's father was one of Houston's cotton merchants, and he had been mayor at the turn of the century. Her own education had included considerable musical training, and she had returned to Houston about 1900, where she led an active social life, including joining the Women's Choral Club. She occupied herself for the next decade making arrangements for the club's many programs. Then, in 1910, she was asked to become manager and booking agent for the new City Auditorium. From this post she became not only Houston's first important concert manager, but also for many years the most successful impresario in the South and

4. An interesting account of Houston in 1910 is given by Charles Orson Cook in two issues of *The Houston Review,* Spring and Fall of 1979, Vol. I, Nos. 1 and 2. His source was John Milsaps's diary, which ran seventy-three volumes.

The Houston Municipal Band gave regularly scheduled free concerts in the city's parks and auditoriums before World War I. Houston has had a tradition of free public musical entertainment since the 1890s, and possibly even earlier than that.

Southwest. She spent about a third of each year in the eastern part of the United States, auditioning performers and attending performances to make arrangements for the following year's season in Houston and other nearby towns.

Mrs. Saunders brought Enrico Caruso to Houston, where he appeared before one of the largest audiences (more than six thousand) in his entire career. Many years later, she recalled the occasion: "We were all sold out, but people jammed the hall anyway, hoping for tickets. Many were Caruso's own countrymen, and I didn't want to turn them away. We opened the doors and Caruso sang . . .with a voice that could be heard by those hundreds on the sidewalks out front."

In the 1930s she started the tradition of bringing the Ballet Russe de Monte Carlo to Houston for Christmas-season performances and the annual round of parties honoring its stars. The company continued this schedule for as long as it was organized under the same managers, for they had developed many friendships with Houstonians, not the least with Mrs. Saunders.[5] She was a strong force in forming Houstonians' taste in

culture, educating and entertaining them for about fifty years. Among the international artists who came under her sponsorship were Fritz Kreisler, Mary Garden, Ezio Pinza, Paderewski, Luisa Tetrazzini, Will Rogers, John McCormack, Grace Moore, the Abbey Irish Players, Kubuki of Japan, Admiral Byrd, Rachmaninoff, the French Army Band, Lauritz Melchior, Marian Anderson, the New York Philharmonic, and Yehudi Menuhin at the tender age of sixteen.

Having mentioned Miss Ima's scrapbooks, one should recognize her again as the single greatest force

5. Nearly fifty years after the first performance by the Ballet Russe de Monte Carlo in Houston, there is still a warm rapport between the city and those dancers. During November 1983, there was a reunion of some of the early Ballet Russe stars, and it was in Houston. The occasion was the Houston Ballet's program, "Tribute to the Ballets Russes," presented at Jones Hall; and the former dancers came from points across the United States and as far away as London and Geneva for the event. As has always been the case, there was a round of parties for the dancers, with the host or hostess being someone who was a personal friend, now living in Houston.

The exterior of the Majestic Theatre, the first "atmospheric" theater to be built by John Eberson.

behind the growth of the Houston Symphony Orchestra. Organized in 1913, the symphony has given concerts under the direction of Toscanini and Sir Thomas Beecham; it has included among its regular seasonal conductors such maestros as Leopold Stokowski, Sir John Barbarolli, Sir Malcolm Sargent, Efrem Kurtz, Andre Previn, and Lawrence Foster. The last two mentioned were in Houston during early parts of their career, Miss Ima and her symphony board having had a special interest in recognizing youthful potential. Her lifetime contributions were augmented by the efforts of General Maurice Hirsch and Miss Nina Cullinan as

well. Houston's growing corporate and trade sectors helped. The HSO concerts were carried by radio over a statewide network for the full winter season as early as 1944, under the sponsorship of the Texas Gulf Sulphur Company. Free Saturday night concerts and later concerts for a dollar were underwritten by the Henke and Pillot grocery stores. In addition to the easy recognition of those who have conducted the Houston Symphony, there has also been a long tradition of outstanding soloists who have appeared for the first time before Houston audiences in concert with the symphony. Some of the symphony's own players have

Ming Yang, graduate student in design at the College of Architecture, University of Houston, worked on a model of what the interior of the old Majestic was like. He studied the old plans and the few extant photographs to build his replica. Photograph by Ming Yang.

May Fetes were an annual event for most school children of German or Middle European ancestry in the Houston ethnic communities. Mothers made their daughters identical spring dresses in pastel colors, while sons would be dressed in fresh white shirts and pants and, if possible, bow ties. Then came the obligatory photograph on the school or church grounds to record the event. This picture shows the relative affluence of the German and Czech communities.

grown in international reputation, partially nurtured by their regular appearances with the HSO. Raphael Fliegel, for instance, made his first appearance while still in high school in Houston, and then for twenty-five years he served as the orchestra's concertmaster. Fine musicians such as Fredell Lack, Drusilla Huffmaster, and James Dick live in the Houston area and have appeared on many occasions with the symphony and in solo recitals.

Recent arrivals to Houston think the evidence for the city's having "come of age" in a musical sense lies in the Houston Grand Opera's premieres of works by Carlisle Floyd and, more recently, by Leonard Bernstein. However, at least two earlier works that are now in the large repertoire for orchestras were also born in Houston. In 1948 Maestro Efrem Kurtz personally commissioned Aaron Copland to compose a symphonic poem elaborating on the music he had written

A partially destroyed but valuable photograph that shows the Houston Mexican community's entertaining Fiestas Patrias celebration in the mid-1940s. While there was a great deal of celebration in this ethnic group, only a few photographs remain to show what it was like.

as the film score for *The Red Pony,* based on John Steinbeck's book. The piece was given its initial performance by the Houston Symphony and is today considered one of the standard modern classical pieces for orchestra. Later, in 1966, for the opening of Jones Hall for the Performing Arts, Alan Hovhaness was asked to compose a new work, and he presented his Houston benefactors with *Ode to the Temple of Sound.*

Other major events, minor incidents, and many people have contributed to Houston's cultural development. Missing from this account are the several steps that led to the establishing of the two major art museums and any recognition of the many smaller ones. While museums of all kinds have been important to Houston, it is difficult to relate a close connection in painting and sculpture created in Houston to

either the larger cultural fabric or the ethnic culture that has made the town what it is. Perhaps there has been some regional or local influence, but it has not yet been isolated or recognized as such; maybe a "Houston school" of art is something still in the future. The major museums do buy from some of the local artists, but a disproportionate part of each budget goes for works that have already made their reputation elsewhere. Houston writers have perhaps fared a bit better. Although not recognized as a Houstonian, William Sydney Porter—O. Henry—did live in the city for a while, writing and doing quite praiseworthy pen sketches for the *Houston Post.* David Westheimer, Garland Roark, Jan de Hartog, Larry McMurtry, and some other writers of national significance have spent considerable time in Houston. More important to the

Maestro Leopold Stokowski brought worldwide recognition to Houston's musical scene when he accepted the post of conductor of the Houston Symphony Orchestra.

Miss Ima Hogg. Oil portrait by Robert Joy. Photograph courtesy of the Bayou Bend Collection, Houston Museum of Fine Arts.

city's posterity, they soaked up the background for much of what they were to create even after they left. In the performing arts, however, Houston has enjoyed its own special limelight.

A City of "Firsts"

When the Astrodome opened its doors in 1965, the world's media rushed to Houston to look and to proclaim, "This is the best!" Not only was the structure so widely photographed that it fast became the city's symbol, but a deeper vein of flattery also became evident as almost every major arena to be constructed after the Astrodome's debut duplicated its functional frill-free design and its enclosed post-free interior. For Houstonians, an error in all the furor over the new facility lay in the idea that Houston had only now arrived as a prophetic builder of entertainment centers. There had been at least two earlier "firsts" that, at the time each had been unveiled, had engendered similar national acclaim.

One was only fifteen years earlier when, in 1950, the Rice University Stadium had been built. Like the Astrodome, the stadium had been constructed at a record pace—this time to accommodate college football fans for an already scheduled season during a decade when Rice had enrolled some razzle-dazzle football heroes. At the same time, the builders had used innovative construction concepts for the massive under- and above-ground structure.[6]

An even earlier attention-getting entertainment center was built in 1923: the Majestic Theatre at 908 Rusk, half a block off Main Street.[7] John Eberson was the ar-

6. The stadium was designed by the combined architectural talents of Lloyd, Morgan and Jones and the McGinty Partnership. Walter P. Moore and Associates, Inc., and Brown & Root, Inc., were the contractors. H. A. Lott, Inc., constructed the Astrodome from architectural designs drawn by two firms: Wilson, Morris, Crane and Anderson, and once again, Lloyd, Morgan and Jones.

7. The theater was *not* located directly on Main Street, as recent accounts in the *Houston Chronicle's Texas Magazine* and the *Smithsonion Institution News* have reported.

chitect, and he was as clever in promotion as in design. He called his creation "the first atmospheric movie palace," and both the catchy adjective and the grandly descriptive noun grew in use across the United States. Eberson and his many imitators went on to design and build more than four thousand motion picture houses during the next fifteen years.

Austrian-born Eberson understood the architectural frou-frou that had been adorning the structures of European royalty for centuries. He especially recognized the fascination that most Americans held for the make-believe world of crystal palaces, Italianate gardens, classical love temples with columns soaring to heaven, gold-leaf plaster, frescoes, and bas-relief Grecian urns. Rather than settle for just one of these decorative devices as a theme for the new downtown Houston theater, Eberson decided to reach for all splendid ornamentations from earlier cultures and climes. He combined recognizable examples of art forms from around the world and across the pages of history. He was unique in his ability to combine this outrageous lot with a sense of fun, so that the effect was one of fantasy and not offense. The suspension of reality that Dr. Samuel Johnson called the first ingredient necessary before a playwright or an actor could transport an audience to another time and place was now, with Eberson's new theater, extended beyond the footlights to include all that surrounded the eye.

The Majestic seemed not to have a roof: there were tiny electric stars in the vaulted dark blue ceiling. Even more wonderful, there were clouds that wafted below the stars, the product of the Brenkert Company's latest invention, a magic lantern that used a strip of negative film pulled across a strong light to form wispy clouds in the "sky." Sculptures of the ancient gods and goddesses were placed in niches and along the many balconies. Gold-leaf plaster was scrolled in mazes. Arbutus vines climbed over the wall areas that had not already been claimed by frescoes or bas-relief mythological animals. The Majestic was make-believe itself as it set the mood for the make-believe motion pictures of a world in another time, another place, with royal stars and their loyal subjects, the fans.

Houston's Majestic was John Eberson's first atmospheric theater, and the local citizenry took considerable pride in his growing fame in designing the atmospherics. From cities far more cosmopolitan that Houston, clients came in a steady stream to see the first theater in this genre. Eberson himself became a celebrity, giving speeches about what he considered to be a new art form. He devised a motto: "Prepare Practical Plans for Pretty Playhouses—Please Patrons—Pay Profits," which was shortened by his contemporaries into "the nine little P's." He reached a zenith with his New York Roxy Theatre, which was billed as the world's largest indoor theater, with 6,214 seats and an orchestra pit for 110 musicians—somewhat larger than a full symphony orchestra.[8]

As the international style of architecture moved to American shores, with the public becoming fascinated first with art deco and then with the sophistication that sought to strike away all ornamentation, the Eberson-styled theaters began to meet the wrecking ball. Such was the fate for both the Roxy and the Majestic. In New York there was an outraged cry of protest, and the Roxy came close to being saved. In Houston the Majestic passed with little notice, yet it was probably the greater loss. By being a "first," the Majestic had earned its rightful place in architectural history, and it deserved to be preserved; but veneration of the old was still some years into the future for Houstonians. An

additional irony was that the Majestic was torn down just before the citizens began to recognize a need for more space in the downtown area for the increased number of live stage productions of drama, ballet, and music. Many cities have found new life for their fine old movie palaces as homes for local and touring stage companies. Not only are such theaters centrally located, but they are also expensively constructed and decorated. Moreover, any remodeling can be achieved at a fraction of the millions of dollars required by new construction today. In Houston, however, the site at 908 Rusk is a well-located midtown parking garage. The only reminder of the earlier tenant is the use of small theater lights spelling out *Entrance* and *Exit,* and the significance of this is probably only accidental.

What Houston's Culture Means

During the public programs that were a secondary part to the several years' research done from 1979 to 1982 on ten of Houston's nearly one hundred ethnic communities, a number of the events presented artists who were best known to members of one particular ethnic group. For example, the program included a number of performers, lecturers, and artists who still maintain close ties to their geographic origins: the touring ink-brush artist who still goes home to Japan; the philosopher who seldom leaves the enclave of Hassidic Jews in New York City; even the resident poet who has recently moved to Houston from his changing Vietnam. Other times, it was those people who carry on the traditions they have learned from their parents and grandparents: the Christmas St. Lucia procession by Scandinavian children with blue eyes and white hair; the 140-year-old Sängerbund of the Germans in Houston; and the melodic songs handed down through black Creole families who have migrated from Louisiana to southern Texas towns. Lustily sung folksongs with new verses added to tell of the events of the day on the job are considered to be a tradition brought to the United States by the Irish who worked to build the Erie Canal; but in Texas such singing can often be the "border songs" that refer to that

8. Hubert Roussel, longtime music critic for the *Houston Post,* wrote the history of the Houston Symphony Orchestra, which was published in 1972. He states that HSO played its first concert in the winter of 1913 in a new vaudeville house, the Majestic, on Texas Avenue. This house was built by Interstate Theaters of Dallas and was renamed the Palace after a few seasons. Those who casually read Mr. Roussel's account might think he had mislocated the theater to Texas Avenue, or—more likely, if they know the truth that he was a careful researcher—that he did know better than other historians would exactly where the Majestic had been built. The Palace (born the Majestic) served the HSO for several seasons. About ten years afterwards, Karl Hoblitzelle of Interstate contracted with John Eberson to design a larger and more modern theater for the new craze, the motion pictures. Once again, the name "Majestic" was chosen, and this is the one that was built on Rusk Avenue.

Texas-Mexican area where men still gather in the cantinas at night to sing and play guitars, their lyrics telling of toiling in the fields and memories of the girls they have left behind. If the verses seem somewhat endless and repetitive, it is nonetheless an accurate description of their lives.

While many people tend to think of the poor blacks' urban experience as being totally negative, a bright young black playwright shows with pathos and humor how it is to live in a world planned and managed by others. Celeste Colson's *The Wrecking Ball* balances the comedy and tragedy found in anyone's daily life with more credibility than far more experienced dramatists have shown. The Houston Center for the Humanities production of this play, directed by Alma Yujan Carriere, was performed by an acting company—amateur only in that its members all hold other jobs during the daytime—that moved the mixed audience frequently to laughter and often nearly to tears. The unusual part of that opening night, however, was the procession Mrs. Carriere used at both the beginning and the ending of the play. The actors, chanting and dancing, traveled in a human chain up and down the aisles. This procession focused the audience's attention on the dramatic energy beforehand; and afterwards, almost all of those who had sat out front joined the chain spontaneously, becoming part of the show as well.

The haunting music of the Greek Orthodox religious services, the strumming of Oriental musical instruments that have been played for hundreds of years, and the staccato of the fiddle in the hands of a Cajun—all of these brought the ethnic message of community to the Houston Center's programs. To those who came to the public programs, the displaying of arts and even household crafts, the demonstrating of folkways and skills, the wearing of ethnic costumes, and the sharing of dance, song, tales, and food caused the greater Houston community to become more aware of the contributions from each of the groups. Culture, in the several definitions of the word, became a viable experience.

In truth, Houston is no different from other cities that have sprung up along the American frontier in the past two hundred years. Where Houston may be unique is in its fortunate tradition of affluence, so that its varied cultures need not be lost in the pursuit of a means for survival. While some newcomers in each immigration wave have obviously been at the bottom of the socioeconomic and political structure, the rapid and steady growth of the city has seen some from every ethnic background rise to the top long before they have forgotten from whence they came or before they have dismissed the pride they feel in their heritage.

Most visitors to Houston describe its people as "friendly." This friendliness certainly carries over to the visiting luminaries who travel to Houston regularly to speak and perform, to instruct and entertain. These special visitors, these artists, meet old friends who now call Houston home; and they make new friends, too. They bring to both groups a shared heritage and a strong bond of mutual interests. Houston's cultural mosaic always has been varied and rich; but it is the special quality of the city and its people that brings to mind that, in Houston, both meanings of the word *culture* are often one.

Southeast Asian Social and Cultural Customs

from *Journal of Refugee Resettlement*, Vol. 1, No. 1

Family

The family is the core social unit in Eastern cultures, and family obligations have traditionally taken precedence over individual autonomy throughout the life cycle. As a result, family relations and functions have been extensively and elaborately defined. Mutually reciprocal obligations join child and parent, husband and wife, household and kin. These customs are changing at present, owing to the involuntary separation of members during flight and resettlement, and also to the acceptability of more independent lifestyles in the American society.

	VIETNAMESE	CAMBODIAN	LAO
A.	***General***		
1.	The family is the basis of society, not the individual.	Same	Same
2.	Up to three or four generations live together in one home.	Same	Same
3.	Within the family, the wife deals with all household matters. The husband deals with the outside world.	Same	Same
4.	The elderly (parents) are supported by married or unmarried children until they die.	Same	Same
5.	Names are written in this order: Example: Nguyen Van Hai Family name —Nguyen Middle name —Van Given name —Hai Family name is placed first as an emphasis on the roots of a person.	Same as Vietnamese Example: Chan Sa Mol Family name —Chan Middle name —Sa Given name —Mol	Names are written in this order: Example: Thonedy Sourivong Family name —Sourivong Given name —Thonedy
6.	Family members cannot use the same given name	Same	Same

7. Traditionally, parents are proud of having a large family.	Parents are proud of a large family.	Same

B. *Marriage*

8. Children live with their parents until they marry. Men marry between the ages of 20 and 30. Women marry between the ages of 18 and 25.	Men marry between 18 and 30. Women marry from age 16 onward. Traditionally, betrothals were prearranged by parents.	Men marry between ages 18 and 30. Women marry between 16 and 22.
9. By tradition (not law) a marriage must be approved by parents from both sides. This is true for persons of all ages.	Same	Same
10. First cousins and their children cannot marry each other up to three generations.	First cousins can marry each other, but an uncle or aunt cannot marry a niece or nephew.	First cousins can marry each other. An uncle from a royal family can marry his niece.
11. The couple prefers to celebrate their wedding at the home of either side, not at the church or temple.	Same, but only at bride's house.	Same as Cambodian.
12. Legally, women keep their own names after marriage. Formally, married women use their husband's name.	After marriage, a woman officially uses her husband's last name. Informally, she can be called by her given name.	Same as Cambodian.
Example: Husband's name—Nguyen Van Hai Wife's maiden name—Le Thi Ba Wife's married name—Le Thi Ba Wife's formal name—Mrs. Nguyen Van Hai	*Example:* Husband's name—Chan Sa Nol Wife's maiden name—Ek Sam Nang Wife's married name—Mrs. Chan Sa Nol Wife's informal name—Mrs. Sam Nang	
13. After marriage, the wife lives with her husband's family. From that day she belongs to her husband's family.	After marriage, the couple can live with either the wife's family or the husband's family.	After marriage, the couple usually lives with the wife's family.
14. Before 1959, Vietnamese men could have more than one wife. Ranking in order of responsibility: First Wife Second Wife Third Wife	Cambodian men can have several wives, but written consent of the first wife is compulsory. All other wives are considered to rank second. In case of death of the first wife, one of the second wives, the oldest in marriage date or in age, gains promotion of rank.	Before 1945, same as Vietnamese.

Note: In coming to the United States, only one spouse may remain married to the husband; second or subsequent marriages must be dissolved. Wives are informally still accepted as family.

15. Divorce is legal but is not common. Family conflict is handled by both sides of the family.	Divorce is legal and is encouraged when necessary, to avoid discord between families.	Same as Cambodian.

C.   Children

16. Boys and girls are not free to do what they want. Girls are under strict supervision. Sex segregation is the common social rule.	Same	Same

D.   Death/Mourning

17. When a person dies, his/her body will be buried underground. If cremation was preferred, the family will comply.	When a person dies, his/her body will be cremated and the ashes will be kept in a pagoda or in the family home.	Same as Cambodian.
18. Elderly love their homes and their land. They want to die at home, not in a hospital or somewhere else.	Same	Same
19. If one of the parents dies, the children traditionally must wait for three years to marry.	Only one year, and a son may become a monk for one week to one year.	Children can marry at any time after the day of the funeral.
20. If the husband dies, the wife traditionally must wait for three years to remarry.	Only one year, but many choose never to marry again.	She can remarry at any time.
21. If the wife dies, the husband must wait one year to remarry.	The husband can remarry at any time.	Same as Cambodian.
22. If one of the siblings dies, the others must wait one year to marry.	Same as Vietnamese.	They can marry at any time.
23. The commemoration of the dead is celebrated every year up to the fourth great-grandparents (ancestor worship). Fifth great-grandparents are believed to have been reborn elsewhere on Earth or admitted to the permanent bliss of Heaven. The eldest son is responsible for the ancestor worship. If there is no	No such custom.	No such custom.

son in the family, then the eldest
daughter will take the
responsibility.

Society

Social customs function to regulate public experience, outside the realm of family life. Harmony is
generally maintained by observance of complementary roles, extending the principle of hierarchical relations to informal and formal encounters. Age, sex,
language, and physical context are keys in determining what role to take in specific occasions. In situations where the individual is uncertain of his/her
proper role, the surest response is to adopt a passive, subordinate position. This mode, demonstrated
broadly in the refugees' acceptance of low-level employment in the U.S., has certain survival value. It can
also lead to frustration, particularly in encounters that
Americans treat as competitive. Again, many refugees
are breaking away from those social traditions that
they do not feel apply to American life. In addition,
the material and institutional supports needed to sustain many customs are not present or permitted in
American communities.

	VIETNAMESE	CAMBODIAN	LAO
1.	Traditional caste system: 1. Scholar 2. Farmer/Fisherman 3. Laborer 4. Businessman	Traditional caste system: 1. King 2. Monk 3. Administrator 4. Technician 5. Businessman 6. Farmer/Laborer	Same as Cambodian.
2.	Traditionally, teachers are more respected than parents for their knowledge and moral virtues.	Parents are more respected than teachers.	Same as Cambodian.
3.	To show their respect, will bow their heads in front of a superior or an elderly person.	Same	Same
4.	To show their respect, Vietnamese use both hands when passing something to a superior or an elderly person.	Same	Same
5.	To salute, Vietnamese join both hands against their chest.	Cambodians join hands at different levels to salute: a. Chest level—between equal persons b. Chin level—to a stranger or older person c. Nose level—to uncles, aunts, teachers, and parents d. Over head—to a monk, or royalty	Same as Cambodian.

6.	While talking, Vietnamese should not look steadily at respected people's eyes.	Same	Same
7.	Women do not shake hands with each other or with men. (Shaking hands has become acceptable in the United States.)	Same	Same
8.	Ladies should not smoke in public.	Same as Vietnamese (up to 35 years old).	Same as Vietnamese (up to 22).
9.	Vietnamese never touch another's head. Only the elderly can touch the heads of young children.	Same as Vietnamese, but only parents can touch the heads of their young children.	Same as Cambodian.
10.	Calling with a finger up is used only toward an animal or an inferior. Between two equal people it is a provocation. To call a person use whole hand with fingers facing down.	Same	Same
11.	No different value between right and left hand, although left-handed people are generally believed to be clumsy.	Right hand is considered noble, left hand is of less or no value. To Cambodians to hand something with the left hand could be impolite.	Same as Cambodian.
12.	Traditionally, a child is not allowed to write with his left hand.	Same	Same
13.	Kissing in public is not acceptable.	Same	Same
14.	Persons of the same sex may hold hands in public or sleep in the same bed without being considered homosexuals.	Same	Same
15.	To eat, Vietnamese use chopsticks and bowls.	Cambodians use forks and spoons. City-dwellers use chopsticks. Villagers use palm leaves as spoons.	Same as Cambodian.
16.	Lunar year. There are many holidays in a year. New Year is in January or February, similar to the Chinese calendar.	Same as Vietnamese. New Year is April 13 each year.	Same as Cambodian.
17.	Time is flexible. There is no need to be in a hurry or punctual except in extremely important cases.	Same	Same

Religion

The religious heritage of every Southeast Asian culture is quite rich. Elements of several traditions are often incorporated in a blend suited to the subtleties of local conditions. The major religions—Buddhist, Taoist, Confucian—are mutually receptive, rather than exclusive, in their common practice. They offer complementary perspectives on human experience (including a vital element of humor!). Elements of Western religion may be accommodated also, as refugees adapt to American ways. There is no fine distinction between sacred and profane: beliefs and rituals that Americans might identify as religious pervade most areas of daily living, while less emphasis may be placed on formal practices. As a result, religious tenets may provide guidance and comfort during resettlement, easing the transitions in family and social life.

	VIETNAMESE	CAMBODIAN	LAO
1.	About 90 percent of the population practices ancestor worship or a loose form of Buddhism (Mahayana School prevails).	99 percent of the population are followers of Buddha (the Theraveda Buddhist sect prevails).	Same as Cambodian.
2.	Besides Buddhism, Animism is also popular.	Same	Same
3.	Belief in the theory of Karma, i.e., one's present life is pre-determined by his good or bad deeds in his previous life. The cycle of life and rebirth for an individual will only cease when he has finally been able to get rid of his earthly desires and achieve the state of spiritual liberation.	Same	Same
4.	Man is supposed to live in harmony with nature, not to dominate nature.	Same	Same
5.	Spiritualism is dominant in the society.	Same	Same

Observations—General Cultural Traits of the Indochinese

From *The Indochinese Refugees,* by Thinh Van Dinh

1. The peoples from Indochina tend to be diligent, intellectually alert, and gregarious. They learn and adapt well. However, they are extremely sentimental as well as unimaginably sensitive. The concept of "face" is very strong among them. To an Asian, especially an Indochinese or Southeast Asian, "losing face" is often something unbearable. You may easily hurt their feelings; therefore, be careful!

Because of language and cultural barriers, they will learn faster if your teaching is detailed and if you are patient. Speak distinctly and a bit slowly, and ask occasional discreet questions to determine whether previous conversation has been understood. The latter is necessary because many Indochinese refugees are very reluctant to admit that they don't comprehend something. Consequently, they will nod their heads as if everything is crystal clear, when actually they may understand little or nothing of what has been said. Don't ask yes-or-no questions! They react better to specific guidance and direction than to generalities. Do not imply. State what is needed to be said but avoid being abrupt or too commanding.

2. Harmonious relationships are very important to the Indochinese. This trait shows up in various ways. For example, they find it difficult to say "No" directly. They usually take an indirect approach in their conversations to dealings, particularly when they involve unpleasant matters. Americans often regard this as unnecessary beating around the bush. In the same vein, the Indochinese will say "Yes" when they really mean "No." This is not deviousness, but a desire not to hurt feelings or cause unpleasantness to retain the above-mentioned harmony in social relations. To the Vietnamese, Laotians, and Cambodians, repeated *excuses* most likely are good clues to polite refusal.

3. They also try very hard to appear knowledgeable or right. They will often say, "Yes, I understand," when they do not really understand. They will answer what they think you want to hear in order not to cause disharmony. To them, "changing the story a little bit" is not lying but is necessary to maintain harmony or to enhance their position. They are unlikely to ask direct questions, even when questions need to be asked. To them, words are silver but silence is golden. And of course, fury may take place after a period of silence.

4. Proper form or appearance is very important to the Indochinese. The ritual of how something is done is often more important than the actual accomplishment. In the gospel framework, they may want to emphasize the letter of the law over the spirit of the law. They often want exact guidance and direction in the tasks that are given. Tea and/or coffee are traditionally a "must," especially when guests are present.

5. The Indochinese do not readily show their emotions. Traditionally, if they have experienced a hurt, real or imaginary, they may wait a long time but eventually they will retaliate. Be careful not to misinterpret laughing or giggling, since these may cover up emotions they do not wish to show. The Indochinese, especially the Vietnamese, always smile or laugh even in distress. A smile may mean tolerance of an error or misunderstanding, submission to an unjust situation, acceptance of guilt, or embarrassment. Indochinese women tend to be embarrassed more easily than men. Sometimes anger or disapproval is covered up by silence. It does not necessarily mean they think that someone or something is funny. Sensitivity is necessary to avoid hurt feelings. Misinterpretation of even a jest may lead to an imagined insult. When you realize they are offended, approach them through one of their trusted family members.

6. The refugees' communication techniques often dif-

fer from those of the Americans. They seemingly resent physical contact of any kind during a conversation. Because the head is considered a sacred part of the body, it is offensive to the Indochinese to be touched on the head or shoulder unless both shoulders are touched. Especially to the Cambodians, putting your arms around their shoulders can only be done by close friends or relatives. A negative response may be considered as your unwillingness to help them. An evasive answer, however, is very acceptable. Direct questions are considered impolite in their cultures. They find the directness and abruptness of the American people rather frustrating and very difficult. They will also become offended if you give more attention to one than another, since they expect to be treated the same as everyone else. They abhor all kinds of discrimination (racial, religious, or cultural). To them, the black, the white, the Indians, the Chinese, or the Indochinese are equal as human beings, because "all men are created equal . . . bestowed with inalienable rights for the pursuit of happiness."

7. Due to cultural differences, gestures and attitudes often convey different meanings to the Indochinese. They consider it extremely impolite to beckon or wave at anyone with upturned fingers. In the motion for someone to come to you, the hand is used with the palm turned down. Waving, beckoning, or snapping the fingers to get someone's attention is considered very impolite. They may not look into the eyes of someone (i.e., their boss or supervisor) whom they respect. Americans feel that looking straight into someone's eyes while we are talking to him is a sign of straightforwardness. Don't expect the Indochinese to do this and don't misunderstand when they don't. Traditionally, in conversation, they don't look into the eyes of those whom they respect or who are superior in rank to them. This is an indication of politeness, not deviousness. Because the feet are considered the lowliest part of the body, it is offensive to the Vietnamese if a person, while sitting, points his foot at another individual. A Vietnamese youngster of Buddhist or Confucian background usually refrains himself from crossing his legs while sitting in front of an adult. Sitting straight with both feet on the floor is a form of respect and being humble.

8. Handshaking has gained wide acceptance among men in Cambodia, Laos, and Vietnam. It is probably best, though, not to shake hands with a woman unless she offers her hand first. Most Indochinese who have been to Europe or have had dealings with Westerners, especially with the French, will always expect to shake hands. When in a home where you are served a drink, no matter how thirsty you may be, the cup or glass should sit on the table until the host or hostess invites you to drink. Many Indochinese tend to nod their heads while shaking hands, or they may shake hands with both hands. This is because they want to show politeness and/or respect. A youth from Laos, Vietnam, or Cambodia will not touch anyone of the opposite sex. Laotians, Vietnamese, Hmongs do not embrace or hold hands with each other in such a manner as may be labeled as "queer" or "gay" in America. However, many Cambodian males still keep the tradition of holding hands and hugging each other as a form of warm greeting.

9. Their ideas about age and classes are different from the American point of view. To the Indochinese, sharing expenses is not the rule. The senior person generally pays all. In a restaurant situation, one member of the party pays for all, since Dutch Treat is not a custom. In any situation, when the refugee offers to pay, the American should let him do so, even if he is obviously less able to afford it than the American. For the American to pay, despite the refugee's offer, would be considered a rejection of the latter's hospitality and a reflection upon his ability to pay. Therefore, when a poor, wretched refugee says to you, "Come on, let's go eat!" he means that he will "cover" your bill. Vice versa when you tell an Indochinese to go eat with you, you had better count your money first!

10. The Indochinese are very responsive to authority. There is a tendency not to question an authority figure, since the people would rather be told what to do and how to do it. Authority figures, as well as elders, are expected always to be right and appropriate in their judgment and way of behaving.

11. Very early in their lives, many Indochinese have learned not to trust anybody. They need to learn that trust is a principle of human behavior leading to true spiritual happiness. Show your trust and respect by listening to their solutions to their problems. Where possible, give them praise for accomplishing what they do. Like most Americans, they love their countries and

they like to hear about the good things and the out-standing characteristics of their native lands. Your showing respect for them and their native lands will help develop their trust in you.

12. Family life is important. The primary loyalty is to the family. In the Indochinese family, the wife and mother has a strong influence in family leadership. Young girls are taught to take over the financial affairs and to run the family from a very early age. The husband and father is never expected to do anything with family finances except earn the money. Sons are rarely expected to do anything around the home. Therefore, don't expect Indochinese young men to sweep the floor for you. The older a child becomes, especially when a new baby takes his place, the less responsibility the parents feel toward him. Small children sometimes run around the house without a shirt, pants, or diapers.

13. The Indochinese tend to live on a day-to-day basis and often daydream about the past. The concept of planning for the future is foreign to many of them. It is difficult for most men to make a decision, especially one that is supposed to be long-lasting and irrevocable. The Indochinese are not slaves to time. Being late or very early at a social gathering does not concern them very much. However, it is amazing to note that those refugees at work always observe punctuality, and their work habits are generally excellent.

14. The dating patterns of Indochinese teenagers are much different from those in the United States. Good social standards and moral purity are strictly observed in their homes. Most Indochinese parents are reluctant to allow their teenage daughters to go out with boys. The fair sex never expects to share the bill when she is dating or "going steady" with a young man.

15. The practice of imposing on another's hospitality is common. They do not think of themselves as an imposition, however. To them, a friendship implies that either party may invoke certain reciprocal obligations without notice.

16. Gifts are often given to gain a favor or a gift in return. This should not be encouraged. When you present them with a gift, they are likely to feel an obligation to give a gift or favor in return. Reassure them that this is not necessary in the American culture.

When you give a gift, they will express their gratitude at the time and probably never mention it again. The gratitude for your thoughtfulness is more meaningful to them than the actual gift. They feel that further mention of the gift would take something away from the close relationship they felt toward you for the gift received. Gifts are given in pairs. It is better to receive two less expensive ones than one nicer one. This is especially true of wedding gifts. Many Indochinese refugees, even some highly educated ones, are still somewhat superstitious.

17. Their eating habits should also be respected. Their way of preparing food is very time-consuming and the smells can be pretty hard for Americans to take. An Indochinese family may leave you and the family member who invited you to their home to eat alone so that you may have special time together as friends. To indicate there was enough to eat and that you are satisfied, leave a little food on the serving platters or bowls. The older person is the first to begin eating.

18. Vietnamese names nearly always consist of a family name, middle name, and given name, in that order. (This is the reverse of the American custom, where the given name comes first and the family name last.) The terms Mr., Mrs., Miss are used with the given name rather than the family name. Again, this is the opposite of the American custom. Thus, Dinh Van Thinh is addressed as Mr. Thinh and Nguyen Thi Oi as Mrs. Oi. Most Vietnamese first and middle names have flowery meanings, whereas family names are derived from the names of ancient kings.

The Cambodians usually have the family name written first and the given name written last. Very rarely do Cambodians have a middle name. Therefore, if a Khmer says his full name is, for instance, Bun Kheng, we should know that his last name is Bun, and Kheng is his first or given name. The same order applies to names of Laotians, Hmongs, and Chinese, although Vietnamese names and Hmong names often have a middle name. Names of Laotian lowlanders are usually longer than names of other nationals. Most Indochinese or Southeast Asians, especially adults, are still used to writing their full names in their own order, i.e., the first name written last and the last name written first. Many still prefer being called by the first name instead of by the last name, for all occasions. Married women are to be called by either their maiden name or their husband's first name, preceded, of course, by the equivalent of "Mrs."

19. Most Indochinese think nothing of asking personal questions, such as your age, your salary, the amount something may have cost, and so forth. An evasive answer should satisfy them. You can show reciprocative interest in them by asking questions about their countries and cultures. Have an understanding heart, seeing eyes, and listening ears. Be sensitive to their needs and frustrations.

Selected Readings

Audric, John. *Angkor and the Khmer Empire.* London: Hale, 1972.

Buttinger, Joseph. *A Dragon Defiant.* New York: Praeger, 1972.

————. *Vietnam: A Dragon Embattled.* New York: Praeger, 1967.

————. *Vietnam: A Political History.* Praeger, 1968.

Duiker, William J. *The Rise of Nationalism in Vietnam, 1900–1941.* Ithaca, N. Y.: Cornell University Press, 1976.

Ennis, Thomas E. *French Policy and Developments in Indochina.* Chicago: University of Chicago Press, 1936. Repr. ed. New York: Russell & Russell, 1973.

Fall, Bernard B. *The Two Viet-Nams: A Political and Military Analysis.* New York: Praeger, 1963.

Halpern, Joel Martin. *Government, Politics, and Social Structure in Laos: A Study of Tradition and Innovation.* New Haven: Yale University Press, 1964.

Hickey, Gerald Cannon. *Village in Vietnam.* New Haven: Yale University Press, 1964.

Kunstadter, Peter, ed. *Southeast Asian Tribes, Minorities, and Nations.* Princeton, N. J.: Princeton University Press, 1967.

Leifer, Michael. *Cambodia: The Search for Security.* New York: Praeger, 1967.

LeMay, Reginald Stuart. *The Culture of South-east Asia, The Heritage of India.* London: Allen & Unwin, 1964.

Steinberg, David J., et al. *Cambodia: Its People, Its Society, Its Culture.* New Haven: Human Relations Area Files Press, 1959.

Willmott, William E. *The Political Structure of the Chinese Community in Cambodia.* London: University of London Athlone Press, 1970.

Zasloff, Joseph Jermiah. *The Pathet Lao: Leadership and Organization.* Lexington, Mass.: Lexington Books, 1973.

A P P E N D I X   C

Public Programs Given Under NEH Grant in Houston, Texas 1980–83.

Blacks

"Black Cowboy, Black Rodeo," Kashmere Gardens, Houston Public Library. Program for students and teachers.

"Meet the Black Cowboy." Same venue and audience.

Opening of exhibit of Houston photographer Earlie Hudnall commemorating Black History Month, Anderson Library, University of Houston Central Campus.

The Wrecking Ball, two-act play by Celeste Colson on the black experience, St. Mark's Episcopal Church Auditorium.

"A Walking Tour of Texas Southern University and Its Art." Artist John Biggers, guide.

"Seminar on Blacks in Houston," by Cary Wintz, University of Houston Central Campus.

Chinese

"Program on the History and Culture of the Chinese in Houston," festival-like program with mass audience, Houston Public Library.

"A Hundred Years of Chinese History in Houston," exhibit, University of Houston Central Campus.

"The History of Chinese Education in Houston," University of Houston Central Campus.

French

"The French in Houston," panel discussion, l'Alliance Française.

"The Cajuns in Houston: Can Their Culture Survive?" Paul Dunn, discussion and music, l'Alliance Française.

Germans

"Easter Among the Texas Germans," exhibit and discussion, St. John Evangelical Lutheran Church.

"German Colonists and Their Descendants in Houston," Dorothy Eckel Justaman, Heights Public Library.

"The Teutonic Texans," singing and festival, Houston Sängerbund Building.

Greeks

"Gia Gia and Pat Pau Tell a Story to Children," program for the community, Annunciation Church.

"Iconography: An Introduction to Byzantine Religious Art," Diamantis Cassis, Annunciation Hall.

"The Role of Women in the Greek Community," panel discussion, Annunciation Hall.

"The Role of Men in the Greek Community," panel discussion, Annunciation Hall.

"Dialogue with the Greek Community," lecture and bread blessing followed by festival-like gathering, Annunciation Hall.

"Seminar on the Greeks," Donna Collins, University of Houston Downtown Campus.

"Seminar on the Greeks," Donna Collins, Hellenic Professional Society.

Indochinese

"The Indochinese Experience in Houston," roundtable discussion, Autry House.

"Vietnamese Housing Problems in Houston," panel discussion, School of Architecture, University of Houston Central Campus.

"Seminar on the Indochinese," Fred R. von der Mehden, SIETAR, Houston Public Library.

"The History of Vietnamese Poetry," Khoi Tien Bui, Autry House.

Japanese

"Health Care and the Aging Population: Implications for Japan and the United States," panel discussion, Autry House.

"Japanese Brush Painting," exhibit and discussion, Tori Hashizume, Houston Public Library.

"Shogun, Fact or Fiction?" panel discussion, Autry House.

Jews

"Jewish Encounters Around the World," Rabbi R. Kahn, discussion, Temple Emanu El.

"A Tribute to Spirit—The Beth Israel Experience," documentary film and discussion, Congregation Beth Israel.

"Student Exchange Trip to Israel Experiences," panel discussion, Autry House.

"Friday Night Sabbath Service" followed by discussion and social gathering, Congregation Beth Israel.

"Book Review of *La America*," Mark Angel, discussion, Jewish Community Center.

Mexicans

"Mexican Americans in Houston," panel discussion, Houston Public Library.

"Mexican Americans at Home," photography exhibit, La Calle de Fulton, Houston Public Library, followed by travel to branch libraries.

"Mexican American Art," exhibit and discussion, Heights Public Library.

"Un Cinco de Mayo," original play by Teatro con Ganas, Moody Park.

"Folklore and Mexican Childrens' Family Histories," St. Joseph's Parish.

Scandinavians

"Danish Music," Hans Jorgen Jensen, cellist, Houston Public Library.

"Exhibit of Danish Art," Bjorn Wiinblad and Nils Obel, Houston Public Library.

"Isak Dinesen: Feminist Writer," talk and discussion, Frank Andersen, Autry House.

"A Swedish Cultural Experience," Moody Memorial Methodist Church, Galveston.

"Christmas in Sweden," discussion and social, Houston Lighting and Power.

"Christmas Lucia Celebration," Houston Baptist University.

Joint Presentations

"Seminar on French and Asian Business in Houston," John S. Ambler and Fred R. von der Mehden, College of Business Administration, University of Houston Central Campus.

"Seminar on the Blacks and Indochinese in Houston," Cary Wintz and Fred R. von der Mehden, St. Mark's Episcopal Church.

"Seminar on the Blacks and Jews in Houston," Cary Wintz and Elaine Maas, St. Martin's Lutheran Church.

"Seminar on the HCH Ethnic Project," Cary Wintz, Texas Southern University.

Six separate seminars on the entire project: Campbell, Cary Wintz, John S. Ambler, Elaine Maas, Donna Collins, Margarita Melville, Louis J. Marchiafava, and Fred R. von der Mehden; University of Houston Continuing Studies.

"Houston Meets Its Authors," five programs cosponsored by HCH, NEH, and CACH, featuring ethnic speakers on Mexican, Vietnamese, and black Creole authors.